The

New

Baby

POST ~ WAR

BABY AUSTINS

A30~A35~A40

Barney Sharratt
Foreword by James Hunt

Published in 1988 by Osprey Publishing Limited
27A Floral Street, London WC2E 9DP
Member company of the George Philip Group

Sole distributors for the USA

Osceola, Wisconsin 54020, USA

British Library Cataloguing in Publication Data

Sharratt, Barney
    The post-war baby Austins.
    1. Austin automobile
    I. Title
    629.2'222   TL215.A9
ISBN 0-85045-710-6

Editor Tony Thacker
Design Martin Bronkhorst

Filmset and printed in England by
BAS Printers Limited, Over Wallop, Hampshire

CONTENTS

Speed merchant James Hunt still gets pleasure from 'pottering' locally in his 34 bhp A35 van. He is seen here with his family at their Wimbledon home. *Courtesy Henry Maslin*

FOREWORD

An old A35 van is a far cry from the sort of cars that I used to drive so I suppose that some will find it strange that an ex-Formula 1 driver should choose a 'humble' A35 van to potter about in as his local runaround. However, I am a great believer in 'horses for courses' and, in any case, I was attracted by both the nature of the thing and the price. Here was a 'classic car' at a price at which one couldn't possibly buy a modern small car in a condition that would offer any ongoing reliability.

My particular vehicle was first registered in March 1967. The bodywork is immaculate and the engine purrs along. The handling is a little lively because I think it is on its original tyres. Barney Sharratt tells me that I really ought to make a 'pit stop' for a set of new radials, but habits die hard and sliding about on cross-plies is rather fun!

I use the van regularly, as does my whole household. A friend of ours often drives it as well and adores it for its 'headturning abilities'. Although I must say that I prefer a low-profile machine and have never noticed his claim! In any case, it gives us all great pleasure and I hope to be using it as everyday local transport for many years to come.

My contacts with the Austin A30–A35 Owners Club have been very enlightening. These little cars obviously engender much enthusiasm and a great spirit of friendship between owners, both here and overseas. As for spares—I had been looking for a replacement steering box for quite a while and without success. My MOT was due to expire so things were becoming desperate. After contacting the club, a brand-new box was delivered to my door in double-quick time. I believe that the benefits of belonging to the A40 Farina Club are similar.

I know Barney to have been a lifelong enthusiast of both pre-war and post-war 'baby Austins'. Many who have already enjoyed his writings as editor of *Spotlight*, the magazine of the Austin A30–A35 Owners Club, have been eagerly awaiting this full history of the Austin A30, A35 and A40 Farina, which is the result of his many years of enthusiastic and painstaking research. As the book unfolds, it takes you 'behind the scenes' to enjoy the full story of the designing, testing and building of these fine little cars. The success the cars had in racing and rallying is not forgotten either, nor are the needs of present-day owners. It is all here.

Enjoy the book and have fun with your baby Austins.

James Hunt

ACKNOWLEDGEMENTS

This book is dedicated to my wife, Cath, because she is to blame for everything, as usual. I bought an A35 for her to travel to work in, joined the A30–A35 Owners Club to learn of spares availability, attended a few club rallies, ended up editing the club magazine and somehow writing this book.

We began our research for the club magazine by visiting BL Heritage (now the British Motor Industry Heritage Trust) and received some excellent leads from Anders Clausager, their knowledgeable archivist. Enquiries at the Austin works at Longbridge, near Birmingham, however, confirmed that the complex history of Austin, BMC, BMH, BL, Austin Morris and Austin Rover, plus the numerous reorganizations that had taken place over the years, had led to the destruction of much archive material. It was clear that the story behind the design and development of the Austin A30, A35 and A40 Farina was likely to be lost forever unless we sought out those who had been actively involved.

All those we contacted were more than happy to help. In no time at all, Cath and I found ourselves engrossed in piecing together a fascinating jigsaw. Over several years, we have spent many delightful days reminiscing with men from 'The Austin'. The nicest thing of all was to find that, in doing so, we had made many new friends.

It was Anders Clausager who first drew our attention to the involvement of an American, Bob Koto, in the styling exercises for the A30. After several years of correspondence, we had the great pleasure of meeting both Bob and his wife, Millie—at their home in Florida and here in Selby. We stayed a night at the Raven Hotel in Droitwich, where the Austin Motor Company had put them up in 1950. Ian Duncan, who had worked with Bob at Longbridge, joined us for dinner. The next day we made a tour of Longbridge with Ken Garrett, who had worked so closely with Ian in devising the structure of the A30. This was a very pleasant way to be studying motoring history. Both Ian and Ken have been most

generous in the amount of help given.

That visit to Longbridge was also enhanced by the presence of George Coates. At 84, George still has a twinkle in his eye and many a yarn to tell—a lovely character whose engineering and linguistic abilities served Austin so well for 49 years.

Roger Lewis, a colleague and friend of George, was another who gave us much assistance. His leads to those who tested Austin prototypes and to those who worked in the research and development departments have unearthed much fascinating information from people like Bob Grice, Gil Jones, Max Oliver, Ben James, Alan Moore, Dan Clayton, Malcolm Gardner, Martin Ostler, Charles Griffin, Jack Daniels, Dr John Weaving, Dr Duncan Stuart, Dr Josef Ehrlich, Fred White, Don Hawley and Norman Horwood.

The morning spent with the late Dick Burzi in northern Italy will always hold happy memories for us. Further information on the styling and design of the cars was also received from Raymond Loewy, Sergio Pininfarina, David Bache, Ben Benbow, Doug Adams, Jack Clare, Harry Wall, Eric Bailey, Barry Kelkin, Godfrey Coates, Barry Wood and Vic Everton.

In researching the background to the birth of the A-series engine, we were fortunate to have met Bill Appleby and to have had extensive help from his right-hand man and successor, Eric Bareham.

On the production and planning side, we learnt much from Joe Edwards, Bill Davis and Dick Perry, while for the shop-floor story we relied on the expertise and knowledge of people like Albert Green, Harvey Williams and Fred Craven.

Much useful help was provided by those who used to be in the press and publicity departments at Longbridge, such as Sam Haynes, Yvonne Hodson, Aubrey Edwards, Ivor Greening and Norman Milne.

The chapter on racing was where Pat Moss-Carlsson, Paul Skilleter, David Lewis, Rupert Jones, Phil Wight and Robert Trevor helped us out, and for Chapter 11 (fresh-air motoring) we turned to Dave Scott, Jack Turner, Gerry Coker, Michael Edwards and John Aston.

Much help of a general nature was drawn from the experience of Stanley Edge, John Wheatley, Ian Elliott, Joe Bache, Stan Woodgate, Ken Wooldridge, Geoff Cooper, Bill Rowkins, Freddie Henry, Stan Johnson and John Hobbs.

It was a pleasure to be able to reunite several Longbridge men who had lost touch over the years. It was also surprising to find that, even in the early days of our research, we were able to enlighten Austin men about happenings in the Longbridge of their day of which they were unaware. We got used to hearing the same stories being related with very different twists. Some stories, quite naturally, depend on the teller's point of view, while others will have altered considerably after a few times round the works and the maturity of a further 30 to 35 years. Many a Longbridge yarn centres on Sir Leonard Lord, later to become Lord Lambury. He is certainly the answer to a writer's prayer, but I hope that the stories recounted here are not seen as a denigration of the fine achievements of the Longbridge which he headed.

I have tried to avoid reproducing information that is obtainable elsewhere, workshop manuals and parts lists, for example, being still available from those who trade in such items. A certain amount of material has been drawn from the road tests that appeared in the motoring press of the 1950s and 1960s. I am indebted to the editors of *Autocar*, *Motor*, *Motor Sport*, *Autosport*, *Commercial Motor* and *Road and Car*, and to the editors of all other publications mentioned, for allowing me to draw from this period material.

In setting the general scene, I have drawn strength from the works of Graham Turner (*The Leyland Papers*) and Bob Wyatt (*The Austin 1905–1952* and *The Austin 7 1922–1939*)—definitely recommended reading.

Wherever possible, the source of diagrams and photographs has been acknowledged *in situ*. Many of the photographs were obtained with the kind assistance of Cyril Comley and John Chasemore in the Longbridge Photographic Department. A large number of them were taken in the days when the late Ron Beach headed that department, and I am most grateful to Austin Rover and BMIHT for permission to reproduce them. Several photographs

were obtained with the help of Les Plowman of Grosvenor Studios, and some of those relating to the A40 Farina were kindly provided by Tim Hinton of the A40 Farina Club.

Much knowledge has been gleaned from members of the Austin A30–A35 Owners Club. Their enthusiasm, friendship and encouragement have been much appreciated over many years. They are simply too numerous to name. Assistance from the A40 Farina Club has been more recent, but none the less thorough. We have swapped club magazines for a long time, but in the final run-up to the book I must have approached all their committee members over some aspect or other, and have always received a quality of help that was above and beyond the call of duty—help that would only be given so freely by true enthusiasts.

For the overseas club scene, we have always had much help from Terry Jorgensen, David James and Dean Solly in Australia, while our many friends in Holland have often recharged our batteries with their infectious enthusiasm. For details of the A40 Futura, we had to enlist the help of Per-Borje Elg in Sweden, and for the Innocenti A40 we were lucky in having the help of Mike Morris of the Fiat Dino Register, Daniele Discepolo of Milan, and Mario Capitani of the Museo dell'Automobile Carlo Biscaretti di Ruffia in Turin.

Recently, we had the opportunity of spending a fortnight with Anders Clausager at Studley, researching the production records of over 900,000 cars. This operation brought a great deal of new information to light, and Anders' expertise and advice was a great help in drawing up our final figures and conclusions. His eagle-eye also helped correct several mistakes in our draft appendices.

The main burden of reading, re-reading and checking the manuscript has fallen to Cath, but I also received much invaluable help and advice from my brother Michael and colleague Jack Watson. Jack is one who knows little about cars but, following his recent indoctrination, he has asked me to give him the nod if I come across a choice A35 for sale. Should this book encourage any others to purchase an A30, A35 or A40 Farina, I doubt that they will be disappointed.

Barney Sharratt
Selby
August 1987

ABOVE 1922. 'When the mechanics had finally completed the car they stood aside and watched with interest as Sir Herbert, complete with bowler hat, took the controls and launched his new protégé out on to the Lickey Road. They watched the little car, with the bowler hat placed squarely amidships, snort away into the distance.' Quote from *Torque*, winter 1951. *Courtesy Austin Rover*

RIGHT June 1945—a six-light, four-door version of the 8 hp saloon. The car was styled soon after the Koto model (seen opposite) arrived at Longbridge, and the front end, in particular, seems to owe something to the American stylist. *Courtesy Austin Rover*

INTRODUCTION

'The Greatest Event in Post-War Motoring'. That is how Austin introduced their new Austin Seven in October 1951. The car was certainly long-awaited. It had been 12 years since a true 'baby' Austin had left the Longbridge production lines.

The original Seven had gained an enviable reputation. It could be bought and run very cheaply, yet seemed to excel in all that was asked of it, being renowned for its ability to keep on going. Conceived by Sir Herbert himself, it became his pride and joy. In 1929, when interviewed for *The Autocar*, he said, 'I look back on the year 1922 as one that marks an important milestone in my life, for it was then that I introduced the now famous Seven. . . . The Seven has done more than anything previously accomplished to bring about the realization of my ambition to motorize the masses.'

The Seven also played an important role in seeing the Austin Motor Company through the difficult times that followed World War 1; times when the official receiver was never very far away; times when Herbert Austin would stand on the canteen steps and encourage the men by announcing that he had purchased two more carburettors or two more magnetos; times so bad that those who were assembling the cars had even plain washers counted out to them.

Sir Herbert's diminutive Seven gradually grew up: a lengthened chassis in 1932, the more stylish Ruby in 1934 and the Big Seven of 1937. In that year, Briggs of America, then the largest independent car body makers in the world, made a bid for Austin custom by sending a quarter-scale proposal for a new baby Austin to Longbridge. Although nothing more was heard of it, the frontal treatment would seem to have influenced the styling of the 8, 10 and 12 hp cars that appeared in 1939. The 8 hp saloon was the new baby of the Austin range—after a production run of some 300,000 examples, the unique and much-loved Austin Seven was to be produced no longer. Thoughts did turn to the design of a completely-new, 500 cc baby Austin along the

Model of a proposed replacement for the pre-war Seven by Briggs Motor Bodies of America and styled by Bob Koto. Opposite sides of the same model offered alternative styling and headlamp heights. *Courtesy Bob Koto*

ABOVE Wooden models of Sheerline and proposed 7 hp saloon stand side by side in the Longbridge experimental department in 1946. The baby car was shelved in order to attack the export market with the A40, but Jack Clare remembers being late for lunch on several occasions while working on that rear-end sweep. Note the large, pre-war-style side lights that would even put in a brief appearance on Dick Burzi's final model for the A30. *Courtesy Austin Rover*

BELOW Platform chassis of the 8 hp saloon, photographed in October 1944. The prospect of attaching independent front suspension to either a platform chassis or a car of unitary construction did not appeal to the design team at Longbridge. As a consequence, the first 'all-new' post-war models returned to the use of a traditional chassis. *Courtesy Austin Rover*

lines of the Fiat Topolino, but World War 2 was about to intervene.

The war saw the factory turned over to munitions. Herbert Austin died in 1941, but in 1937, when war with Germany seemed inevitable, he had had the foresight to contact the Ministry of Defence and obtain contracts for ambulances, trucks and cars. This ensured that wartime production would range not only from jerry cans and tin helmets to Hurricane fighters and Lancaster bombers, but would also include sufficient vehicles to allow a certain amount of development work to take place. Austin got car production swiftly under way at the end of the war by reintroducing their 8, 10 and 12 hp range, strengthening it with the addition of a 16 hp saloon, which had an overhead-valve engine originally intended for a jeep. The new engine apart, this range was only seen as a stop-gap arrangement until their completely-new designs were ready for release.

A new baby car was well down the list of priorities. There was no choice but to go in search of the dollar to relieve the pressure on our battered economy. The British Government was determined that the meagre supplies of steel should be channelled towards production for export. A baby car was hardly ideal dollar-bait.

In 1946, just over a year after becoming Chairman of the Austin Motor Company, Leonard Lord explained to his shareholders why a new baby car did not figure in his immediate plans. He was convinced that the best strategy was to aim at those parts of the American market which were not catered for by Americans themselves. He saw two possibilities: there ought to be scope for selling a small (but not *too* small) economical car of lively performance, and a well-finished larger car of distinctive appearance.

Cars to satisfy these requirements had been on the drawing-boards for some time. Barry Kelkin, now manager of feasibility for trim and hardware at Austin Rover, was a youngster in the styling department during the latter part of the war. He spent most of his time holding sweeps for those at work on the drawing-boards or acting as office boy by running their errands. These errands took him into all the 'no-go' areas of the plant, and he remembers the work already being done on the Sheerline and Devon in his first year—1943.

By September 1947, the Sheerline, Princess, Devon and Dorset had all been launched—the export drive could begin in earnest. The A40 Devon and Dorset were attractive cars for their day. Pleasantly styled, they also offered independent front suspension and a lively, efficient overhead-valve engine. Good though they were, the question was whether the Americans would buy them in sufficient numbers to make operations over there viable. Leonard Lord was determined to find out, and his visits to the USA in 1947 were to good effect. Of the 1200 cars imported into America in February 1948, 1053 were Austins. By November 1950, over a quarter of a million A40s had brought $70,000,000 to Britain.

There is little doubt that Lord was correct to assess the 1200 cc A40 as quite small enough to offer to the Americans. Even so, articles appeared in their motoring press which explained in detail how to approach the 'difficult' jobs of getting into and out of the car.

The A40 tag was used to indicate the car's approximate brake horsepower. Other new Austin models would follow suit. I remember the A90 Atlantic as one of the highlights of the 1948 Earls Court Motor Show. To a young lad, the A70 Hampshire announced at the same time was not quite so impressive, and that Morris Minor did not seem very important at all! Being a youngster, I was not in a position to purchase anything, but then neither were most of the other half-million or so visitors to this first British motor show for ten years—unless they were from overseas.

Over 75 per cent of production was being exported, and visitors from overseas could order a car with the knowledge that it would be waiting for them at their port of arrival. It was a little different for potential UK owners. Delivery dates were being quoted in years—if quoted at all. One wag of a dealer drew attention to himself by advertising: 'If you want your name to go down to posterity, order your Austin now.'

Longbridge presented a very busy scene in those early post-war days—days in which management attempted to set the tone by striding rapidly about, their bodies set at something like a 30-degree forward lean to signify the urgency of the tasks in hand. Even senior management could be found helping to push completed cars off the assembly lines to keep them moving at full tilt and not keep the ships waiting.

The ships certainly were waiting. *The Autocar* of 17 November 1950 declared, 'Demand from all over the world has led to a record year for the Austin Motor Company Ltd, which showed a profit of four and a half million.' Commonwealth countries offered ready markets. In 1949, Austin were shipping 2000 cars a month to Canada, and in that same year a third more Austins were registered in British Columbia

Austin prototype—June 1947. An A35 grille badge shows that had this car been put into production it would have been the first A35. It had a 1000 cc, short-stroke version of the A40 engine and was 3 in. narrower than the A40. It clocked up a considerable mileage before the idea was dropped. Note the 'artillery' wheels of the 8 hp series.
Courtesy Austin Rover

than any other make of car. Austins also easily out-sold all other cars imported into Australia during 1949.

However, *The Motor* of 12 October 1949 gave voice to the feelings of many in Britain: 'Once again there was a notable absentee from Earls Court. Everyone seems to want a motor car of some sort as soon as possible, and very cheap because there are not many pennies about. . . . A latter-day Austin Seven is what many people yammer for.'

1

REPLACING THE PRE-WAR SEVEN

Although 1950 would see another Earls Court Show without a baby Austin, the car had been on its way since 1948. It was then that Ian Duncan had arrived at Longbridge in a small, prototype car boasting many advanced features. Known as the Duncan Dragonfly, it had been produced by Duncan Industries (noted for their Duncan-bodied Healey and Alvis cars) with the specific intention of offering it to a large-scale manufacturer.

Armed with his home-made brochure, in which the features of this 'Economy Car for World Markets' were explained, Ian had taken the car to both Jaguar and BSA (the latter had provided two free engines for the project), but both manufacturers turned it down. It was only when Duncan arrived at Longbridge that the merits of the car seemed to be appreciated fully. First, he took the chief tester, Lou Kings, over the customary short test route; after that, Johnnie Rix, chief designer, and finally it was Len Lord's turn. They managed to outpace an A40 over the Lickey Hills. Lord was impressed. After 15 minutes' discussion, they agreed on a price of £10,000, part of the deal being that Ian Duncan himself would work a three-year contract at Longbridge.

Obviously, Lord had seen the car's potential, but it is uncertain whether he purchased it with the serious intention of putting such a car into production, or whether keeping the design and designer out of the hands of his competitors was uppermost in his mind. Perhaps he was simply backing two horses; he was certainly taking no chances, for Ian Duncan was handed the cheque and sent home in an A40, while the Dragonfly remained at Longbridge.

It is easy to see why Lord was impressed with the car. Its unitary construction was advanced enough for its time, but it also had a transverse engine with front-wheel drive to Mini-type wheels. Its rubber suspension had been worked out in conjunction with Alex Moulton, a colleague of Duncan's during their days at the Bristol Aeroplane Company. The

500 cc, overhead-valve, air-cooled twin was placed forward of the front wheels, aiding the car's remarkable stability. No doubt, Sir Alec Issigonis would have approved of many of Duncan's ideas, but at the time the Issigonis Mini was still 11 years away.

Whatever Len Lord had in mind, Ian Duncan was given the impression that he had been taken on at Longbridge to produce a four-seater version of his revolutionary car—the prototype took three abreast at a pinch— and he set to work in an office in South Works, adjacent to that of the chief designer, Johnnie Rix. Both Rix and Lord had already come to the conclusion that the way ahead in car design would involve producing vehicles of truly chassisless construction. In Ian Duncan, they had found a man with more experience than most in this field. At about the same time, they managed to obtain the services of Ken Garrett, who had also been in the aircraft industry and had the necessary knowledge of stressed-skin construction.

Ian Duncan was only at Longbridge for three years, but he is remembered by some of those who were there as a very lively and advanced engineer of the Issigonis mould. Ken Garrett still rates him as one of the most able design engineers he has ever met. Ian was, and is, quite a character. To see him at Longbridge in his hefty flying jacket, brushing out four inches of snow from his Duncan-bodied (but completely topless) Allard before he tore off in it, was 'a sight to behold'.

Initially, only Ian and Ken were involved with the new project. They simply 'borrowed' draughtsmen, as and when necessary. It was not all plain sailing, however. The layout of the car was completely new to Longbridge, and there were those who had managed to accept the radical move of eliminating the chassis, but who had begun to get cold feet about front-wheel drive and rubber suspension. In fairness, it must be said that this early attempt at rubber suspension suffered from excessive wear after about 5000 miles, and as it appeared that the only quick

RIGHT The Dragonfly
stands in the
experimental
department at
Longbridge in early
1949. *Courtesy Austin
Rover*

THE DUNCAN DRAGONFLY

LEFT Photograph taken from Ian
Duncan's 'home-made' brochure
for the Dragonfly. *Courtesy Ian
Duncan*

BELOW Detail of the Dragonfly's
rubber suspension and front-
wheel drive. *Courtesy Ian Duncan*

LEFT May 1949. Perhaps the
Dragonfly inspired this Dick
Burzi proposal for a new Austin
Seven, although Dick had already
experimented with a Topolino-
like car before the war. Here, the
first signs of the A30 are
beginning to creep in. Are those
Morris Minor hub caps? *Courtesy
Austin Rover*

cure was to fit shock absorbers as well, the system had lost its attraction.

In any case, things were about to change. Ian Duncan was soon to discover that the project, in its original form, had been abandoned—the news was broken to him by the tea boy! An agreed merger with Morris had just fallen by the wayside, and a much-aggrieved Len Lord decided that the new baby Austin should no longer be a 'hole in the corner' operation. It would be given priority so that it could challenge the Morris Minor.

Although this meant that, in future, all decisions would go through the accepted Longbridge channels, it did not mean that Ian Duncan and Ken Garrett were surplus to Austin's requirements. Indeed, the car was still to be chassisless, so their skills were much needed. However, those very skills were to produce a somewhat delicate situation. At times, they found themselves talking a different language to their established superiors. Their talk of shear flows, wagner beams and tension fields was a little disconcerting to men who had spent their lives building traditional motor cars. The resulting tension and divergence of opinion was probably exacerbated by the clumsy way in which appointments were sometimes made at Longbridge. Ken Garrett, for example, was appointed by Johnnie Rix and passed straight on to Jim Stanfield, the chief body designer who, unfortunately, had not been consulted at all.

There were other reasons why Duncan and Garrett found their immediate superiors reluctant to stick their necks out in championing too much radical innovation, and why technical decisions were not necessarily based on a logical assessment of the possible alternatives. Leonard Lord was considered by many to be a production engineer without equal, and in that respect some would even place him in a similar category to Herbert Austin. No one could possibly deny the great achievements during his time in charge at Longbridge, nor is it hard to find those who will testify to personal kindnesses received at his hands, but you do not have to speak to many Austin men to realize that he could be a very hard taskmaster with an abrupt style, often quoted as verging on crudity.

Stories abound of those who did not measure up to Lord's standards—like the superintendent who had returned from a short absence from his office to find his belongings stacked in the corridor and someone else occupying his chair. Lord could arrive at the works in a gloomy mood and announce quite openly, 'I feel just like sacking some bugger today.'

Dismissal could be swift and brutal. When Lord's trilby was pushed to the back of his head, it was more than likely that sparks would fly—if you wanted to survive, you kept your head down. There are those who argue that Lord had difficulty in persuading his designers to be more adventurous, but it is hardly surprising if they were a little wary of being too innovative in case any failure should incur his wrath.

The decision to put the proposed new car on to the official drawing-boards meant that it came firmly under the wing of chief designer Rix, and it was through him that the new Seven was to have a direct link with the pre-war car. Much of the pre-war baby was designed by Stanley Edge while he was still in his teens. He undertook the work in the privacy of Lickey Grange, the home of Herbert Austin. In conversation with Stanley, at the Longbridge dinner celebrating the Diamond Jubilee of the Seven in 1982, he told me, 'When the Seven went into production, Johnnie Rix (known as Jack to his pre-war colleagues) was with me putting my comparatively scrappy, pre-production details into a form more acceptable to production methods—we became close friends.' Rix is remembered as an engineer who was able to 'talk with his pencil' to those involved as he made his daily rounds of the drawing-boards. He toured all departments twice every day, and expected the leader of each section, for example Bill Appleby on engines, to tour the department with him. If there was a weakness in the system, it was that each component of a car tended to be treated in isolation. Ian Duncan found that it was frowned upon if a body man took it upon himself to mull things over with, say, a chassis man; everything had to go through Rix.

The A30 project was discussed at monthly meetings which were chaired by George Harriman, Lord's deputy, although Len Lord himself was determined to oversee the project. The meetings were also attended by Bill Appleby (chief engine designer), Jim Stanfield (chief body designer), Dick Burzi (chief stylist) and Dr John Weaving (in charge of research and development). Discussions became quite heated when the various compromises were being thrashed out. The research department sometimes saw things quite differently from one of the production departments and, with lively minds eager to prove their point, tempers could get frayed. Such rifts were not always healed by adequate apologies, either—'I apologize for calling you a bloody fool in front of the men, but not for calling you a bloody fool', is hardly a phrasing that will settle differences!

To demonstrate their proposals for the basic structure, Ian Duncan and Ken Garrett built a quarter-
scale model from cartridge paper and glue. The
model consisted of the floorpan, front and rear
wheel arches and flitches, the rear seat back and the
dashboard, as well as all the suspension mounts. The
fact that the car was to be chassisless meant that all
the components had to be mounted on relatively
thin-gauge metal, which had been shaped or supported to take the loads involved. The loading
applied to the structure had to be analysed carefully
so that adequate strength could be obtained with the
minimum of metal. Ken devised the basic structure,
while Ian built the car around it to suit the requirements of engine, suspension, passengers and
luggage.

Although Duncan and Garrett were not responsible for the external shape of the car, they did have
to take account of any styling decisions. It was not
long before they learnt that Lord was employing an
outside stylist. The contract had been awarded to
American industrial designer Raymond Loewy. It
seemed that Lord was really pushing the boat out
for the new car—Loewy was already famous for his
efforts to integrate art and engineering in the design
of mass-produced goods. Even by 1950, Loewy had
been involved in a vast number of design projects
that ranged from duplicators to refrigerators, from
cigarette packets to Coke bottles, and from locomo-
tives to motor cars—aesthetic appeal was fast
becoming a major factor in marketing.

With his eye on the American market, Lord had
been impressed with the job Loewy had done on the
early post-war Studebakers, cars with such novel
styling that people maintained it was impossible to
tell if they were coming or going. They set the
fashion for a 'three-box' style, where the boot was
about as large as the engine bay.

Loewy had offices in New York, Paris and
London, but to fulfil the Austin contract he sent
Holden 'Bob' Koto to Longbridge from America in
the summer of 1950. This was quite a coincidence,
since Briggs' pre-war proposal for an Austin Seven
had been styled by Bob, too. He left Briggs in 1939
and, after a spell at Hudson, he had joined Raymond
Loewy in 1943. By this route, he found himself styling an Austin Seven replacement for the second time.
A letter, received from the late Raymond Loewy in
1982, describes how he rated the man he had put
in charge of the project: 'I consider Bob Koto as
amongst the foremost automotive designers of our
time. Bob has innate good taste and talent and an
international reputation. To have him on my team

RIGHT **Clay mock-up for an alternative front end.** *Courtesy Bob Koto*

BELOW **Bob Koto's quarter-scale model. Note the alternative styling for the grille. The mitred and recessed framing to the side windows was one feature from Bob Koto's quarter-scale model that appeared in the final Burzi model for the production car.** *Courtesy Bob Koto*

at Austin was a great asset because he fully understood that I wished our mock-ups to have flowing,
sensuous lines that would get us away from the
squarish "shoebox-type" of design.'

One can imagine how this influx of 'slick, col-
ogned Americans', as one observer called them, must
have caused further ripples among the established
design teams at Longbridge, but Loewy's men
enjoyed themselves immensely. They were treated
quite royally by Lord, who installed them in luxury
at the Raven Hotel in Droitwich and provided a
chauffeur to take them to and from the Longbridge
works each day.

When Bob Koto arrived at Longbridge, he was
furnished with the 'package' by the engineering
department. This detailed the overall dimensions
and seating space, his brief being to style a small,
low-priced car that would emulate the pre-war
Seven. He began by making a few sketches and soon
translated these into a quarter-scale model. This was
simply a stage in developing the full-sized model,
but it also served the purpose of keeping Raymond
Loewy up to date with progress. Photographs of it
were sent to him as the work proceeded. With
Loewy's approval, a start was made on the full-sized
clay mock-up. The wood shop provided the
armatures that formed the base for the clay, and
when the model was completed it was sprayed with
a special paint, brought over from the USA, which
would adhere well to clay.

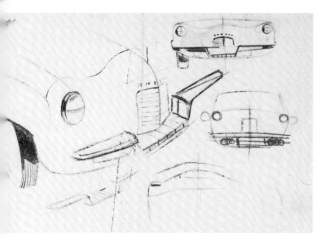

ABOVE Ken Howes, who later styled the Sunbeam Alpine, assisted Bob Koto at Longbridge. While there, Ken designed a lounge for Ian Duncan. On the reverse of the design for the lounge, they began sketching how the new baby car might look if it had to be traditionally Austin. The rough frontal view at middle right was Ian Duncan's 'talking paper', while the remainder represents Ken Howes' immediate thoughts. *Courtesy Ian Duncan*

CENTRE **Full-sized clay model by Bob Koto.** *Courtesy Bob Koto*

Both Leonard Lord and George Harriman seemed very impressed with the finished model. Lord, pointing to a model which Dick Burzi had been working on for about two years, said to Bob Koto, 'Look at what you've done in only four months.' Bob left England feeling very elated and met Raymond Loewy in Paris. Loewy had heard of the results and, naturally, was very pleased. However, both were surprised and disappointed when, eventually, they saw the production car. It had been altered so much that they did not recognize it. Neither Loewy nor Koto could understand how Austin management could spend so much money on hiring outside help and not use it. Loewy got in touch with Longbridge, and could hardly believe it when Leonard Lord told him that he had simply wanted to expose Austin to the newest designs Americans could produce so that Longbridge could counter them. Lord went on to say that Austin preferred a more traditional 'English look'. Loewy was none too pleased, but Bob Koto looks back on his time at Longbridge with great pleasure. After a lifetime in automobile styling, he will still tell you that he had the most fun when he came to England for Loewy. He had brought his whole family with him: his wife Millie, daughter Barbara and son David. Bob recalls philosophically, 'Doggone it, they didn't come out with the job, but living there in England was such fun; the English people were just great to us.' He also recalls, 'When Raymond Loewy sent Clare Hodgman and myself to design the Hillman Minx in 1953, the production model was exactly the same as our full-sized model.' Those who look carefully at the Minx (of 1956) should have no difficulty in spotting the '53 Studebaker influence.

While at Longbridge, Bob Koto was in close touch with Ian Duncan. At one stage, Bob had suggested moving the seats and engine about 4 in. forward to obtain better styling proportions. Ian liked the idea too, and put it to Len Lord. Although Lord agreed, he referred him back to the others and, as Ian was unable to convince Johnnie Rix of the merits of the proposal, the idea was abandoned.

Ian Duncan is in no doubt about the beauty of Bob Koto's design: 'It was very attractive indeed and would have sold like wildfire, as it would have had very exceptional style for such a small car.' It seems, however, that Lord and Harriman tended to relate the cost of a car directly to its length. Bob Koto had stuck to their original dimensions, but after he left Longbridge they decided to shorten the car by $4\frac{1}{2}$ in. Duncan says that this entailed placing the rear seat above the axle, and he feels that the resulting

LEFT Leonard Lord quite fancied himself as a stylist. Here he scrutinizes a Dick Burzi proposal for an Atlantic-like A40. Looking at this photo, one can see why Lord was sometimes referred to as 'Spiky' at shop-floor level. *Courtesy Austin Rover*

RIGHT October 1951. An A30 prototype, produced from Dick Burzi's final model, stands in the new styling studio at Longbridge. Note that the As on the hub caps are still camouflaged with tape. This early prototype has the fuel filler on the nearside. *Courtesy Austin Rover*

increase in height rather spoiled the original design. The increase in height also meant that some of the metal saved by reducing the length was simply put back in height. Bob Koto's only regret was that he could not have worked with Ian in developing the shorter version: 'Our proposed shift of the seats, allied with front-wheel drive, but keeping the same design, could have made a beautiful baby Austin.'

The styling of the shortened version of the car, which still used the basic structure determined by Ian Duncan and Ken Garrett, was undertaken by Dick Burzi, a delightful character, who had arrived at Longbridge in 1929, speaking little English and sporting a green felt hat, complete with feather.

Although Argentinian by birth, Burzi had been working for Lancia in Italy until things got rather warm for him there after he had drawn some cartoons for a newspaper opposed to Mussolini. Vincenzo Lancia saved the situation by moving Dick to his Paris coachbuilding firm. Furthermore, a recommendation made by Lancia to Herbert Austin, when they met each other while travelling to America on the Queen Mary, led to Dick moving to Longbridge. His real name was Ricardo, but he was soon known as Dick by one and all. He was responsible for all Austin styling from the mid-1930s onwards. Until that time, Herbert Austin himself had kept a tight rein on all the design work, and he intimated to Dick that many of his proposals were much too advanced for the conservative British. In later years, Dick was to find that Len Lord fancied himself as a stylist too. By all accounts, Lord was a remarkably good draughtsman, and he certainly enjoyed claiming that he always made the preliminary 'roughs' for any new model.

Dick Burzi was a highly respected member of staff, very capable and very likeable. His colleagues felt for him at times when, for example, Len Lord returned from a lengthy trip abroad and decided to 'knock a couple of feet' out of the middle of a car, 'just as though he was cutting butter', or when he tore up Dick's drawings in front of others. Dick had a famous drawer where he kept such designs 'for another day', but it seems that these events never altered his genial character or his determination to go ahead with his own styling. Indeed, in his eighties he looked back with particular pleasure to the years he spent at Longbridge. With a smile, the most he would say of the problems he faced in getting his ideas into production was, 'By the time the engineers and management had finished with my designs, there was only that much of me in any car.' What 'that much' meant was depicted by holding his thumb and forefinger about half an inch apart. He even agreed that the Koto designs for the A30 were of better styling proportion than the actual production car, but pointed out that the decision to lop off the tail of a car was a common occurrence. In the case of the A30, it meant that he had to restyle the car to fit the new constraints on length and to produce a version with more family resemblance to other Austins.

After making a quarter-scale model and receiving Lord's go-ahead for the full-sized version, he found that he was still asked to alter it several times. It was obvious to all that Len Lord saw the car as his baby Austin—the successor to Sir Herbert's famous Seven. One senior member of staff put his foot in it by asking Lord if the large, pre-war-style side lights that sat on top of the wings of the Burzi model

were to be left there in the production version. 'I'll leave them where I bloody well like,' said Lord, but shortly afterwards the lights were slimmed down to their final, torpedo-like shape. Considering all the constraints that were placed upon him, Dick Burzi did well to produce a car with such pleasing lines and attractive detail—not an easy thing to do in so short a car.

David Bache, the renowned stylist of many successful cars, including the Rover 2000, Range Rover and Rover SD1, and known for his work on the Metro and Maestro as head of styling at BL from late 1975, worked in the Burzi studio in those early days. In conjunction with Smiths Instruments, he produced quite a sophisticated styling mock-up for the fascia of the A30. David's mock-up was not used, essentially being an exercise, but he remembers the controversy over the Koto and Burzi styling. His own impression was that opinions were fairly equally divided, but that Koto's design was well liked and would probably have carried the day had there been such a thing as a vote. Bob Koto just laughs about it today: 'I bet Dick Burzi was laughing his socks off. He'd be saying to himself, "Here's this American guy thinking he's going to have a car out on the road", but of course Dick must have known that that was not to be so.'

While all these styling deliberations were taking place, Ian Duncan and Ken Garrett had carried on with their work on the internal structure. They knew that the mechanical layout would be vastly different from Ian's original ideas, but this did not affect their plans for the basic structure. The overall design was proving to be extremely economical in steel and the extra weight added to the bodyshell

ABOVE A happy reunion at Longbridge in August 1985. From left to right: Bob Koto, Ian Duncan and Ken Garrett stand on the steps of the Longbridge 'Kremlin', some 35 years after they last worked together. On the far right is George Coates, who worked at 'The Austin' from 1919 until 1968

CENTRE Bordighera, northern Italy, in August 1981. The author's wife (left) chats with the late Dick Burzi and his wife, Anna, about some of the photos reproduced here

by the reinforcements, which fed the loads into the structure, was extremely small.

The basic structure consists of two side-members (each comprising front wheel arch, dashboard side, sill and rear wheel arch) running either side of the vehicle, between which are three main cross-members. In addition to forming part of the structure, each cross-member was cleverly devised to perform a specific function. The rear cross-member, for example, carries the rear spring hangers; further forward, the heelboard acts both as a cross-member and as a support for the forward ends of the rear springs; the toeboard transfers the vertical loads from the front suspension into the sills; and the cross-member at the very front of the car supports the radiator.

The metal of the rear-seat squab was shaped to clear the telescopic dampers that were fitted to the first prototype. Later, it was found easier to mount the lever-arm type of damper, but the shaped squab was retained as it was thought to add to the comfort of rear-seat passengers.

A shear-force and bending-moment diagram was used to determine the dimensions required for the sills and to obtain an approximate idea of the necessary proportions for the rest of the structure. Naturally, the heaviest bending loads would be taken by the sills, and although the propshaft tunnel and the roof would relieve some of the bending moments, the calculations were based on the assumption that the sills were to take all these loads. This was so that a convertible version could be made from the same tooling, although in this case the thickness of the inner sill would have been increased to 18 swg (standard wire gauge) from the 20 swg of the rest of the body.

The calculations to check the strength of the entire vehicle's structure took about three months to complete. To shorten the work, many approximations were made and a fair margin of safety allowed. This car was breaking new ground at Longbridge, and there was much discussion about how to attach the independent front suspension to a chassisless car. Billy Ellcock, who as a chassis man was still responsible for the suspension, felt that a body built from pressed panels would give neither an accurate nor a strong enough location. A separate front subframe was mooted and even tested, but eventually Duncan and Garrett carried the day. They managed to demonstrate that provided the body panels were suitably supported and stiffened, their relatively large depth produced a far stronger and stiffer structure than could be obtained by using a chassis.

It was mid-1952 before the final front suspension mounts were devised. This assembly, photographed in June 1952, had been marked for some remedial welding. *Courtesy Austin Rover*

A separate frame to support the front suspension was not the answer. This one, photographed in July 1951, had fractured badly. *Courtesy Austin Rover*

In late 1950, with the first prototype ready for the road, it fell to Johnnie Rix to be the first to take it out. After an initial trial run, he showed obvious relief that the new car was so pleasant to drive. The ride had astonished him. He was used to expecting a certain amount of deflection in the body, as this was quite normal in a car with a separate chassis, but this first chassisless Austin felt very solid. Ken Garrett remembers his exact words: 'This is a small car with a big-car ride.'

The prototype, in its dull brown paint, was taken on a hush-hush test trip to Wales, but at an enforced stop one curious Welshman was heard to exclaim to his companion, 'Oh, it's a Duncan, see.' He was pointing to the decoy badge that had been hastily added to the grille of the car from the stripped-down Dragonfly that now stood forlornly in the corner of Alf Depper's shop.

The new Seven, then, had had a rather uncertain birth, fraught with much indecision, but now it was ready to be put through its paces. The question was, would it fulfil the hopes of providing Austin with another 'Car for the Masses'? Only time would tell.

2

THE BIRTH OF THE A-SERIES

Bill Appleby, who was later to become chief designer of engines and gearboxes for BMC, was the leader of the engine design section at Longbridge. Although he was in charge, and must take much of the credit for steering the ship in the right direction, it is clear that most of the detailed design and layout for the new Seven engine was carried out by his deputy and successor, Eric Bareham. Indeed, most of the instructions that Eric received came direct from the chief designer, Johnnie Rix.

War was still raging when Eric laid down the preliminary dimensions for a new, 7 hp side-valve engine. In fact, it was June 1942, a date drawn from the notebooks in which he calculated the various fits and limits of the engines on which he was working. Later in the same year, an overhead-valve version of the 8 hp side-valve engine was laid out, but it was never built.

Experiments were also carried out with a three-cylinder engine that had been produced from the 8 hp unit. They had a devil's own job trying to balance it, though. According to Bill Appleby, 'When the gear-lever knob vibrated in resonance with the engine, the knob could scarcely be seen.'

By the mid-1940s, however, Len Lord had just about made up his mind that all future Austin engines should be of overhead-valve design. That he wavered a little before deciding on an ohv unit for the A30 was quite understandable. If it was to be a true successor to the pre-war Seven, simplicity and cheapness were essential considerations.

A look at Eric Bareham's notes shows that on 24 May 1949 a side-valve engine was still in the running. On that date he detailed a design specification for an SF (small four) 7 hp, 800 cc side-valve engine, for which it was stipulated that weight and cost should be kept to a minimum. To this end, it was proposed that thermosyphon cooling be used and that the distributor be placed on the front of the block to eliminate the need for a camshaft skew gear. A question mark was placed against the need for a petrol pump, although it seems that gravity-feed was never considered too seriously. It was also suggested that further economies could be made by combining the oil filler and dipstick, and by using the dynamo and starter motor from the A40. It was not long, however, before this proposed engine was abandoned.

In the end, of course, the A30 was to borrow much more than the odd ancillary from the A40's 1200 cc ohv engine. The unit was proving so popular and reliable that it seemed sensible to consider basing the new engine on a scaled-down version, the cost of which would fall somewhere between the £28 for an A40 engine and an estimated £18 for a new 7 hp side-valve unit.

By July 1949, the preliminary fits and limits had been calculated for an 800 cc overhead-valve engine which was to bear a close resemblance to the larger A40 unit. This meant it was to be a conventional four-cylinder, in-line unit, but by careful attention to detail, the designers hoped to achieve considerable gains in efficiency. The team was hoping to achieve these gains without forsaking the Austin tradition of producing an engine that was very flexible over a wide speed range and that pulled well, even at low revs. Much thought was to be given to the features that produced these characteristics: a comparatively heavy flywheel, large valves and well-researched valve timing. During its design period, it was to be known simply as the 7 hp or AS3 engine. It was only much later that it became known as the A-series.

The A40 engine had been such a success that it was decided to employ the same stroke/bore ratio of 1.3:1, using a stroke of 76 mm and a bore of 58 mm. As this ratio was slightly higher than normal, it helped to minimize the engine's length. The water pump helped in that respect too; it was designed so that its rotor lay inside the cylinder block.

A great deal of the credit for the efficiency of the engine must be attributed to the cylinder-head

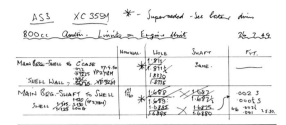

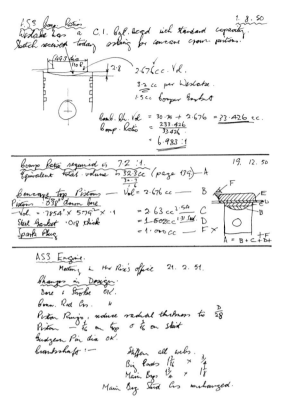

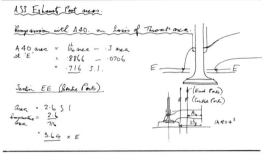

ABOVE Extracts from Eric Bareham's notes, showing the first line or two of his calculations for the fits and limits of the 803 cc engine. Other snatches clearly show how the A40 engine was used as a starting point for many of the calculations. We can also see some of the calculations relating to Weslake's suggestion of using pistons with concave crowns

LEFT The late Bill Appleby, outside his Cheltenham home in 1981, inspects the engine bay of the author's A35 saloon

LEFT Eric Bareham, Bill Appleby's deputy and successor. The man responsible for putting the engine for the 'New Seven' on to the drawing-board

design, which had been evolved by Harry Weslake. Most of the cylinder heads of the period were of simple 'bathtub' design, but Weslake's philosophy was to 'look after the gas'. His cylinder heads incorporated a heart-shaped combustion chamber which directed the incoming gas towards the plug. A high gas velocity was maintained into the chamber by running the wall of the chamber very close to the back of the inlet valve. This also created considerable swirl, which seemed to stratify the charge and give a richer mixture near the plug, leading to more efficient burning and improved fuel consumption. Zenith, the manufacturers of the carburettor, remarked several times that combustion in this little engine was more constant than in any other they were testing at the time.

Dr John Weaving, who was in charge of research and development at Longbridge, gleefully recalls how they tried to improve on Weslake's design by cutting off the protuberance in the combustion chamber, familiarly known to them as the 'Weslake tit'. Try as they might, they had little success, since any alterations tended to cause pinking. Eric Bareham points out that Weslake's design features determined not only the shape of the combustion chamber, but also the valve-port shapes—a point not usually recognized.

John Bishop, who was responsible for the stress-analysis work that was done on the engine, had also developed the cam profile. The shape of the cams had been determined mathematically. The idea was to produce a cam that eliminated any sudden changes in acceleration of the entire valve mechanism while a valve was opening or closing. This reduced wear on the moving parts and, at the same time, permitted higher valve lift and better engine breathing. The part of the cam profile which takes up the clearance between the tappet and the end of the valve stem is known as the ramp. Bishop designed this so that at the point of contact between the tappet and the end of the valve stem, the ramp would only be moving at about a third of the velocity of a conventional ramp. This resulted in extremely smooth valve operation, but it is worth noting that if the tappet clearances are not adjusted correctly, the velocity at the point of opening or closing may well be three or four times the design speed.

As with the earlier ohv Austin engines, the camshaft and pushrods were on the same side of the engine as the inlet and exhaust ports. This gave rise to nicely-placed, well-cooled spark plugs, but to avoid passing the pushrods through the water jacket, or through the ports themselves, siamezed inlet ports and a siamezed centre exhaust port had become necessities. Bill Appleby's contention was that while a siamezed exhaust port did call for first-class exhaust-valve materials, they never found any disadvantage in using a siamezed inlet port. In fact, he claimed it to be an advantage because the reduced volume of the induction system allowed for a quicker response to the accelerator.

Another bonus of the design was that all the electrical equipment, including distributor, plugs, starter motor and dynamo, was on the opposite side of the engine to the carburettor. This kept any potential sparks away from possible petrol drips as well as removing all the electrical gear from the heat of the exhaust manifold.

Even the exhaust heat was put to good use. With both the inlet and exhaust manifolds on the same side of the engine, it was a simple matter to produce an inlet-manifold 'hot-spot'. Thus the fuel mixture would vaporize more readily and endow the engine with its quick-warm-up characteristics.

The oil pump was unconventional, being driven from the end of the camshaft. The reason for this was to eliminate the cost of providing an extra gear to drive it, but it did mean that the pump was well above the oil level in the sump and required priming after an engine strip-down. Bill Appleby was unhappy about this arrangement, but Johnnie Rix insisted that it was a necessary economy. In fact, the pump has proved to be very successful, and you could not have a cheaper or neater assembly. A threaded plug in the crankcase wall could be removed to prime the pump after an engine rebuild, although later pumps were found to provide about a 3 ft lift when dry, so the priming plug was omitted from the design. An attempt had been made to phase the rotors of the pump in relation to the cams so that they had a damping effect on camshaft vibration.

Another point worthy of note, even though it was standard Austin practice, was the use of four rings per piston. The three compression rings, in conjunction with a lower oil-control ring, were found to give very satisfactory oil consumption and kept blow-by to a minimum. In later years, this must have been instrumental in helping the engine cope with the increasing legislation on pollution.

Once under way, the design work progressed speedily. By late 1949, components that had been made from experimental drawings were beginning to appear from the machine shops. In early 1950, a start was made on assembling the first engine. The end of March saw the engine completed and installed on a test-bed. Over the next month or two, other

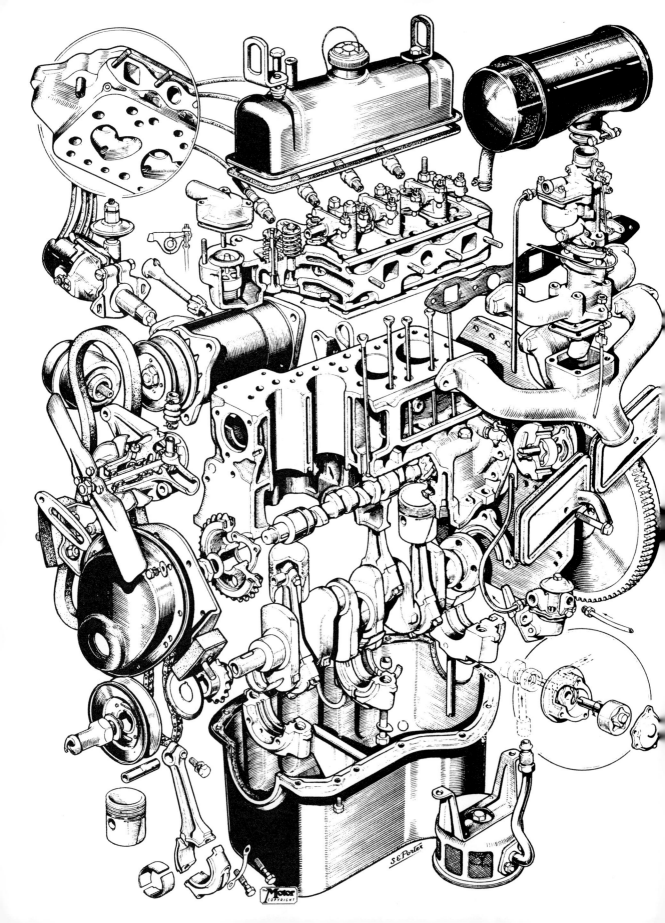

S.E. Porter

The Motor
COPYRIGHT

engines were completed and, like the first, they were subjected to endurance runs of 100 hours to test the crankshaft bearings as well as the valve gear and all the ancillaries.

Max Oliver, then in the experimental department, remembers how Alf Depper had asked him to assemble the first AS3 gearbox by handing him a box of bits and saying, 'I'd like you to put that together, Max.' There were no drawings or build instructions—in that department you had to know how to go about things and were expected to check on the fits and limits as a matter of course. Apparently, it went together with very little trouble, and in Max's words: 'George Coates had just returned from one of his merry trips abroad, so the pair of us put the gearbox on to one of the first AS3 engines and installed it in the old 8 hp. It was quite impressive—something we'd never felt before, and it was a much better gearbox.' George has his own memory of that same occasion: 'Well, it was nice to be able to set the tappets without getting your knuckles burnt. Ah, yes, that was another advantage of the overhead-valve engine.'

Eric Bareham's notes inform us that the engine for the first car was completed on 24 November 1950, and five days later it was installed in an A30 prototype.

The very earliest engines, including the one fitted to this first prototype, had an aluminium cylinder head, but the production version had a cast-iron head. Cast-iron was chosen not only because it was a familiar and reliable material, but also because it avoided any problems that might have occurred as a consequence of fitting valve-seat inserts to an aluminium head.

Weslake suggested the use of pistons with a concave crown to ensure a compact combustion space with its largest dimensions at the centre of the piston. This alteration in design meant that the compression ratio would have dropped to less than 7:1 if the original aluminium head had been fitted, and to 6.77:1 if the standard cast-iron Weslake head had been used. This was too low, but as only pool petrol was available at the time, the compression ratio

could only be raised to something like 7.2:1. This was achieved by using a Weslake cast-iron head that produced a total combustion-chamber volume of 32.3 cc. The calculations required for this head are noted in Eric Bareham's diary of 19 December 1950, and it would seem that this arrangement, along with the concave pistons, was used from engine number seven onwards.

As the bench tests continued and the early prototypes were put through their paces, one or two weaknesses began to show up which necessitated small changes in the design. At a meeting in Johnnie Rix's office in February 1951, it was decided to stiffen all the crankshaft webs and to increase the size of the bearings. The main bearings were increased from the original $1\frac{5}{8} \times 1$ in. to $1\frac{3}{4} \times 1\frac{1}{8}$ in., and the big-end bearings were increased from $1\frac{1}{8} \times \frac{3}{4}$ in. to $1\frac{1}{4} \times \frac{3}{4}$ in.

In August 1951, this engine, known as the Type II, was given 100 hours of bench testing, cycling from 2800 to 4800 rpm. At the end of the test, the con-rod bearings were found to be in bad condition and the centre main bearing was also badly worn. It was decided that a satisfactory solution would be to increase the width of the main bearings from $1\frac{1}{8}$ in. to $1\frac{3}{16}$ in., and the size of the con-rod bearings from $\frac{3}{4}$ in. to $\frac{7}{8}$ in.

During the first continental road test of the A30 at the end of November 1951, Johnnie Rix had complained from the South of France that the sump was hitting the ground on rutted roads. He requested that it be raised by 1 in.

In May 1952, an engine that was stripped after covering 35,000 miles showed signs of wear in both the oil-pump driving pin and spindle. This led to an increase of $\frac{1}{32}$ in. in the diameter of the driving pin, giving more width to the flat. The limits on the pin and pump-spindle slot were tightened to reduce the backlash that was thought to be adding to the wear. The slot in the pump spindle was also shortened to reduce any tendency for it to open out. At the same time, the oil-pump cover was stiffened because leaks had been occurring due to distortion of the cover when it was being tightened.

In production form, the engine developed 30 bhp at 4800 rpm, and it was clear that there was plenty of scope for development. It was to prove a remarkably efficient engine—even at its launch it was producing 75 per cent of the A40's horsepower, yet weighed 33 per cent less, even though the dynamo, starter and distributor were the same for both cars.

Most small cars of the day were still being turned out with primitive side-valve engines (which, in

An exploded drawing of the A30 engine which appeared in *The Motor* of 24 September 1952. The 'hot-spot' arrangement can be clearly seen where the inlet manifold bolts on to the exhaust manifold

The 803 cc engine and gearbox in October 1951. Note the mounting rubber encircling the rear end of the gearbox and the disposable oil filter. All the electrical equipment can be seen conveniently grouped on one side of the engine. *Courtesy Austin Rover*

Ford's case, would carry on for almost a further decade), so this brand-new ohv unit was a considerable factor in the new car's favour.

Few could have guessed, however, that the engine developed for the A30 (and those derived from it) would rank as one of the greatest small engines ever produced. Its history runs through a long series of Austin, BMC, BMH, BL, Austin Morris and Austin Rover cars: from the A30/35 and Minor, through the A40 Farina, Sprite, Midget and Mini, on to the 1100, 1300, Allegro and Marina, and finally (in its A-Plus form) to the Metro, Maestro and even the smallest Montegos of 1984. With this pedigree, we can see why the late Bill Appleby, shortly before his death, was prepared to agree that perhaps he and his designers 'had just about got it right'.

3
THE BUILDING AND TESTING OF PROTOTYPES

The transition from model to prototype took place in the various shops of the Longbridge experimental department.

Eric Bailey had come to Longbridge from Vanden Plas, and one of his first jobs, under Arthur West in the body design office, was to help produce the full-sized drawings of the A30 on linen-reinforced paper. The 6 ft high roll of paper was fixed to a drawing-board some 30 ft in length, soaked with water and left to shrink, producing a parchment-like finish. Then it was divided into 10 in. squares. There was much checking to avoid inaccuracies.

Several projections and views ended up on the one sheet of paper, and six or seven people would be working on it at once. The lines had to be drawn very fine indeed because they worked to an accuracy of $\frac{1}{64}$ in. As Barry Kelkin explains, 'It just had to be right. There was a superb inspector of patterns—Billy Turton—"two-thou Turton", we called him. He was a great fella, but didn't let anything go by.' The finished drawings contained not only the feature lines, but also the smoothing lines which determined the exact contours of any particular area. The propshaft movements and the steering and bump movements of the wheels were also added. The more senior draughtsmen did the layout work and the juniors the detail drawings. Barry Kelkin remembers working on the fascia of the A30 as well as the front and rear seats: 'They were the most slender seats we had done at the time, and that rear door, well, we were amazed at how small it was. We wondered if it would actually make a door.'

From the detail drawings, solid hardwood models were made of each panel. These could be bolted together on a central frame to produce a 'stacking model' of the car. Then, the pattern makers produced slightly oversize models of each panel in either softwood or plaster. These were used as patterns for casting the heavy dies for the press tools that would punch out the metal panels for the production cars.

Each rough-cast die was set up next to the mahogany model of the same panel so that a Keller profile copying machine could traverse both surfaces, milling the metal die to the shape of the mahogany. The final smoothing of the dies was done by hand.

The first prototypes, however, were built from hand-made panels, and some of this work could be speeded up by getting Billy Bedford to do the initial forming on his rubber press, a machine that had been of great service during the war. A former was placed on the lower table with the metal sheet above it. Down came a big, flat slab of hard rubber, some 15 in. deep, that forced the metal into shape. Then, the semi-formed panel could be finished by hand.

The panel beating and body building took place in Dick Gallimore's shop. Dick's only interest was his work, and he took a pride in letting nothing beat him. You had to get to know him, though, before you understood his ways. Those arriving at his elbow while he had a job in progress could talk to him as much as they liked, but he would only acknowledge their presence when he had finished. He gave his total concentration to whatever he was doing. Once, Eric Bailey approached Dick with a particular job and made a suggestion or two as to how it might be done. He soon learnt that this was not the way to approach Dick. 'Tell me what you want, but not how to do it,' was Dick's attitude. However, once you had gained his confidence, he would work wonders for you without batting an eyelid.

Many remember Dick drawing with his thick pencil on even thicker sheets of plywood to produce a pattern for whatever they had requested. This apparently haphazard approach invariably produced faultless results, and it was a situation in which Len Lord seems to have revelled. He visited the shop so frequently that they built him a special stool, and he would sit there chatting about the possibility of lopping a bit off here or there, or even of adding 3 or 4 in. to the centre of a car to produce a new model. The A70 Hampshire was one car so

produced. Lord, who obviously enjoyed bypassing his designers and stylists, was even known to ask those responsible for body design at Pressed Steel to produce him a body, saying, 'Tie in with Dick here, but don't mention it to Stanfield [his chief body designer!] if you happen to bump into him.' Fortunately, Jim Stanfield was used to Lord's tactics and when, eventually, he learnt of such projects, seemed able to take it well.

Doug Adams, who became foreman of Dick Gallimore's shop in 1959 and took over its running on Dick's retirement, was one of those who worked on the hand-beaten panels for the first A30 prototypes. Most of the panels were plain sailing for men skilled in this fascinating art, but the shaping of the bonnet and grille surround did present problems. This complex panel, with its many curves, had been designed in one piece, and with only a small bonnet opening, to add as much stiffness as possible to the box-like structure which supported the front suspension. Doug Adams remembers only too well that if you made the area on either side of the grille too deep, there was no way you could sort it out — you simply

had to start all over again. About six prototypes were built of hand-beaten panels, and they were motorized in Alf Depper's shop. Then, it fell to Bob Grice, as chief experimental and development engineer, to see them through the prototype stages.

Much of the early testing took place on the *pavé* and washboard at MIRA, the Motor Industry Research Association's test track near Nuneaton. Each car has a critical speed on the washboard; it was 25–30 mph for the A30, so instructions were given to test for 1000 miles on the washboard at this speed. Then, it went on to the *pavé* for a further 1000 miles. It was estimated that 1000 miles on either *pavé* or washboard was equivalent to the full life of a car under normal road conditions. The dust tunnel was used to find where dust might enter the car in the more extreme conditions of some potential export markets.

Running a prototype with sandbags in the boot soon showed the need for slightly beefier rear springs. The brakes were tested for fade by braking hard from 50 mph for 20 consecutive stops, and many different linings were tried to obtain the best

anti-fade results. Prototypes were regularly taken into Wales, and the brakes were well tested again by much hard driving round the Welsh mountains, particularly at Bwlch-y-Groes and Alt-y-Bady.

For a while, excessive wear of the front tyres caused much concern, and it took many testing sessions before the problem was cured by sorting out the steering geometry. The prototype dampers were adjustable, and when satisfactory settings were achieved they were put on test rigs to establish the readings from which the production dampers could be made.

The cross-shaft which operates the clutch used to knock badly. Bob Grice remembers packing the bushes with heavy grease to see if it would help. It was to no avail, so the oval plates that retain the bushes were made of heavier-gauge metal to hold the bearings more firmly. At chassis number 13,675, the solid inner bush was replaced by a rubber one that had a brass lining with shallow pockets to help retain the lubricant and provide quieter operation. It is no surprise that the clutch pedal rattled, and still does rattle on a car that has perished engine

mounting rubbers or which is not in perfect tune. A glance at the two slots in the panel through which the pedals pass reveals why. The brake pedal, which has no lateral movement to allow for, passes through a wide slot, while the clutch pedal, which rocks sideways in unison with any vibration of the engine and gearbox, passes through a narrow slot. Somehow, between the drawing stage and the production stage, the arrangement of the slots seems to have been accidentally transposed.

There was close liaison between the Longbridge experimental department and the major suppliers of components such as brakes, dampers, carburettors and clutches. In those days, the department had such an enviable reputation that the senior representatives of all the component firms spent much time collaborating with them. At times, it seemed that Longbridge was doing much of the donkey work for the trade in general.

The first continental road test of the AS3 took place in November and December 1951. Two AS3s, LOP 855 (right-hand drive) and LOP 854 (left-hand drive), were accompanied by three A40 Somersets for a complete test in France, Spain and Belgium. The Longbridge party was led by Harry Broom and included Gil Jones from development, George Coates, Roger Lewis and Max Oliver from experimental, and Arthur West from design, as well as representatives from Zenith, Lockheed and Armstrong Patents. Bob Grice was in charge and he, Johnnie Rix and Jim Stanfield flew out to meet the test party at certain points on the route.

When Bob Grice hears people recounting examples of Len Lord's stubbornness, he is reminded that on this trip it almost certainly saved his life. Bob's plane had touched down in France before crossing the Pyrenees, so he had taken the opportunity of phoning Lord to discuss a matter of some importance. Lord kept him talking, saying, 'Forget your plane, there'll be another one.' When, eventually, Bob crossed the mountains by night, he noticed a large fire—the plane he would have been on had flown straight into the side of a mountain.

The main party sailed from Newhaven to Dieppe, travelling south through France to Bordeaux and carrying on through the Pyrenees into Spain, where extensive testing took place. They made use of the Rio Tinto area to carry out dust trials by selecting circuits that consisted of dirt and secondary roads. The high-altitude testing took place in the Sierra Nevada, where they could reach over 11,000 ft on Europe's highest road. The return journey was made through France and Belgium.

It was hard work. For four of the six weeks, it meant a different bed each night. Trying to fit in a bit of sightseeing took some doing, by the time they had seen to the cars and written any necessary reports. Those keen on some night life managed it, of course, but paid for it the next morning when they had to be up at the crack of dawn to prepare for the day's run. In those early post-war days, however, they were considered to be among the privileged few—staying in the best hotels and eating foods that had not been seen since before the war.

The continental test confirmed that the chassisless baby Austin could tackle the worst of roads without any obvious shake or deflection of the structure. The test also did its job in highlighting the weak points of the prototypes.

The steering felt noticeably light, but under the heavily-laden conditions of the test the cars steered quite well and were found to be particularly good on mountain passes and when manoeuvring in traffic. The mistral, blowing through gaps between the pines on the roads of southern France, did make things a little tricky. George Coates stopped the con-

voy when he found the wind taking charge of the steering. Johnnie Rix was sceptical at first but, after trying the car himself, had to agree that considerable concentration was needed to keep the car on the desired path and prevent it from wandering perilously close to the oncoming traffic. Work continued on solving this problem when they returned to England. A slightly wider rear track, allied with an improvement in the front dampers, helped things somewhat by decreasing the roll effect caused by sudden gusts of wind.

Draughts from the front doors were one of the worst features of the car. They came from around the edges of the removable door casings and from the top and bottom edges of the windows. There were also draughts from the outer edges of the doors themselves. During the main part of the journey there was little entry of dust, but in the Rio Tinto area the dust blew in freely when the windows were dropped about 3 in. Closing the windows kept out the dust, but neither passenger nor driver could carry on without ventilation from an open window. The heater was satisfactory, but the draughts from around the front doors meant that the occupants were warm on one side and cold on the other.

The front spring pans became buckled in a similar manner to those in previous tests in England, but this was put right by a minor modification that prevented concentration of the load on the inner edge of the pan. The rear springs were too long in relation to body clearance and were fouling at the rear shackles.

The most serious trouble occurred with the road wheels. Fractures appeared after the wheels had been subjected to repeated side thrusts when cornering in the Pyrenees. Well into the mountains, Harry Broom shouted for George Coates to stop. After crossing a gulley, as they ran downhill they had heard a pronounced click, followed by a continuous tinkling noise from the rear of the car. On removing a hub cap, they found that the wheel was split all the way round. Further inspection showed others with signs of cracking too. They had no option but to roll gently down to the next village where they managed to sort out some $\frac{1}{2}$ in. rod, stripped off all the tyres, and welded hoops over the cracks. On reaching Madrid, they sent for new wheels and tyres, and as a result of the test, a heavier-gauge metal was chosen for the wheels.

Max Oliver remembers it was a little unnerving to be dashing around mountains on suspect wheels. One day, in the Sierra Nevada, Gil Jones was really stepping on it, with Max in the second A30 doing

Pictures from the first continental test of the AS3. Clockwise
from top left: a prototype being hoisted aboard the
Newhaven–Dieppe ferry; a stop for refreshments near Jerez
in Spain; a Somerset and two AS3s in the French Pyrenees;
the cars in the Maritime Alps; en route from Malaga to
Madrid; an A30 high in the Sierra Nevada (this photo was
taken on a later trip). *Courtesy Bob Grice*

LEFT Wheel trouble in the Pyrenees. The test party inspect the cracked wheels, while Roger Lewis (far right) does what a man has to do! It is definitely Roger. His wife, Sylvia, says she would know that stance anywhere! *Courtesy Gil Jones*

ABOVE A member of the test party checks the knocking big-end on Gil Jones' car. From left to right, we can make out Bob Grice, Harry Broom and Johnnie Rix. *Courtesy Gil Jones*

LEFT October 1951. Bob Grice uses a pre-release prototype to demonstrate how the 'Flying A' motif is used to open the bonnet

his best to keep up. After 15 or 20 miles, the three A40s had dropped far behind. The sheer drop on one side and the rock face on the other meant that motoring was not for the faint-hearted, but Gil continued to bat along, even after one of his rear wheels had commenced its customary wobble. It took a great deal of light flashing by Max to convince Gil that everything was not quite in apple-pie order. When, eventually, he stopped, he was a little shocked to find his offside rear wheel collapsing under the car.

Wheel problems apart, the ride seemed remarkably good, although the dampers did lose considerable resistance in the warmer climate. High-velocity bumps caused a fair bit of bumping-through, and this pointed to the need for a substantial improvement in damper performance.

The gearboxes had not performed well at all. The synchromesh was poor and there had been much jumping out of gear. However, they were not of the latest type that had stronger synchro springs and a modified synchro cone angle.

The rear axle on LOP 855 was quite noisy on both drive and overrun. In the main, this appears to have been caused by slackness in the threads of the set screws holding the crown-wheel assembly to the differential case.

The brakes were thought to be perfectly satisfactory for all normal conditions, but had required high pedal pressures when heavily laden in the mountains. Both cars had carried a heavy load of driver, passenger, luggage and spares. Some 35 years after the test, you could still see the impression made by the spare wheel on George Coates' case due to the weight that was packed upon it. Even so, third gear was the lowest necessary for negotiating the majority of hills. Second gear was only used when climbing the very steepest hills or when speed was lost on hairpins. They found 50 mph to be a comfortable cruising speed, and fuel consumption averaged out at 40 mpg.

A con-rod bearing failed on LOP 854 after 4700 miles, but neither car had the latest type of engine with larger bearings. It was Gil Jones who ran the bearings. Some of the others were not too pleased with him. However, Gil was undeterred—he was there to put the car through its paces and discover its weaknesses.

One reason for Gil's unpopularity was that they were carrying no replacement shells, so the car had to be towed all the way home from southern Spain. Thus, Gil found himself on the end of a tow rope behind a prototype A40 for several hundred miles,

attempting to maintain the required concentration while peering through a spray-covered screen.

The damaged car was driven carefully through the towns, not only because this was easier than towing it in traffic, but also because it simply would not have done for the new Austin to be seen in such difficulties. Eventually, the others persuaded Gil to let them give him a break. Soon after Max Oliver took over, the wipers packed up. Harry Lad of Armstrongs came to the rescue, managing to wipe the screen as they were towed along by trapping a cloth behind the long T-spanner which he used on the dampers.

The day they arrived in Angoulême had been a tough one. Being extremely hungry, Max Oliver and Roger Lewis changed for dinner in record time and made their own way to the dining room instead of waiting for the others. During dinner, Harry Broom made it obvious that he was none too pleased with them, and it became even more obvious when, afterwards, he asked the pair of them to fit a new set of shells to Gil's car. Heaven knows where he had obtained them. Having wined and dined well, Roger and Max simply put on their overalls over their best suits, crawled under the car and set to work. George Coates was then asked to give the car a test run, only to return ten minutes later with the bearings gone again. The job had probably been unsuccessful due to working with insufficient light and without any compressed air to blow out the oil passages in the crank. Towing was resumed with Brussels as the eventual destination.

A new engine and gearbox were waiting in Brussels, and Max Oliver and Roger Lewis installed them on arrival. They suggested transferring the old engine number as well, to keep the customs happy, but Harry Broom told them to forget it. If only he had listened. The bonnet was raised by a customs officer at Dover and the ill-fated car was unable to complete its journey back to Longbridge—it was impounded for six weeks until the original engine had been shipped back to Dover.

When the cars returned to Longbridge, they were stripped completely and all parts checked for wear. The oil consumption of LOP 855 had been rather high at 1200 mpg. Although some was leaking from the front sump cork and from the region of the tappet cover, the amount of smoke emitted from the exhaust suggested that most of the oil was being consumed in the engine. The oil-control rings and their grooves had worn more than expected, and the gaps in the rings were found to be excessive, as were the piston-skirt clearances.

Until the bearing trouble, LOP 854 had returned an oil consumption of 2000 mpg, apparently due to smaller skirt clearances and the fact that the compression rings were a better fit. However, this engine showed more wear, the cylinder bore wear being an average of 0.002 in. after 4700 miles, compared with 0.0016 in. after 9000 miles on LOP 855. Maximum bore wear occurred in no. 1 cylinder, and this appeared to be linked with water-circulation problems. Excessive distortion was found on the heads of the two centre exhaust valves, but the trouble was overcome by producing a head with modified water circulation between the two centre valves.

Timing-chain rattle had been very noticeable on LOP 854 and quite bad on LOP 855. The final inspection showed excessive slackness in the chains, but the noise seemed to be due to misalignment of the camshaft and crankshaft sprockets, causing side contact between the chain and sprocket teeth.

On 31 December 1951, Ben James set out on a further continental trip in an AS3 with all the weaknesses attended to. Accompanied by a Somerset, he travelled through France and Italy as far as Pisa. The return trip involved much driving through snow, particularly over the mountains between Pisa and Bologna and between Bologna and Altdorf. Back at the works, however, the car was found to be in good shape and there was nothing unusual to report.

Much day and night testing took place in the UK to see what happened as the miles accrued. Dick Perry, the present chief executive of the car division of Rolls-Royce and an Austin apprentice during 1948-52, is remembered by many for knocking up phenomenal overnight mileages in an A30. As chairman of the apprentices, he spoke at their annual dinner in December 1951, congratulating the management on their foresight in 'entrusting the apprentices with a Seven to be run to death'. Using a car that would have already clocked up about 400 miles during the day, he and his co-driver would add at least another 400 miles between 7 pm and 7 am by driving to Anglesey and back, via a circuitous route. Dick still managed to become such a regular at one pub en route that he even made it into the local darts team.

At least two cars were to cover 50,000 miles of testing in three months of 1952. An incident which took place in Wales during those particular tests reminded ex-apprentice Malcolm Gardner that the very early A30s had bolts securing the wheels, as opposed to studs and nuts. They found that the nearside rear hub cap would fly off after about 200 miles due to the bolts unscrewing themselves. After tightening things up, they would simply set off again. The design department did not agree to their suggestion of fitting studs and nuts because it would have cost a few extra pence per car and they were working to a very tight budget. Instead, they produced a wheel spanner that gave more leverage, allowing 230 miles to be covered before a hub cap flew off! One day in Wales, the wheel itself came off and the car overturned. Luckily, there were no injuries and only minor damage was sustained. The wheel had come off because continual slackening and retightening had caused the holes in it to become larger than the retaining bolts. The usual early-warning system of a departing hub cap had become inoperative, as the cap could remain on the departing wheel! After that incident, it was accepted that studs and nuts were the best solution.

The testing of the A30 prototypes was drawing to a close. Bob Grice, who is still remembered as a 'very professional, no-nonsense head of testing', was satisfied that the car was ready for the road.

4

THE LAUNCH OF THE NEW BABY

It was common knowledge that a new Austin Seven was on the way, but as all the testing had taken place in remote areas or under cover of darkness, the details of the car had remained secret.

It was not that the press had not tried. As the launch date approached, they haunted the area surrounding the works. One newspaper had even used a light plane in its quest for a scoop, but the official pre-release photos were taken in a special session arranged at Longbridge.

Much was made of the new car's links with the past. Publicity by Smiths Motor Accessories was typical: 'My! How you've grown', ran their advertisement in *The Autocar*, '. . . but you still use Smiths. What car ever won the hearts of motorists so completely as the first, friendly little Austin Seven did, from the moment it was introduced? Smiths instruments were a part of its endearing reliability then—and recorded its impudent performance. Now the Austin has come back to us, transformed in everything but the virtues that have kept its memory warm; and of course, Smiths are in it again, very proud to be there, and very happy to renew the old friendship.'

The Austin Magazine of November 1951 told its readers that 'The first faint whispers of the possibility of the reintroduction of this famous car aroused such widespread public enthusiasm, and the numbers of enquiries for more information which have poured into Longbridge from all parts of the world have been so enormous, as to leave no doubt about the potential popularity of this comeback.' The same magazine went on to proclaim, 'At last the long-awaited day has dawned! The Austin "Seven" is once more on show, and this "baby" has everything—all the qualities of its predecessors plus. . .!'

There is no doubt that the car was one of the highlights of the 1951 Earls Court Motor Show. A new Seven, after so many years, was quite an event. Besides, there was little else new to be seen. Apart

ABOVE **Thirty years of progress. Bob Grice and Roger Lewis assist the photographer in comparing the 1922 model with that for 1952. The 'New Seven' still awaits its Austin badging. Before a similar photograph was published in** *Worldwide*, **the number plates were doctored to read 'New 7' and 'Old 7' in order to hammer home the point.** *Courtesy David Lewis*

TOP **October 1951. Still under wraps, the new car makes its way down the test-hill inside the works.** *Courtesy David Lewis*

The Motor Show

October 1951

Making its bow—the new Austin Seven, taking pride of place on the Austin stand.

The new Austin Seven engine and gear box unit partly sectioned. The sump extends up to the centre line of the crankshaft. The depth of the gear box is reduced by placing the shafts side by side and putting the selectors on the side of the box instead of on top. The water thermostat is housed in the cylinder head casting.

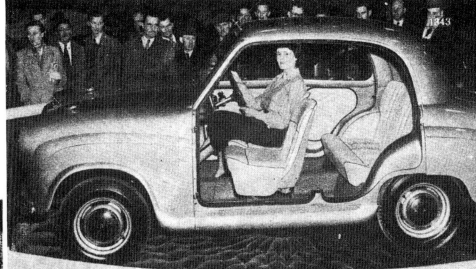

Doors and centre pillar are removed from one side of the Austin Seven saloon to reveal details of the seating accommodation. This is one of the Show's most popular exhibits.

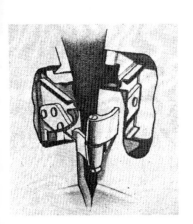

To avoid the use of a thick door, the new Austin Seven has external hinges. The forming of the sheet steel at this point is interesting.

There's a fence round it, so can't try what it feels like to be a driver. A pity, because the new Austin Seven . . . just about the right size.

ABOVE Another way in which the public were reminded of the car's pedigree. Harry Austin, Herbert's brother, was brought in on the act. The line-up consists of a 1909 single-cylinder 7 hp Austin, a 1922 7 hp Chummy and a 1951 A30 Seven. The 'Austin of England' sign on the new car assembly building provides a suitable backcloth. *Courtesy Austin Rover*

LEFT Photographs from the Earls Court Show which appeared in *The Autocar* during October 1951

from Vauxhall's Velox and Wyvern, you had to go into the realms of Daimlers and Healeys to find other major changes.

The car 'completely stole the show', claimed *Worldwide*, and was 'undoubtedly the outstanding novelty', said *Automotive Industries*, while the technical editor of *British Automobiles Overseas* proclaimed that 'An event eagerly awaited in all parts of the world has come to pass with the reintroduction of the Austin Seven.'

Motor Industry of 17 October 1951 offered the compliment that 'undoubtedly the Seven is the nearest approach yet made to the perfectly scaled-down big car', and in an article entitled 'Once More an Austin Seven', *The Autocar* of 19 October developed this theme: '. . . there is about it a fineness of line which is not easily achieved in small cars. So well proportioned is the little Austin that it does not give the appearance of being small; yet it is. . . for the wheelbase is but 6 ft 7 in. . . the overall length 11 ft 4⅝ in. and height 4 ft 10 in. Within these small dimensions, however, clever designing has made the utmost use of the passenger space, so that four adults can be quite comfortably accommodated. Moreover, they are seated within the wheelbase, for the squab of the rear seat is approximately in line with the centre line of the axle.'

Although the car was launched in October 1951, it was not scheduled to go into production until May the following year, and as the prototypes had not yet undertaken their continental testing, they could hardly be made available for road testing by the press. For the time being, they would have to make do by describing the car as they saw it and by detailing its specification.

It was natural that much was made of Austin's first essay in unitary construction, and those who had taken time to scrutinize the details were obviously quite impressed. Even the exposed door hinges were accepted as a clever way of reducing door thickness, and the efforts which had been made to eliminate soldered joints in the body were much mentioned.

As the mechanical specification of the car was quite orthodox, there was little for the press to do but pass on the details. The four-cylinder engine, clutch and gearbox were all seen as following designs that had already been well proven on other Longbridge products. The independent front suspension, of wishbone and coil-spring variety, and the semi-elliptic springing at the rear were accepted in the same light.

Something a little different could be found in the braking system, where a normal hydraulic set-up at the front was combined with a unique idea at the rear. On depression of the brake pedal, the rear brakes were applied by a hydraulic cylinder mounted in a frame that was linked mechanically to the rear brakes. The handbrake cleverly utilized the same mechanical linkage but quite independently of the footbrake.

With no test cars available, it was hardly possible to compare the car with its competitors, but in his 'Report For The Man With The Smaller Pocket' in *The Autocar* of 26 October 1951, Michael Clayton did try to remind readers of the range of small cars available. Of the new Seven, he wrote: '. . . the advent of the new Austin Seven must be an occasion for jubilation. Those who have been thronging the appropriate stand at the Show will have noticed so many points which can never be really appreciated without a personal inspection. Predominantly, delight is registered because the car is in the real Seven tradition. Everything, although comfortable, is simple: the seats are light and neat; there is room for four, and four only, without an inch of waste space. . . .' He continued: '. . . but what about the appearance? Photographs tend to suggest that it may

ABOVE The 'New Seven' as the centre-piece in the 'old showroom'. By applying to their supervisor, employees could obtain a ticket to view it. Over 20,000 took the opportunity. At one stage, there was a queue six or eight deep which stretched way up the Bristol Road and well into Longbridge Lane. *Courtesy Austin Rover*

ABOVE October 1951. Bob Grice demonstrates the carrying capacity of a prototype's boot. The boot lid was designed to swing upwards and outwards to clear the bodywork. On a wet day, any water on the lid's surface was deposited on to the luggage. Halfway through AS3 production, the lid was given external hinges which allowed a wider boot opening and ensured that most surface water was displaced into the drainage channels. *Courtesy Bob Grice*

ABOVE The combined door handle, door-pull and window lock was designed so that no handles protruded into the passenger space. Access to the window-lift mechanism was easily obtained by removing the millboard panel from its rubber surround. *Courtesy Austin Rover*

BELOW Drawings from *The Autocar* of 19 October 1951, illustrating the dimensions and full details of the 'New Seven' construction

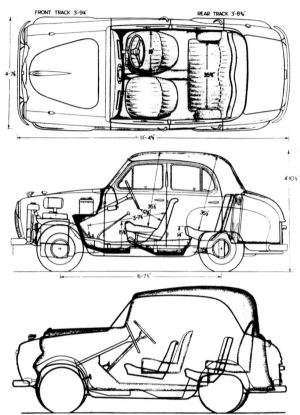

The bonnet-opening of the A30—adequate in size, yet kept to a minimum in an effort to produce a strong front-end structure. This prototype (in November 1951) is devoid of the new Austin 'winged-wheel' badge which was placed just above the grille on the production AS3. *Courtesy Austin Rover*

November 1952. Early AS3s had no boot handle. The boot was opened by inserting a T-key below the 'Austin of England' badge. Note that the prototypes and early production cars had a single rear light. Subsequent changes in lighting regulations saw the introduction of twin rear reflectors, followed by twin rear lights. *Courtesy Austin Rover*

be too much in the modern manner for such a small car, with many a moulding in a short span of car. When seen, however, this does not prove to be so, because all the mouldings are small and shallow and entirely in keeping.'

Clayton went on to look at other small cars which, 'Although suffering from the glamour of the new Austin's arrival. . .are formidable performers which have already shown their paces.' The Morris Minor, of course, was one of these, and he wrote of it, 'The Minor is most famous for its superb roadholding, which enables almost any reasonable bend to be taken at speeds limited only by traffic conditions and the power available. This quite exceptionally good behaviour is assisted by the steering, which combines lightness with exceptional accuracy. . .it handles even better than some less comfortable chariots which fall under the sports car heading.' How would the new Austin compare? With competition like that, it would obviously need to be quite a car if it was to achieve the standing of its illustrious predecessor, but the only comparison which could be made at that time lay in the pricing of the two cars. With purchase tax included, a two-door Minor stood at £519 10s 0d, and the four-door at £569 5s 7d. The early A30 was only available in the four-door version, undercutting both Morrises at £507 5s 7d.

However, the selling price did not bear too much relation to production costs. In *The Leyland Papers*, Graham Turner tells us of Len Lord's determination to emerge the winner in the Austin/Morris rivalry stakes. He also tells us that Joe Edwards, who was later to become managing director of the British Motor Corporation, is reputed to have said, 'We always had our cars within £10 of Nuffield. Len would ask, ''What's the A30 going to cost?'' ''Ex-works £300, selling price £525,'' somebody would say. ''What's Nuffield's bloody figure then?'' Len would ask. ''£515.'' ''Right, make ours £510.'''

The old Ford Anglia, of course, was still soldiering on, and would do so in the guise of the Popular for several years yet. Although the Anglia was way behind the Austin and Morris in terms of roadholding, performance and petrol consumption, it was on offer at £480 and had a reputation for extremely-low overall running costs.

Import restrictions saw to it that, for some time, there would be little competition from foreign cars. In any case, we still believed in the high quality of British cars, and the days of buying a foreign car and then justifying the decision by telling all and sundry how marvellous it was, while forgiving it not

ABOVE **This left-hand-drive AS3 was photographed in May 1953, but the changes it shows had all taken place at body number 2006 in the autumn of 1952. The trafficator switch was moved to the extreme right or left of the fascia to suit rhd or lhd cars, a blanking plate covering the hole used previously. In the earliest cars, the switch for the optional heater was placed on a separate bracket below the fascia, but it would now use this blanked hole. The ignition switch was operated with a key.** *Courtesy Austin Rover*

TOP **Early AS3 (June 1952) fitted with optional radio. There was no ignition key, simply a turn button marked 'I' to the left of the circular speedometer. This photo also shows the position of the trafficator switch on the earliest cars. The 70 mph speedometer included a fuel gauge as well as warning lights for main beam, low oil pressure and lack of charge. The horn button is on the end of the lighting control arm seen to the right of the wheel.** *Courtesy Austin Rover*

only its faults but also the expensive servicing and catastrophic depreciation, were not yet upon us.

Even so, very few of the early A30s would reach the home market. Canada was the favoured destination initially, 100 of the first 1000 cars ending up there. Austin had been proud to announce that, in the previous three years, they had received £17,000,000 from their Canadian subsidiary. A reminder of those times is their claim that this was 'enough to pay for the meat ration for the entire nation for 11 weeks.' It was hoped that the new Seven would add to these achievements.

Although launched as a 'New Seven', the little car was gradually weaned from that name. For a while, it was referred to as the A30 Seven, but eventually was allowed out into the world in its own right as the Austin A30. Whatever it was called, we can positively classify the first production run as the AS3 series, of which 30,036 examples were built.

Between October 1951 and May 1952, about a dozen pre-production prototypes had been put through their paces. Only then did normal production commence. Car 114, in Cotswold beige, was the first produced. It went undated in the records, but it is recorded that car 118 passed its final inspection on 3 May 1952; thus a May start is attributable to the production cars. Car 139, in Powder blue, was the first car produced for the home market, but the vast majority of the first 5000 were exported.

Just the ticket! The police department in Medford, Massachusetts, USA, found this A30 a handy little vehicle for checking parking violations. *Courtesy Austin Rover*

They did not go to Canada alone. Car 241 went to Helsinki to be used by the British Olympic Team, along with some A40s and A70s. This was a useful piece of international publicity. A30s were soon being dispatched to countries as numerous as those from which the athletes had come.

By the end of 1952, only about 4000 A30s had been built, so an A30 first registered in Britain in 1952 is rare indeed. Cars 2702–2749 went CKD (Completely Knocked Down) to Dublin, where they were assembled by Lincoln and Nolan. By the spring of 1953, shipments of CKD A30s were going to South Africa, Australia and New Zealand in quite large numbers.

The British public had to wait until October 1952, a year after the initial launch, before *The Autocar* was able to bring them their first road test of the new Seven. Their report considered the performance to be quite satisfactory, and under test a mean speed of 62 mph was achieved. The car managed to hold its own with other small cars on the road, and the engine was lively and flexible, although on the car tested there appeared to be some transmission vibration. Slight difficulty was occasionally experienced in engaging both first and reverse gears, but the clutch was found to be very smooth and sweet, requiring only a very light pedal pressure.

The suspension was said to provide a stable and comfortable car in both the one-up and fully-laden conditions. This was acclaimed as 'no mean feat' in so small a car, where the variable load is a much greater proportion of the total car weight than it is in larger cars.

We can see that the A30 was still a very scarce commodity, because *The Motor* was to test the same car (MOK 420) the following month, and *Motor Sport* would have to wait until May 1953 before it got behind the same steering wheel. As *The Motor* said in November 1952, 'Comparatively few people outside the immediate trade circle have had an opportunity of sampling the car for themselves', and observed, '. . . it can be said right away that this new example of the Seven is a car which will exactly fit the bill for many thousands of motorists and potential car users, both in this country and abroad.' The car was said to 'offer a surprising combination of comfort and compactness. . . in every way a very roadworthy little car.'

Whereas *The Autocar* had found that 'at the top end of the speed range there is a definite impression that parts of the little engine are moving very quickly', *The Motor* thought, '. . . it propels the car at comfortably over the mile-a-minute mark when

This opening and closing A30 created a great deal of interest at all the major motor shows during 1952–53. It is seen here in Geneva. *Courtesy Emil Frey*

required and it reveals no sign of distress when driven flat-out for considerable periods.' They also commented on the flexibility of the engine, finding that the car would travel comfortably at speeds as low as 12 mph in top gear in a slow stream of traffic. It was suggested that petrol consumption could be expected to be around the 40 mpg mark under normal driving conditions.

Clutch operation was considered a great improvement on the delicate touch required with the prewar Seven, but once again engaging the lower gears while stationary was found to be rather difficult.

Handling qualities were thought to be most satisfying, making for a car that 'is particularly easy to thread in and out of traffic, while retaining a very pleasant degree of roadworthiness when being driven fast in the open country.' Rolling was said to be almost entirely absent, and this feature was thought to be 'particularly praiseworthy in view of the modest track.' There was more praise for the suspension, and they felt that, taken together, 'the handling and suspension qualities of this car can be classed as good by any standards, and particularly good for a model of such compact dimensions, where the provision of roadworthiness and comfort offer very much more difficult problems for the designer.' The very effective handbrake also received due praise.

The controls did come in for some criticism, particularly the difficulty a long-legged driver had of holding the throttle in the half-open position over a long period, and the fact that to reach the dipped headlight position, it was necessary to go through the full-beam position first.

The report agreed with others in its liking of the driving position, excellent view of the road and the extremely comfortable front seats for a car of this size. It continued: 'The back seats, too, earn praise for the good all-round support which they offer and, whilst knee room is naturally limited, this Austin Seven will very definitely carry four full-sized occupants in comfort.' Luggage accommodation was thought to be surprisingly good, considering the overall size of the car.

In short, the new Seven was considered to offer a fully-fledged car to a section of the motoring public to whom economy was of paramount importance. The only real criticism was a valid one: 'The rather unusual handles inside the four doors, which move one way to secure the counter-balanced window panes and the other to release the door catch, can easily open the door when it is intended to simply unlock the window. There are no markings to explain their dual function and they only escape classification as dangerous because the doors are hinged from their forward edges.'

Motor Sport was known to give any new car quite a searching test, and that could be one of the reasons why it took them so long to obtain the same car. However, after covering 594 very varied miles, they were able to report that no oil or water had been required and no trouble experienced, except that a knob had come adrift from the radio. Indeed, they wrote, 'Our outstanding impressions of the current Austin Seven are of an excellent road performance from its very game engine, accomplished with a high degree of smoothness and lack of fuss, outstandingly good brakes, and very pleasant steering.'

They did think that the car was 'not strictly the economy car we all require', nor did they think it a true four-seater; they thought it fell between the two. Mind you, they did concede that it scored 'as a 40 mpg plus car which is priced competitively, and which possesses acceleration and speed which make main road journeys anything but tedious.'

The report was compiled by Bill Boddy, and it was quite a compliment to the car that he should write, '. . . the A30 cruises silently and smoothly at 45 mph and, with no more indication of fuss than a slight intrusion of engine noise, will hold a speedometer 60 mph, or slightly more, as a matter of course. Not only this, but there is a real surge of acceleration available from 20 to 50 mph in top, and the Austin will tackle very steep hills without a change of gear . . . the engine gains full marks as a very smooth and lively one.'

A question mark was placed against the gap between third and top gear, but it was thought that 'forward visibility could not be better', and even the pedals were said to be 'of adequate size and well placed'.

The Lockheed brakes received high praise, being considered 'well nigh perfect, calling for only light pedal pressures in normal usage, yet being extremely powerful, and pulling the car up silently in a dead straight line in emergency with no fade tendencies. The right-hand handbrake holds well on hills and is convenient to use.'

They did find the handling a little less than perfect, however. As Bill Boddy put it: 'In a car which goes along so very willingly, handling qualities are of considerable importance. It must be said at once that the Austin Seven does not possess such good controllability as its near-relation, the Morris Minor. It has a narrower track and is higher, so that steering it on a wet road in a strong crosswind, or at its terminal velocity downhill, is rather like we imagine tightrope walking to be—alright if you keep going straight. The suspension is soft, giving a comfortable, pitch-free if somewhat lively ride, but this induces considerable roll-oversteer which spoils the cornering properties. In extreme conditions the roll is sufficiently excessive to lift an inside back wheel. Very pleasant high-geared steering largely offsets

this, and perhaps the fairest way to express the matter is to say that the A30 is controllable but not enjoyably so.'

To sum up, it was suggested that the A30 would represent very good transport at a moderate purchase price and that it was the best model in the existing Austin range.

With that *Motor Sport* report we begin to see comparisons being made with the already legendary roadholding of the Morris Minor. Perhaps the management's preoccupation with the idea that the new Seven must emulate the old had led to excessive constraints being placed on its designers. The width of the A30 had been arrived at as the minimum which could be used to seat two abreast without undue discomfort and with the tenor of the pre-war Seven very much in mind. As we have seen already, the same 'minimum dimensions' thinking led to the A30 being shortened by some $4\frac{1}{2}$ in. when well into the design stage, resulting in an overall increase in height. This, allied to the narrow track, was not a recipe to enhance its roadholding or to allow full use of the excellent performance that was on offer.

Issigonis had purposely designed the Minor with torsion-bar front suspension and rack-and-pinion steering, and he had placed the engine well forward to ensure a very stable car, but its excellent roadholding must also have been enhanced by the free hand he was given throughout the design process. How they determined the width for the Morris is well related by Paul Skilleter in his excellent book, *Morris Minor*. He quotes Issigonis: 'I wasn't very happy with the final version of the Morris Minor. So I went to the shop one evening and I told my mechanics to cut the car in half. Then I went in the morning and we moved it apart—ah, too much; ah, too little—no, a bit more that way—that's it!'

It appears that when the car had been widened by 4 in., Issigonis felt the proportions to be right. The increase in width, from 57 in. to 61 in., must have been instrumental in imparting a considerable extra measure of stability to the car. The A30, being some 6 in. narrower, was going to be hard pressed to compete in this respect.

That was not all. Once again, mergers were in the air. Finally, in July 1952, the merger between Austin and Morris took place. The days of the British Motor Corporation (BMC) had arrived. It was more than a little ironic. The A30, Len Lord's competitor for the Minor, had just come into full production. The merger meant that it would share its greatest asset, the lively and economical overhead-valve engine, with its chief rival.

5

THE A30 – MIDST MERGERS AND MISGIVINGS

Yes, it was a very young A30 that was asked to share its engine with the Series II Minor. Many Austin men were more than a little perturbed to see the opposition gain such benefits but, for their part, the Morris men were not necessarily impressed by Austin's generosity.

The rivalry between Longbridge and Cowley had become almost a tradition. Len Lord was at Austin, but in the mid-1930s he had made his name at Morris until a row with Nuffield brought about his departure. Meanwhile, it seems that Herbert Austin had been quietly noting Lord's achievements and took this opportunity of acquiring his services. Bob Wyatt, in his book *The Austin 1905–1952*, suggests that 'Austin had chosen Lord partly for his undoubted organizing and engineering ability, but also because he knew Lord would do everything in his power to beat Nuffield as a car maker.' Lord certainly relished this opportunity, declaring that he would now take Cowley apart, 'brick by bloody brick'. No wonder the merger that formed BMC left Morris men a little dismayed. An avowed opponent of Cowley would now be able to have his way with them.

Lord or no Lord, such a merger was bound to be difficult, and the proposal to install the A30's engine in the Minor produced one of the first of many post-merger arguments. There had been plans to replace the Minor's outdated side-valve engine, which it had inherited from the Series E Morris, by an overhead-valve version that had been developed for the Wolseley Eight. Paul Skilleter, writing in his book on the Minor, tells us, 'Preparations for the use of the Wolseley engine were quite advanced. . . . Then Austin arrived, and in the name of rationalization it was decreed that the new Minor would be getting the A30's 803 cc ohv power unit. This was a sad blow to many of those in the engineering team at Cowley, who saw their Wolseley-engined car sink without trace.'

Others have suggested that the decision to use the 803 cc Austin engine in the Minor was not only a Leonard Lord decree, but one taken with arrogant relish. How we see things, of course, depends very much on our point of view, and although Austin men were all too aware of Len Lord's temperament, they have rather different stories to tell of events after the merger. Joe Edwards, for one, is in no doubt about how and why the Austin engine ended up in the Minor. Soon after the merger, a costing exercise was done on all major components, such as engines, gearboxes and back axles. The different units were laid out in the basement of the 'Kremlin'* at Longbridge and each was labelled with its component costs. It proved an interesting exercise. The cost of producing similar items within the newly-formed group was found to vary enormously. So too did the cost of buying in identical items from the same source, depending on who had negotiated the purchase and in what quantities. Joe Edwards explains that after this exercise, he found himself having to persuade George Harriman that the 803 cc engine should go in the Minor.

Bill Appleby was asked to submit a power unit, comprising engine and gearbox, to the Cowley experimental department. He recalled: 'They accepted it after lengthy testing. We were all aware that the 803 cc engine was small for the heavier Morris Minor. I saw the drawings of the 918 cc Morris ohv engine at Engines Branch, Coventry, but at that time they were not in a position to produce the necessary quantities.'

Even Sir Alec Issigonis was to tell Paul Skilleter, '. . . the A-series was already in full production, so Harriman very rightly said, look, there's no point in tooling up for your engine, use the A-series, so we did. And it gave the car a new lease of life.' Production figures for the Minor bear out Sir Alec's

*It is uncertain who dreamt up this name for the impressive administration block at Longbridge. Whoever did would no doubt be delighted to know that the name caught on and has been used by one and all for over 35 years.

statement. In the first full year of the ohv-engined Minor, there was a 50 per cent increase in production over the last full year of the side-valve version. Engine designer Eric Bareham remembers having 'an entirely agreeable liaison with the Cowley engineering staff. Some rivalry and mutual criticisms there certainly were, but as engineers we all spoke the same language and, having been set problems, proceeded to solve them in the only way we knew.'

A fair amount of criticism was levelled at the A30's gearbox, particularly in relation to its use in the Minor, but as Bill Appleby saw it: 'Bill Ellcock, who was superintendent of chassis design at Austin, was responsible for the gearbox. I never had occasion to question the ratios. Billy Ellcock was a highly-experienced designer, commanding great respect for his engineering knowledge. I do not believe he would get the ratios wrong for the majority of drivers, but doubtless they could have been better for the high-speed driver who liked to keep his car moving near maximum speed. The ratios in the Austin gearbox followed standard practice. Austin cars sold exceptionally well in hilly areas such as Scotland, Wales, Cornwall and Devon, whereas Morris cars, with their high ratios, sold well in flat country. Certainly, the performance of the side-valve MM on a long steep hill was pathetic, so a change was desirable.'

Harry Gardner, under Bill Ellcock, was really the man responsible for the A30 gearbox, and a yarn still persists of the day a Morris man took him out for a run in one of the first Minors to be fitted with the A-series engine and gearbox. On descending Rose Hill, the chap from Morris depressed the clutch pedal and then let his foot slip sideways off it, so that the gears re-engaged with a wallop. Harry was affronted. 'What did you do that for?' Back came the reply, 'Well, our gearbox can stand it. Can yours?' It did stand it, that once at any rate, but we shall soon see how the use of the A30's power unit in the heavier Minor was to play its part in the further development of both these BMC babies.

Of course, if BMC were to reap the full benefits of the merger, they would have to address themselves to more serious matters. Was it sensible, for example, to be producing two baby cars that competed so directly with each other? If not, which car should be taken out of production? How would the powerful Austin or Morris distributors react to these questions? Could their interests be safeguarded by producing the Morris, say, with an Austin power unit and transmission, and marketing it under both badges? Although such things would come to pass eventually, the initial shock waves from the merger had obviously provided enough animosity and headaches to be going on with. Many important questions went either unasked or unanswered. The status quo prevailed, but not without Austin having to deny the rumours circulating in 1953 that the A30 was about to be cancelled.

Meanwhile, the design teams had been kept busy with routine development work. At Len Lord's instructions, an A30 was sent to Cowley and a Minor brought to Longbridge to see if economies could be made in the trimming of either car. It did not lead to anything, but the experimental department at Cowley could not resist the opportunity of testing the torsional stiffness of the A30's body. In Jack Daniels' words: 'We had built up a full history of the torsional stiffness of all sorts of cars. It was a fairly simple and crude test for twisting and bending, but we were staggered to find that the A30 body had a torsional stiffness of about 13,000 lb ft per degree of deflection. The Morris Minor gave a figure of only 4500 lb ft per degree, and we considered that more than adequate.'

At first sight, these figures would appear to suggest that the A30 was considerably overbodied, but it is a fact that the body of the truly chassisless A30 was not directly comparable with that of the Minor, which was of integral or unitary construction. Ken Garrett points out that the stiffness of the Minor was derived mainly from the frame that was welded into the body, rather than from the body panels themselves, and this leaves the car more liable to flex. In Ken's words: 'With the A30, the whole depth of each body panel was fully effective in resisting torsion and taking the static and dynamic loading.' He is justifiably proud of the strength they had built into the A30 while using the minimum of metal, and adds, 'Only if we had had modern computer-aided design facilities could we have reduced the weight of that body. Even then, I doubt whether much could have been taken out of it. Indeed, it would be very interesting to put the A30's structure through a CAD programme to see how it compares with modern cars designed on the basis of the same or similar programmes. Perhaps some technical college might be persuaded that it would be a useful exercise for its students.'

In the A30, Ken Garrett and Ian Duncan had managed to ensure that the efficient use of metal produced not only a strong motor car, but one with an excellent power-to-weight ratio. No doubt, a small saving in metal could have been made if the original calculations for the A30 body had not ignored the strength of the roof, but as Ken Garrett puts it: 'That decision was based partly on the desire to make the structure adequate as a base for producing a convertible, and partly because no one at that time had any idea as to precisely how much the roof contributed to the strength and stiffness, since it depended to a major extent on how the glazing was done and how tightly the doors were secured by their locks.'

Perhaps the only real question is whether there could have been savings in weight and cost if Austin's desire to produce a 'large car in miniature' had been relaxed just a little. On so small a wheelbase, might it not have made sense to produce only a two-door version of the car? Access to the rear seat from two larger doors is little worse than through those tiny rear doors. With a reduction in the effective length of the sill, an equally strong structure could have been produced from less metal. Assembly would have been simpler, tooling costs reduced, and the power-to-weight ratio improved marginally. Apparently, Ian Duncan did press for only two doors for these very reasons, and Ken Garrett believed that he was right to do so, but Ken points out: 'A salesman would say that many people will reject a car because it only has two doors, whereas few indeed will buy one because it has two doors. The only reason why a two-door car sells at all is because some customers cannot afford or do not wish to pay extra for a four-door one.' However, when a two-door A30 was eventually produced in late 1953, it proved to be very popular. Of the first 27,000 saloons produced after its introduction, only 5000 were of the four-door variety.

In early 1953, a rather strange three-door AS3 stood in Dick Burzi's studio. A four-door saloon had been modified on one side only to assess the feasibility of producing a two-door version. Doug Adams remembers being asked to produce this mock-up at very short notice. Hoping to save time, they cut through the driver's door of the four-door car and added 6 in. to its middle. As the door was being welded, it sank in on them, so they had to begin again, making a complete outer skin of the correct size. This meant burning the midnight oil to ensure that all was ready for the meeting at which the proposals for the car were to be finalized.

The two-door A30 was first shown publicly at Earls Court in October 1953. With a basic price of £335 and purchase tax of £140 14s 2d, the total came to £475 14s 2d, which was about £20 cheaper than the four-door version.

Under the model number A2S4, the two-door car incorporated several other modifications which

28 August 1953. This two-tone, two-door A30 (A2S4) saloon, used in publicity shots, had been hand-built from an AS3 body. It had the new larger grille but retained the winged badge. The latter item would not be found on the production cars. *Courtesy Austin Rover*

were introduced on the four-door (AS4) version at the same time.

The fascia had been redesigned completely. Below it was a full-width parcel shelf and automatic courtesy light. The horn push was incorporated in the centre of the steering wheel, and it was at this time that the trafficator control was moved to its final position above the centre of the dashboard. An optional fresh-air heater replaced the previous recirculatory type.

More luggage space was obtained by moving the spare wheel to the left side of the boot and standing it in a depression in the floor. The petrol tank was moved further to the rear of the car, and an increase in the diameter of the filler pipe, which now emerged through the rear panel, provided it with self-venting properties.

LEFT As *Auto Age* put it in December 1953: '. . . to lower the front windows is a simple matter: just place a pinky or two on the raised glass bar and pull down.' *Courtesy Austin Rover*

CENTRE LEFT The two- and four-door saloons introduced in October 1953 retained the small rear window of the AS3. A peep through this one shows the more conventional door handle of the new model. *Courtesy Austin Rover*

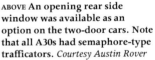

ABOVE An opening rear side window was available as an option on the two-door cars. Note that all A30s had semaphore-type trafficators. *Courtesy Austin Rover*

LEFT The boot of the hand-built two-door saloon shows the new position for the spare wheel. Note the AS3-type petrol filler and cap which emerge at an angle from the back panel. The production version of the car had a larger-diameter pipe emerging at right angles. A patch on the rear-seat back would seem to indicate that experiments had already taken place to pass the Rotodip pole through the A30 body rather than underneath it. *Courtesy Austin Rover*

ABOVE January 1954. Yvonne
Coates (now Yvonne Hodson)
models the rear seat of a two-door
A30. Not a lot of spare room for
adults, but quite good in so small
a car. *Courtesy Austin Rover*

RIGHT A30 speedometer and
instruments, November 1953. The
new speedometer was quite a
distinctive feature of the car.
Above it is the direction-indicator
switch in its final resting place.
Ignition, heater, wipers and panel
light were now all controlled
from a separate panel in the
centre of the full-width parcel
shelf. *Courtesy Austin Rover*

Increasing the length of the rear spring shackles reduced the angular movement of the shackle for any given deflection of the spring, effectively lengthening the life of the rubber bushes.

The seating had been altered to give more room in the rear, as well as more comfort in the front. Separate interior door handles were fitted in response to the criticism that the previous combination of door and window opener had been a hazard.

The first AS3s had a 7/36 rear axle, that is, seven teeth on the bevel pinion and 36 teeth on the crown wheel, giving a gear ratio of 5.143:1. Although the earliest parts list for the AS3 states that an 8/41 axle, giving a ratio of 5.125:1, was used from car 1019 onwards, the production records do not concur. The first car not to have its build record rubber-stamped with a 7/36 axle ratio was car/chassis 30,372, which was an early A2S4. There was an overlap in the production of AS3s, AS4s and A2S4s. Some of the very late AS3s, which were produced after the introduc-

tion of the AS4 and A2S4, had their build records stamped with an 8/41 rear-axle ratio, while a few of the early AS4 and A2S4 records were stamped with the 7/36 ratio.

However, checks made with owners of early A30s seem to indicate that the parts list is likely to be correct. Whoever was wielding that 7/36 rubber stamp may simply have become attached to it, because no car with a 7/36 ratio has yet been found after C 1016, although this is not to say that some do not exist!

Chassis number 25,631 belonged to an experimental AS4 (recorded as having a 7/36 axle ratio), which was built for the Earls Court Show of 1953. Continuous production of AS3 ceased at car/chassis 29,897, but after that 228 CKD AS3s went to Australia, and a further 12 AS3s were completed on the Longbridge production lines.

Road testing the two-door A30 in December 1953, *The Autocar* commented: 'It settles down well on a long journey and its ability to pull from low speeds

enables a very satisfactory average to be obtained. Towards the maximum speed of 63 mph there is a tendency for the engine to indicate that it is turning over rapidly and it seems happiest cruising between 40 and 50 mph. At the higher speeds a transmission rumble was evident, which was not lessened by the car tested having a somewhat noisy rear axle.' Even so, they felt a long journey could be undertaken happily because 'the comfort and performance of the Austin enables one to load it to capacity and sally forth with the knowledge that one's destination will be reached in a very reasonable time and at a minimum of expense.'

The Motor of 6 January 1954 found that the larger doors of the two-door version gave easier access to the front compartment and that the hinged front seats made access to the rear 'quite tolerably easy'. They also thought that the two-door version would appeal to those with young children, because the internal door handles were now safely out of the reach of rear-seat passengers. They did gently criticize the gap between third and top gear: '... for overtaking other moderately brisk traffic, the gear ratios are not ideal but doubtless the majority of customers will gladly accept this limitation in order to be able to surmount very considerable gradients without needing to make a further downward change into second gear.'

Continuing their report, *The Motor* said, 'Handling qualities, which initially seem slightly peculiar, very soon come to be accepted as quite pleasing after some miles have been covered in this car.' With this sentence, they had summed up one of the weaknesses of the A30/35. Although the cars become a pleasure to drive when you know their ways, they can be a little off-putting initially. Not necessarily a car to be highly recommended after the short acquaintance of a road test.

The Motor made the usual commendation of the excellent forward vision together with the usual criticism that diagonal vision was impaired by the combination of the windscreen pillars and quarter lights. The steering-column switch for the lights, which replaced the earlier horn/light switch, was considered an improvement, although a rather more sensitive action was thought desirable.

The Light Car of May 1954 gave the two-door A30 an excellent write-up in almost every respect. They considered that the designers had succeeded well in providing 'multum in parvo' and that the few extra inches available here and there had produced a genuine four-seater with a surprisingly capacious luggage compartment. They thought that 50 mph was a comfortable cruising speed, and they obtained a fuel consumption of 45 mpg at a constant 40 mph.

It seems that the Swedes would have argued with that description of the car as a full four-seater. It was not that they had anything against the little car—they nicknamed it 'The Meatball' and bought it in large numbers— it was simply that they experienced difficulties when both the driver and front-seat passenger got into the car in their bulky sheepskins and then attempted to shut the doors. They persuaded Joe Bache (of the Austin Export Corporation) that the car would have greater appeal if it could be widened. Joe, in turn, got Lord's approval to build a one-off A30 with a 3 in. strip added to the middle. Joe was delighted with it. He told Len Lord it would triple the sales in Sweden and elsewhere, but Lord declared, 'It wouldn't pull

LEFT An A30 two-door saloon photographed in June 1955 at Moreton. Note the fixed rear side window in its rubber surround. *Courtesy Austin Rover*

RIGHT Elegant-Reliable-Comfortable-Economical. In 1954 Emil Frey, Austin distributor for Switzerland, offered this A30 as a ten-lap sprint prize at the first six-day cycle race to be held in Zurich. The car is seen on show in the centre of the track. *Courtesy Emil Frey*

the skin off a rice pudding.' The car ended up in the 'Kremlin' garage and was never put into production, although the list of all the pressings that would have had to be altered is still in existence today.

Of course, it is impossible to please everyone, but it could be argued that the British motor industry was trying too hard to do so. The Americans found amusement in the range of cars on offer. The A70, A40 and A30 were seen as something akin to a set of Toby jugs of ever-decreasing size. To them, they were all baby cars. In 1954, Stanley Edge met Johnnie Rix in America. Rix, who was there in an attempt to sell the A30, both to agents and to anyone who might wish to make it under licence, told Stanley that the Americans were derisive about Austin having different models with only some 3 in. between them in width. Pointing to the A30, they had asked, 'What's this narrow one for? Is it for narrow people?'

Kay Petre, racing driver, motoring correspondent and lady extraordinaire, had also been observing the American scene. She noted that they were employing women as colour stylists in the belief that it was often the lady of the household who had the final say in the choice of a car. Kay managed to sell Len Lord the idea that colourful cars would help to win sales. Her appointment as the Austin colour consultant was soon being used in Austin advertising. Lighter pastel colours were introduced into the Austin range, but the prevailing view was that British motorists would require a gradual weaning from their beloved blacks and greys.

However, in late 1953 and early 1954, several A30 two-door saloons were produced with a contrasting roof colour. A two-door saloon in Coronet cream with a red roof was used in all the brochures which covered the A2S4 and AS4. The colour options for the two-tone, two-door cars are given in Appendix 4, but these cars were not produced in any great numbers.

From 1953 onwards, many more cars began reaching the home market. Not only were materials in better supply, but it was also becoming more difficult to export to countries determined to have their own motor industries. In early post-war days, 75–80 per cent of production was being exported. By 1954, this figure had dropped to around 40 per cent. At home, the days of second-hand cars being worth more than twice their original purchase price had gone. The A30 was selling steadily; nearly 60,000 saloons were sold in 1954, and over 63,000 in 1955.

The original AS3, which had a rear-axle ratio of 5.143:1, had given 12.62 mph per 1000 rpm. The change to a ratio of 5.125:1 had provided 12.66 mph per 1000 rpm. In the spring of 1954, a new 8/39 differential produced a ratio of 4.875:1, which gave 13.30 mph per 1000 rpm. This latter change had helped to keep the car abreast of the times, but even so the A30 was beginning to fall short of what some people were demanding.

Among the buyers of small cars, there were those who were expecting 'longer legs' than cars like the A30 possessed. A report in *Road & Track* of August 1954 illustrates the point: 'While the A30 may meet the needs and desires of the British marginal motorist, it seems ill-suited to American requirements. Barely able to keep up with normal "easy-going" traffic, the tiny engine must be revved unmercifully... an 800-mile trip was an unhappy experience. The comfortable cruising speed is no more than

50 mph and above that the engine is neither quiet nor vibrationless. . . . There is rear axle noise, engine noise and even suspension noise—all blended into a cacophonous highway harmony. When the wind noise joined in with the others there were those who indicated they thought they'd rather walk instead. While the British motor journals call the performance of this car "brisk", our test crew did not concur and were of the opinion that the A30 might lose a stop-light "drag" race to the newpaper boy on his bicycle. Even more to the point, we wondered what state of repair the engine would be in after a full year of struggling to stay up with the traffic.'

This American view may well have been somewhat extreme, but they were right to consider the engine's health. Even in Europe, little allowance was being made for the size of the car. On continental motorways, and on our own improved trunk roads, cars large and small were regularly being asked to sustain very high speeds over long distances. Under these conditions, the temperature of the oil in the A30's engine would rise dramatically, leaving the white-metal bearings very much at risk. The heavier Morris Minor was helping to prove the same point. Her bearings were at even more risk. It was not just that the Minor was heavier than the A30. With its superior roadholding, it could be driven to the limit on even secondary roads. Many drivers did just that, so it is not surprising that there were instances of premature bearing failure. Discussing these failures, Bill Appleby pointed out, 'The big-end bearings of the 803 cc engine were designed to the usual formula for white-metal bearings, so they were not undersize for the load. However, as there was only a bypass oil filtration, it is possible that owners who neglected to change their oil at the stated mileage would experience trouble. Also white metal, while accepting a small degree of embeddability of foreign matter, would crack up under prolonged high-speed hammering.'

With roads improving, high-speed hammering was becoming an everyday occurrence. Something had to be done.

6

THE A35 – PERFORMANCE AND ECONOMY COMBINED

By the mid-1950s, British cars were cornering a smaller percentage of both home and overseas markets. The charge had been made, said the editorial of *The Motor* for 24 October 1956, that 'some British cars were outmoded in style and deficient in performance', but they were pleased to see that 'Britain's largest selling small cars had been given a performance superior to their rivals.'

They were referring, of course, to the newly-announced Austin A35 and Morris Minor 1000, the shared power unit of which had been cleverly redesigned. The new unit transformed both cars completely. When *The Motor* compared the power-to-weight ratio of British and continental cars of less than a litre, they found that the A35 topped the lot with its 'remarkable figure of 40 bhp/laden ton'.

An increase in engine size had been under discussion since early 1953, when bore and stroke calculations were made for several engines which varied in capacity from 848 cc to 998 cc. At the end of October 1953, a 1000 cc engine with siamezed bores was under consideration. Basically, it was this engine, with its bores reduced by $\frac{1}{16}$ in., that became the 948 cc engine. This had a bore of 2.478 in. (62.94 mm), but it retained the 3 in. (76.2 mm) stroke of the 803 cc engine.

By this time, higher-octane fuels were available, but they called for higher compression ratios. The A30's white-metal bearings were already stretched to the limit at a ratio of 7.2:1. The problem was solved by the use of lead-indium bearings, which had been tried experimentally in the 803 cc engine from as early as 1952. These consisted of a steel-backed copper/lead bearing with a very fine coating of lead indium. Not only does indium have a very low coefficient of friction, but it also renders a bearing less liable to corrosion and fatigue.

The 948 cc engine was improved further by increasing the size of the big-end journals from $1\frac{7}{16}$ in. to $1\frac{5}{8}$ in. With the loss of the embeddable qualities of the white-metal bearings, it was thought

prudent to introduce full-flow oil filtration to reduce any risk of the harder bearings leading to scored crankshafts. Full value could now be wrung from premium fuels by raising the compression ratio to 8.3:1. The new engine developed 34 bhp at 4750 rpm.

During the development stages, there had been concern that the siamezed bores might cause bore distortion. This concern seemed to have been well-founded when the first engines showed considerable distortion, but there was much relief when the cause was traced to the new copper-and-asbestos cylinder-head gasket. Reducing the thickness of the gasket solved the problem.

Alan Moore, of the experimental road test department, remembers his first experience of a 948 cc engine installed in an A30. Gil Jones had asked him to do a set of figures on it at MIRA. He also completed a 200-mile test route, averaging 35 mph and 50 mpg, and could not believe the figures he was getting: 'Here was a car with a top speed in excess of 70 mph that was giving 50 mpg on the road. There was nothing in the world to touch it!' Alan was surprised to find that nobody seemed to be taking any notice of the results he had obtained, until Don Hawley, from power unit development, asked him about them. Not long after that, the new engine underwent reliability trials in both A30s and Minors on the German autobahns.

With the coming together of the two test teams in this first joint Austin/Morris (BMC) test, there was much debate as to who had the best test procedures, and socializing was pretty much at arm's length. Be that as it may, they certainly got down to the testing. With Stuttgart as a base, they used much of the same autobahns as Hitler's troops did when they put over $1\frac{1}{4}$ million miles (50,000 miles per car) on to the VW Beetle prototypes.

The BMC cars were not to be tested quite so extensively, but it was still no picnic. Each car clocked up over 25,000 miles in the space of a few weeks.

They maintained an average speed of more than 60 mph, and the 260-mile return trip between Stuttgart and Munich was frequently completed in only four hours and ten minutes, with only a ten-minute stop for refuelling. Each car did between 600 and 800 miles a day, six days a week. Servicing and maintenance took place on Sunday mornings.

The testing confirmed the abilities of the lead-indium bearings to withstand considerable hammering, and the full-flow oil filtration system passed with flying colours. In spite of the harsh treatment, the 948 cc engine returned between 36 and 40 mpg and would shortly become renowned for its successful combination of an almost cheeky liveliness with exceptional economy. The test cars were fitted with a new remote-control gearbox with revised ratios which helped considerably in making the A35 much more pleasant to drive than the A30. A new 9/41 (4.55:1) final-drive ratio provided the 'longer legs' now demanded. In top gear, the road speed was 14.26 mph per 1000 rpm.

RIGHT Cars taking part in the first Austin/Morris combined test in 1956, seen here on the autobahn between Heilbronn and Munich.
Courtesy Austin Rover

In August 1951, when an experimental engine had shown excessive wear after 100 hours on the test-bed, Eric Bareham had made a disapproving note in his diary: 'Still not fully balanced.' To keep weight and cost to a minimum, only very limited balancing had been allowed on the 803 cc engine. In August 1956, Eric was much happier. The fully-balanced crank of the 948 cc engine was definitely a great improvement.

It was not only the A30's mechanical specification that had been under scrutiny. Since 1951, a number of styling exercises had taken place and a variety of face-lifts considered—some more radical than others. In the end, however, the mechanical changes already discussed were the main differences that transformed the A30 into the A35. The roof line was cleaned up by running the drip channel down the front screen pillars, a chromed slipper formed the base for the side lights, and the semaphore-type traf-ficators were replaced by flashing indicators. The chromed grille of the A30 was replaced by a painted

ABOVE **The test personnel after the cars had attended their Sunday-morning service (!) in Stuttgart.** *Courtesy Austin Rover*

BELOW **The 948 cc engine and gearbox, November 1956. Note the remote-control gearchange and the full-flow oil filter.** *Courtesy Austin Rover*

May 1953. One of several clay models produced by Dick Burzi for an update of the A30. This is probably the finest he did, and it would seem to owe something to Bob Koto's earlier models, as well as showing quite a resemblance to later Austins. *Courtesy Austin Rover*

This model, which was completed in January 1954, shows how, by that time, the proposals for restyling the A30 had become much less adventurous. *Courtesy Austin Rover*

The styling changes eventually decided upon were even less adventurous than that last 'fish-mouthed' offering, but they were certainly more pleasing. This advance publicity shot, taken in September 1956, shows an A35 sporting Metropolitan bumpers and overriders. It still has the A30's small 'Flying A' plinth, too. *Courtesy Austin Rover*

ABOVE Publicity shot of the production version of the two-door A35 saloon. *Courtesy Austin Rover*

BELOW American stylist Bob Koto with the author's A35 in August 1985. This was his first opportunity to take a close look at the lines of the Burzi car

LEFT The A35 fascia and controls were the same as the A30's, apart from the 80 mph speedometer and stubby gear lever. This photo shows a carpet fitted in the front, but towards the end of 1956, after the production of 4500 two-door A35s and 630 four-door A35s, a one-piece moulded rubber mat was used in the front with carpet in the rear. The mats were in blue, red or green. De luxe cars had ashtrays, overriders and, on the two-door model, hinged rear windows. Heater and radio were extra. *Courtesy Austin Rover*

RIGHT A35 luggage compartment. This also shows the arrangement of the rear lights and flashing indicators. Flashing indicators became a legal alternative to semaphores in January 1954. That pear-shaped cut-out in the seat back was to allow the Rotodip pole to pass right through the car (see Chapter 10). *Courtesy Austin Rover*

LEFT A35 four-door interior, showing rubber mat in front and carpet in rear. A blanking plate on the central door post covers the recess for the A30's semaphore indicators. *Courtesy Austin Rover*

grille with a chromed 'horseshoe' surround, the latter being arrived at in typical Len Lord fashion—he drew it on the floor of Dick Gallimore's shop.

Dick Burzi determined the size and shape of the larger rear window when he formed the new outline in black tape on the rear of an A30. The Swedish distributor, Hans Osterman, had beaten Austin to this change. Previously, he had written to Longbridge, suggesting that a larger rear window be fitted to the A30. When it was not forthcoming, he converted the cars himself during a six- to eight-month period prior to the launch of the A35 in October 1956.

The press gave the A35 a friendly reception. *The Motor* of 21 November 1956 thought it 'no overstatement to say that the new engine and gearbox have transformed this smallest Austin completely . . . it remains the likeable little car it has always been, but with an added liveliness that now makes it one of the quickest point-to-point means of transport in big towns that has ever been produced. On the open road, the difference is even more marked because the improved acceleration and hill-climbing place it in an entirely different class, especially in the matter of easier overtaking. Greatly added facility in this respect, coupled with an ability to cruise at higher speeds without worry, make the new A35 a distinctly quick form of point-to-point transport on country roads as well as in towns.'

The same report spoke well of the new gearbox and its sports-car-like, remote-control gear lever, which provided a positive action that was 'altogether delightful'. Third gear was found to provide a possible 58 mph 'within easy everyday scope', and although the indirect gears were 'by no means inaudible', the noise level was thought to be very

acceptable, even though the test car's rear axle was 'not as quiet as it might have been'.

Once again, the *Motor* report told us that the car took a little getting used to: 'The handling qualities of the A35 may be classed as good, although the characteristics brought about by the short wheelbase, narrow track and a rear anti-roll bar strike a strange driver as somewhat unusual. On corners, there is surprisingly little roll, but a definite feeling of weight transference from the inside to the outside rear wheel produces the impression of a pronounced oversteer which does not truly exist. Once the driver becomes used to this, corners can be taken fast with confidence and if the speed should prove to be slightly exuberant, a quick twitch of the light and high geared steering immediately puts matters right.'

They thought that the brake pedal needed surprisingly high pressure, but overall 'the A35 represents an extremely good example of conventional design in minimum four-seater size at minimum cost. At unaltered price and with greatly improved performance, it should make more friends than ever.'

The Autocar of 28 December 1956 noted that the performance of the car was now a match for some 1½-litre cars. They found that the 10 mph addition to the maximum speed, plus the extra 16 mph available in third gear and the car's ability to accelerate away in top gear from about 12 mph, made the A35 a nippy car for commuting as well as one that could make good times on long journeys without undue noise or stress.

They, too, were a little concerned with the heavy pedal pressures required to slow the car from speed and advocated that an increase in power output of any new model should be matched by an improved braking system.

Although the effect of strong winds on the car was mentioned, roadholding was thought to be pretty good, and they concluded, 'There is little doubt that this latest version of an outstanding small car will prove more popular than its predecessor—and that is high praise. Its economy—an outstanding feature—makes it particularly desirable where fuel is scarce and expensive.'

The best comparison of the A35 with the A30 was probably made in *The Motor* of 21 November 1956, when it gave the following figures: 'Taking fuel consumption at constant speeds first, the A35 showed a gain of 2.6 per cent at 30 mph with the very notable figure of 60 mpg. At 40 mph the improvement increased to 4.8 per cent, whilst at 50 mph and 60 mph there was nothing to choose between the two, with the very minor gain of 1.3 per cent at the former speed and an equally small loss of 1.4 per cent at 60 mph. Thus the balance is appreciably in favour of the new model for the sort of cruising speeds many drivers of this type of car adopt, with a small margin in hand for those who wish to take advantage of the improved acceleration of the new model without sacrifice of economy.'

With regard to speed and acceleration, they remarked, '. . . the gains shown by the new model are very pronounced indeed. With a maximum mean speed of 71.9 mph, the A35 is 11.1 per cent faster than its predecessor, whilst acceleration figures from a standing start show improvements ranging from 20 per cent in the times taken to reach 30 mph and 40 mph to a gain of nearly 29 per cent in the 0–60 mph figure. As for acceleration in top gear, the

smallest gain (from 20 mph to 40 mph) was 18 per cent and the largest, which, as might be expected, is in the 40–60 mph figure, is no less than 33.7 per cent.'

When it gave details of the Austin range for 1957, *The Motor* of 10 October 1956 gave comparative power outputs for the A30 and A35 as follows: '. . . the new unit develops 21.4 per cent more power at a slightly lower peak speed, the output having gone up from 28 bhp at 4800 rpm to 34 bhp at 4750 rpm. Even more important, where normal road behaviour is concerned, is the increase in torque. Here the improvement is no less than 25 per cent, whilst the speed at which it is developed is materially reduced; thus the new engine has a maximum torque of 50 lb ft at 2000 rpm compared with the 40 lb ft at 2200 rpm of the A30.'

They thought that the new gearbox with its higher third gear, in conjunction with the higher final-drive ratio of 4.55:1, would allow the characteristics of the new engine to be used to the full so that the A35 'should easily equal or surpass anything which the best continental small cars can offer in ability to withstand continuous hard driving over long distances.'

In the A35, Austin were offering the public a baby car that combined first-rate performance and reliability with exceptional economy. It was now up to the advertising department to sell the idea to potential buyers.

They beat the economy drum first. In November 1956, all the major daily newspapers carried advertising based on an unsolicited letter the company had received from a Captain Hosack. He had given much praise to the remarkable and economical performances of his A30 on some quite extended journeying. In the advertising, it was promised that even better things could be expected from the new A35. We will never know exactly how effective that advertising was in encouraging new sales, but it prompted numerous owners to bombard Longbridge with tale after tale of the economical and reliable motoring feats their little A30s had performed. Reading those letters leaves one in no doubt that they were very proud indeed of their baby Austins.

Many of the writers were to claim well over 50 mpg, and it is quite obvious that they were getting exceptional results. However, it must be pointed out that most A30/35 odometers (in line with most other cars, of course) read high in miles covered to the tune of some 6 per cent, and this should always be taken into account when one wishes to calculate a true figure for mpg.

It was not long, however, before Austin were to demonstrate that results such as this were easily attainable with an A35. The RAC were asked to observe the car over a 500-mile run. Joe Lowrey of *The Motor* was persuaded to drive the car, and Leslie Webb was appointed by the RAC as their official observer.

Leslie selected a car from the assembly lines at Longbridge, and it was handed over to Ben James of the road test department who ran it in under supervision. The car had to be kept absolutely standard. Only normal servicing was allowed, and the recommended tyre pressures had to be adhered to. Austin's aim was to prove that a standard A35, driven carefully, but without any coasting, could

ABOVE The 1956 Economy Run. Leslie Webb, of the RAC, keeps a watchful eye on the A35 as it is filled up at the start of the run in Fulham. Note that the tank had been modified so that it was easy to fill it to within an inch of the top of the vertical filler pipe inside the boot. *Courtesy Ben James*

BELOW This outdoor poster was offered free to dealers. It bills the A35 as Britain's most economical four-seater

clock up at least 50 mpg over a varied test route. They even accepted Joe Lowrey's suggested route, which commenced in London and encompassed Lyme Regis and Lincoln before returning to London. During the two-day test run, they experienced high winds and torrential rain, but the result was an average speed of 31.6 mph and a very useful petrol consumption of 53.7 mpg. By now, it was December 1956, the time of the Suez Crisis, and as petrol rationing was about to be introduced in Britain, the results of the test were particularly newsworthy, receiving a great deal of coverage in the press. In the spring of 1957, when the sales of medium and larger cars were in decline, production of the A35 and Morris Minor had to be stepped up to cater for the increase in demand.

In 1982, the aforementioned Economy Run was restaged by the A30/35 Owners Club. Once again the run was strictly supervised (even down to tyre pressures) by Leslie Webb and the RAC. Odometer readings were ignored, the true distance covered being used in all calculations. The author's A35, the cylinder head of which had never been removed in its 25-year life, achieved the highest figure for an A35 at 49.75 mpg. Other 'spoils' were interestingly shared, Anders Clausager of BMIHT obtaining the best A30 figure of 47.23 mpg and Jeremy Sinek of *Motor* squeezing a remarkable 57.92 mpg out of his 'modified' A35.

Further publicity for the A35 was based on an attempt to demonstrate its reliability over many thousands of miles at high speed. The idea had originated in Cambridge rather than Longbridge. Gyde Horrocks, of the Cambridge University Car Club, had approached Marcus Chambers to see if the BMC competitions department would supply them with a car in which they could attack some of the long-distance records for cars of 750–1100 cc. A distance of 10,000 miles in 10,000 minutes was generally accepted as proof of the reliability of any car, but it had never been done by a car in the smaller-engined category. Both the Minor and A35 were considered as possibilities, the A35 being chosen due to its relative lightness. The car was prepared at Abingdon and the run took place at the Montlhéry circuit near Paris. It seemed that a slightly modified car would be able to take the most records, so it was prepared with International Class G records in mind.

The bodywork was virtually standard, except for a bonnet louvre and an extension to the front apron, which was simply to tidy up the front after the bumper had been removed. The major modification was the fitting of a 3.9:1 differential, while the stan-

ABOVE **The Australians had to do without an A35. The A30 soldiered on into 1957, but was offered with this 'gay two-toning which adds a new look to the baby of the Austin range.'** *Courtesy Terry Jorgensen*

RIGHT **The A35 at Montlhéry in 1957, about to begin its run of seven days and seven nights, clocking up over 12,500 miles at almost 75 mph.** *Courtesy National Motor Museum*

dard engine was carefully rebuilt and its carburettor exchanged for a 30 mm VIG downdraught Zenith. Other changes included a larger-diameter downpipe from the exhaust manifold, an oil cooler, an SU petrol pump and harder brake linings. A larger petrol tank was also fitted which could be filled very rapidly from inside the boot. Temperature gauge, oil-pressure gauge, tachometer and Halda Speed Pilot completed the additions.

The record attempt took place between 1 and 8 July 1957. A rear spring shackle was the only failure, but it was repaired swiftly. The main hardships seemed to be due to the intense heat of that summer and the notorious roughness of the Montlhéry track. It was not possible to combat the heat by driving with the windows wide open, because the extra drag on the car required a noticeable increase in throttle opening. Ice-cold drinks soon became too hot to consume, but the car seemed to take the heat in its stride, requiring very little in the way of water. In the evenings, flies, that would have clogged the radiator, were blown out with an air line.

The 10,000 miles were clocked up in less than 8000 minutes. In the seven days and seven nights, the car had travelled over 12,500 miles at an average

speed (including stops) of 74.9 mph and had established seven Class G records in the process. Austin were justifiably proud of the car's achievements and, quite naturally, the advertising department had a field day.

The A35 was exported worldwide, Sweden being the biggest export market by far for fully-assembled cars. They would usually be sent there with an 82-degree thermostat and often with white-wall tyres. Large numbers of CKD kits went to Wellington, Capetown, Dublin and Brussels. However, no A35s were assembled in Australia, although a few did eventually reach the country by direct import.

Different export markets made different stipulations. The steady trickle of cars which went to Paris required laminated screens. The flashing indicators of those going to America had to be white at the front of the car and red at the rear. Cars went to a variety of places with wooden rims on their wheels to escape duty of up to 300 per cent that was sometimes levied on imported tyres. March 1957 saw the beginning of safety and other regulations that were going to make matters more complicated in certain markets. From that month on, cars going to New Zealand had to be fitted with a plastic 'Flying A'; Denmark and

Switzerland soon followed suit.

In the UK, the A35 was chosen by several organizations as an ideal means of transport for their local representatives. Orders from the Milk Board surpassed all others. From 1956 onwards, their staff were buzzing round country lanes in little black A35s, checking on the cleanliness and quality of milk. Remember those Weathermaster and Town & Country tyres? Nearly all Milk Board cars were fitted with those as standard before leaving Longbridge.

By August 1959, when production of the A35 saloon came to an end, 129,000 examples had been assembled at Longbridge. Over 100,000 of these were of the two-door variety.

There cannot have been many cars as 'honest' as the A35. Its ability to provide economical and reliable motoring in such a lively package meant that the post-war baby Austin was proving itself a worthy successor to the pre-war Seven. Its giant-killing exploits on the racetrack are dealt with in a later chapter.

The A35 saloon deserved more than a three-year production run, but progress demanded otherwise. We were heading for the swinging sixties.

7

PUTTING ON THE STYLE - THE A40 FARINA

'Driving along the dual carriageway into Brum, I noticed heads turning, eyes staring and quite a few fingers pointing at this new sleek shape which must have come from the Austin factory. What new model was this? It looked different from the traditional Burzi-designed shape which had characterized most Austins cruising along the Bristol Road, running down Low Hill Lane or flogging up Rose Hill since the end of the war. Was it really an Austin, or something else?' Thus, Norman Milne, then engaged in press and public relations work at Longbridge, remembers his first drive in an A40 Farina. At the end of the pre-release press day in September 1958, Reg Bishop, BMC director of publicity, had asked him to take one of the editorial guests to Birmingham's New Street station.

It is understandable that the car caused a stir and that its Austin parentage was doubted, for this was a completely new departure in Austin styling. What had brought it about?

Well liked and respected though Dick Burzi was, there had been those at Longbridge who were not altogether happy with the cars that, supposedly, had been styled by him but which also bore the unmistakable heavy hand of Len Lord. There was a general feeling that, as long as Lord was in control of styling, they would never get a top-flight range of cars. When one brave soul made this point to George Harriman, with a suggestion that 'they should take the A30 to Italy to see what they could do with it', he was told that he simply must not talk about the company chairman in those terms.

It was a time when Italian stylists in general, and Farina in particular, had been making a name for themselves, not only for their production of exotica, but also for their ability to add a touch of classical style to even mass-produced cars. Joe Bache was another who liked what he had seen of such developments, and he was bold enough to suggest to Len Lord that their cars would probably be much more popular on the Continent if they commissioned

Farina to do some styling. Lord replied, 'We don't want any more damn foreigners, we've enough of them already.'

Nevertheless, the seeds of discontent had been sown. At the 1955 Geneva Show, George Harriman took all his senior men around the stands, pointing out the features that he wanted to see on future Austins. Then, he packed them off home to get on with it. Several of them even missed the Austin dinner, held every year in Geneva under the auspices of Emil Frey, the Swiss distributor. It was at this dinner that George Harriman confided to his close associates that he had commissioned Farina to do some styling.

Another factor had played a part in the decision. BMC were about to go in for 'badge engineering' in a big way. The idea was to achieve further economy of scale by producing far fewer basic designs. Dealers would be supplied with their own particular marque by adding the appropriate badging and trim to an otherwise identical vehicle. Employing an outside stylist was seen as a means of reducing the conflict between the Longbridge and Cowley drawing offices as to whose designs should go into production.

The decision to engage Farina would not be common knowledge for some time, and Lord received at least one more suggestion that he should take the course of action he had already embarked upon. In December 1955, Longbridge had an important visitor. The day seemed to go well, except when the guest was in the presence of Lord, whose abrasive and off-hand manner did not quite fit the occasion. Obviously, the visitor was finding it a little difficult to contain himself. Having viewed everything that Longbridge had up its sleeve by way of future models, he asked if Lord thought they would stand up to the foreign competition. Of course, when he went as far as asking Lord if he had heard of the work Farina was doing, Lord was able to reply, 'Yes, I'm meeting him tomorrow.' The chap who had been asking the leading questions was none other than the Duke of Edinburgh.

What of Dick Burzi in all this? What of his status and pride? Poor Dick had never really been given any official status anyway and, of course, there was still a faint hope that Len Lord would relent. After all, they had been through this before in the days that led up to the A30.

This time it would be different. Easy-going though Dick was, he did admit to feelings of disappointment when, in September 1956, his proposals for an A35 replacement were turned down in favour of Farina's efforts. Although, inwardly, he had known that was how it would be, he had not quite resigned himself to the fact. Nevertheless, things turned out quite well for him. The major part of the styling would be Farina's, but overall it was a joint affair. At least Dick was working with someone with whom he had already had friendly associations; someone whom he respected. At least Len Lord would have to be more careful how he referred to Burzi in future. If he continued to call him 'the ice-cream vendor', it might no longer be clear to whom he was referring.

During the period in which the details of the car were being finalized (under the Austin drawing office code, ADO 8), Farina made almost monthly visits to Longbridge. In theory, he had been given a clean sheet of paper; in practice, much was already determined. The car would be a replacement for the A35 and, as such, would have to make use of all the original running gear. It was, in effect, a packaging problem, to which Farina would bring considerable flair.

The initial approaches to Farina were made at the time when Len Lord's proposed Minor replacement had been relegated to its role as the Wolseley 1500, and Lord definitely gave the impression, to Barry Kelkin and others, that Farina's first job would be to style a replacement for the Minor. Only when the first model arrived at Longbridge did they realize that it was to be a replacement for the A35.

Such words as crisp, clean and classic were all justifiably used to describe the neat, simple and uncluttered lines devised by Farina. Barry Kelkin recalls the day they stood waiting for the first Farina prototype to be unloaded at Longbridge: 'As it came off the transporter, we thought it was just great. It looked quite something with its black roof and in the colour that was later to be known as Farina grey.' The extended roof line gave it the appearance of being a much larger car than it actually was. Although the wheelbase was some 4 in. longer than the A35, the car was still almost 4 in. shorter than

1956—Farina's first offering for the A35 replacement. It was light and airy, but those slim roof pillars would have required a strong underbody, leading to a heavier car.
Courtesy Pininfarina

September 1956. Reflected in the front hub cap of Dick Burzi's proposed A35 replacement is an A35 saloon, not yet launched! Dick had tried to produce a style which would suit pick-up, saloon, or Countryman versions. That rear end somehow manages to conjure up a floating feeling. *Courtesy Austin Rover*

October 1956. The cleaner lines of the Farina model are more convincing. The designer seems to have been clear in his aims from the outset. Fortunately, the idea of fitting A30 side lights under the main headlamp cowl was dropped in favour of a new uncluttered look. Note the A35 badging. *Courtesy Austin Rover*

March 1957. Still designated as an A35 in the records, this was to be the final model. The tape shows where templates were being taken to put it on the drawing-board. Then it was decided that Farina's attempt to satisfy the Longbridge desire for a more 'traditional' grille had made the car even more Italianate. His original proposal for a horizontal grille was reinstated. *Courtesy Austin Rover*

October 1957. ADO 8 prototype, labelled as an A35 in the Longbridge records. A year before the launch and almost there. The eagle-eyed will notice the smoother flasher lenses and the slightly different 'Flying A' to that on the production car. *Courtesy Austin Rover*

the Morris Minor. In those terms, it was still a baby Austin. The rearward extension of the roof line meant that, even in this small package, it was possible to provide adequate headroom for the rear-seat passengers and to increase the luggage-carrying capacity considerably.

In the detail of the roof and rear of the car, we can see how a distinguished outside stylist was able to have his way where an in-house designer might have been overruled, either due to protests from the production engineers or on considerations of cost. Had the roof been extended to the very rear of the vehicle, it would have produced a very effective estate car, but Farina was able to compromise by incorporating an inclined rear window which allowed a much more graceful line. He was also able to insist on retaining his proposed wrap-under of the roof's rear edge. Detail such as this, though very effective in giving the roof a neat and solid look, called for expensive tooling to produce an otherwise simple panel.

Although Farina's styling produced a roomy car with greatly increased glass area, it only weighed some 90 lb more than the A35 and was still about 170 lb lighter than the Minor. This had been achieved by using the roof to take more than its usual share of loading by way of the screen, door pillars and double-skinned panels on either side of the rear window. Careful stress analysis of the component parts of the bodyshell had shown this to be feasible. As with the A30, strength had also been built in by using deep sills.

As most of the mechanical components came straight from the A35, there was no need for lengthy testing and development work. Apart from the normal tests on the torsional strength of the body, over 2000 miles were covered on the *pavé* at MIRA, where the cars also endured the switchback, water splash and dust tunnel. Other prototypes clocked up more than 60,000 miles over a variety of test routes.

As one would expect with such well-tried components, the cars performed well. The heelboards did tend to bend a little, so a stiffening channel was added to the pre-production cars in March 1958. Underneath the car, extensions were added to the rear frame side-members so that their forward ends met the heelboard fully. In June 1958, the prototypes had their gearbox tunnels modified to provide more clearance in this area.

The car was about to be launched as the new A35 when, at the eleventh hour, it was decided that the fuel shortage, caused by the Suez Crisis, warranted the continuation of the original, smaller and more

An ADO 8 prototype in disguise? Not really—simply an attempt to stop the rear window getting dirty during the mud-splash tests of January 1958. A variety of mudflaps and extensions to wheel arches and roof were also tried in an effort to cure what is now accepted as one of the hazards of estate-car design. *Courtesy Austin Rover*

economical model. The new car would have to be called an A40. This caused some embarrassment for those producing its brochure. Already fully laid out, the brochure stressed that the new car was a 'Big Austin A35' with 'the Big interior' and 'Big advantages'. There was only time to insert 'A40' instead of 'A35', so the new brochure boasted how big this new A40 was—although it was smaller by far than any yet produced.

Battista Pininfarina and his son Sergio were both in attendance at Longbridge for the unveiling ceremony. It was a proud day. The cars were bold and colourful—the unusual black roof emphasizing their new lines. The press had assembled from far and wide. Harold Dvoretsky recorded his views in the Australian magazine *Modern Motor* of November 1958, declaring the lines of the body to be 'almost severe in their simplicity—gone are those twiddly moulded curves and vignettes, apparently beloved by Austin's own design staff. The stressed-steel, two-door bodyshell looks neat, purposeful and very practical.' After trying the car out in the factory grounds, he wrote, 'I found the A40 as sprightly as the A35, despite its extra 100 lb weight. . . . There wasn't enough straight and level territory to time higher speeds, but around the Exhibition Hall curve, in full view of BMC chairman Sir Leonard Lord, Australian director Jim Kirby, designer Pinin Farina and his son Serge—I did manage to raise 65 on the speedo before going into the roundabout. There was a slight roll, but the A40 seemed perfectly safe all the way. A few minutes later Sir Leonard Lord told me 65 mph was nothing—Alec Issigonis manages 70 mph on the same section. And, as if to prove his boss's claim, Alec came hurtling round the curve at

A40 display in the Longbridge exhibition hall—September 1958. *Courtesy Austin Rover*

a terrific bat and tossed this good-looking car into the roundabout with plenty of verve—it didn't give an inch!' Apparently, Jim Kirby commented, 'This'll be a winner in Australia.'

Something of the new car's attributes can be seen from the way it was billed. In America, they offered it as 'The Gayest Economy Sedan Ever', though probably would not do so today. In Switzerland, it was graphically described as a small car *'mit dem grossen Innenraum'*.

The A40 made its public début in October 1958 at the Grand Palais in Paris, and the British public got their first look at it at Earls Court later the same month.

The first three production cars were built on 2 June. The first went to the experimental department, but the second was dispatched to Capetown before the end of July. This was well before the car's release but, no doubt, it anticipated their early assembly of CKD A40s. The first CKD shipment left for Capetown on 1 October, and that same day similar shipments were dispatched to both Sydney and Dublin. A little later, the A40 would also be assembled in Holland, Belgium and New Zealand, and in November 1958, a CKD pack of a dozen cars was to find its way to Mexico.

Towards the end of the year, six Tartan red cars, all with black roofs and white-wall tyres, were shipped to the USA to be used as press demonstrators in Jacksonville, San Francisco, New Orleans,

Charleston, Houston and New York. Obviously, they had the desired effect, because in the next few months large numbers went to the USA. Orders soon tailed off, but the A40 had definitely made more of an impression on America than had the A30 or A35.

The plan was to produce 650 A40s a week by the end of September. Production of the A35 saloon had been running considerably higher than that, but after the A40's launch, it was expected that the two models would be produced in equal numbers until at least the end of the year. In practice, A40 production got going a little more slowly than expected. In the last quarter of 1958, only about 400 a week were being built, while the A35 saloons were being turned out at about twice that rate.

At the launch, it was emphasized that the new A40 did not replace the A35 or any other model in the BMC range. This decision not only reflected the fuel situation at the time, but also the uncertainty of how the new car would be received. Its 'two-box' style was, after all, a completely new approach. It had been felt that estate-type vehicles would be even more popular than they had already become if their styling could be made more acceptable. Did the A40 have the answer? Would this compromise between an estate and a family saloon find a ready market? Indeed, had it gone too far upmarket to be able to replace the A35? Certainly, it seems to have gone rather further upmarket than was the original intention. At £676 7s 0d, it was £106 more than the corresponding two-door A35, and if you did not want to perish in winter, you had to find a further £20 or so for a heater. If money was not a problem, you could specify a de luxe model which, for an extra £13, came equipped with a passenger's sun-visor, opening rear side windows and overriders, as well as windscreen and window surrounds made of stainless steel.

It is interesting to see that the A40 Farina was immediately recognized as a vehicle which would have considerable influence on the future design of the smaller family car. In *The Autocar* of 31 October 1958, Harry Mundy prophesied, 'When the 1958 Earls Court Exhibition is farther behind us than at present, it will be regarded as quite a landmark in the evolution of the passenger car.' He was not referring solely to the new A40, but did say, '. . . it would appear that a new breakthrough has been achieved in the conception of the small car, as exemplified by the new Farina-styled Austin A40—the first of a new line of BMC models.'

It was natural that every account and every road test of the car would dwell, initially, on the departure in both styling and accommodation. The general feeling was that Austin were to be commended for their bold attempt to combine practicality with style. Farina and Austin had united successfully to produce a fresh and interesting package, even though the engine, gearbox, differential,

ABOVE **August 1958. ADO 8, complete with production flashers, but minus its grille badge, stands outside the styling studio one month before launch day.** *Courtesy Austin Rover*

TOP **Outside the exhibition hall on announcement day, 18 September 1958. From left to right: Leonard Lord, Battista Pininfarina, George Harriman and the stylist's son, Sergio Pininfarina.** *Courtesy Austin Rover*

BELOW **A40 details as revealed in** *The Motor* **of 24 September 1958**

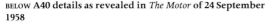

steering gear and suspension had all come almost directly from the A35. Thus, they had kept tooling and development costs to a minimum. By now, the dealers and distributors were well versed in servicing the mechanical components of the car and already held the majority of the mechanical spares.

The braking system retained the rear hydro-mechanical brakes of the A35, but offered increased efficiency at the front from new 8 × 1½ in. drums. New pendant-type pedals operated the brakes and hydraulic clutch, which meant that the fluid reservoirs and master cylinders could be placed under the bonnet in a much more accessible and protected position than the under-floor arrangement of the A30/35.

The Autocar of 19 September 1958 found the driving characteristics to be similar in many ways to the A35, allowing for the fact that the greater weight made it less lively on acceleration. The ride was thought to be fairly comfortable, if somewhat noisy, and the visibility was classed as excellent all round. Even the lift-up windows were seen as a sensible economy.

With hindsight, we can see that the conversion of the rear compartment had not had quite enough thought given to it. Even the earliest road tests picked this up, and some gave suggestions as to how it might be improved upon. *The Autocar*, for example, noted that 'the rear seat squab folds forward to enable luggage to be carried on it, but it is not horizontal in this position and the cushion does not hinge forward to protect the front seat squabs . . . there is no firm barrier to maintain loads in position during heavy braking . . . there are no clear surfaces for sliding luggage into position, as the spare wheel, in its plastic cover with a hard top, occupies most of the floor space.'

In one of their previous reviews, it had already been suggested that the spare wheel could have been placed under the floor and the fuel tank repositioned behind one of the wheel arches. Austin were to provide their own answers to the criticisms, but for now let us see what else was said in the first *Autocar* test of the A40.

It spoke of achieving 'quite high average speeds on long journeys' and of the ability to 'cruise indefinitely at about 60 mph without excessive noise or fuss'. At 65 and 70 mph, a variety of vibrations were mentioned, but the flexibility of the engine was said to allow for 'leisurely driving without frequent gear changing'. For the size and performance of the car, the fuel consumption was considered remarkably low: 'Only when the maximum performance can be used continuously is the mpg brought below 40; the minimum figure of 38 . . . was recorded after a 200 miles' run of hard motoring on open roads and in city traffic. In gentle driving in the country, the excellent figure of 51 mpg was recorded.'

The Motor tested the A40 on the Goodwood track at the Guild of Motoring Writers' Test Day in 1958. Their account of 5 November compared it with a Minor in which they had just done a few laps of the circuit: 'At first the A40 felt a much softer car than the Minor but experience seemed to show that one could drive in Minor fashion without anything untoward occurring once one had grown accustomed to the different feel. It was certainly noisier than the Minor when travelling at speed, but not unexpectedly so with that type of body.'

The road test of the car in the same issue of *The*

The first Austin to be built in the Netherlands was a Mk 1 A40 Farina. It is seen here, in the spring of 1959, outside J. J. Molenaar's assembly plant at Amersfoort, where Morris cars were already under construction. *Courtesy Dick van Arum*

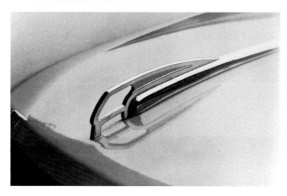

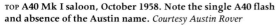

TOP **A40 Mk I saloon, October 1958. Note the single A40 flash and absence of the Austin name.** *Courtesy Austin Rover*

CENTRE **A40 fascia, October 1958. The speedometer has come straight from the A35, but the padded edges and dished steering wheel show the beginnings of concern for the safety of occupants.** *Courtesy Austin Rover*

BOTTOM **A stylish 'Flying A' to suit a stylish car. Safety regulations in other countries meant that it would soon be removed.** *Courtesy Austin Rover*

TOP **August 1958. The interior of ADO 8 was perhaps a little spartan. Note the contrasting piping on the seats. The front seats tip forward for easy access to the rear.** *Courtesy Austin Rover*

CENTRE **An under-bonnet shot, taken in December 1958, showing the arrangement of the heater as well as the reservoirs for the A40's hydraulic brakes and clutch.** *Courtesy Austin Rover*

BOTTOM **A single strap supported the boot lid on early cars. Plenty of luggage space, but rather difficult to load heavy objects**

Motor began with a mention of the 'boldly unconventional styling' and the 'competent performance' of the engine and gearbox. Then, they elaborated on the noise levels: 'With rather flat steel body panels carrying little or no sound damping material, this car does not by any means conceal from its driver the fact that a hard-working engine is running at 1000 rpm for every $14\frac{1}{4}$ mph of car speed.' The fact that the noise disappeared when coasting suggested to them that 'sound deadening treatment of the scuttle structure and bonnet top should allow those undeterred by a few extra pounds weight and cost to quieten an A40 very usefully.'

As for the steering and suspension, it was their view that 'The Austin A35 has proved itself a remarkably well-sprung car; the A40 which uses much the same components but has $3\frac{1}{2}$ in. added to the wheelbase and $2\frac{1}{4}$ in. added to the track is a little better still . . . . There is some degree of body roll on corners which are negotiated fast, but not so much as to prevent the A40 being driven very quickly along a winding road even when passengers with non-sporting ideas about cornering speeds are being carried.'

The seating arrangements and general comfort were to pass as adequate, but the planning of the load space was brought into question again: 'This is a saloon car which can on occasion move an oversized load, rather than a true "station wagon".' The pull-down windows were only seen as a 'tolerable but not very attractive simplification'. Nor did they like what they described as the 'weirdly-shaped speedometer dial from the A35' or the fact that self-cancelling indicators were not provided. However, they did think that the steering-column lighting switch was a 'welcome inheritance from the A35' and that the use of the ignition key to control the starter was a 'welcome refinement'. They finished off in complimentary mood, saying that 'the Austin A40 is a fresh-looking newcomer which seems assured of success, offering as it does an extremely well-balanced combination of comfort, carrying capacity and safety, with economy and speed.'

Bill Boddy of *Motor Sport*, having tried the car at the Goodwood Test Day, was not too enthusiastic. In *Motor Sport* of December 1958, he wrote, 'Remembering all the pre-Motor Show "hoo-hah" about the new Austin A40 we had a go in one of these, noting that the side windows are of sliding, not wind-up type, wondering whether the recesses on the doors are intended as ash-receptacles or "pulls", and disliking the painted "tin" fascia with crude loudspeaker slots. This little car *goes*, and is light to handle, while forward vision is excellent and the bonnet length implies a larger engine. The pleated upholstery is amusing. But on the whole the appearance, particularly from full astern, is nothing to prate about, the clutch action was horrid and first gear really troublesome to engage.'

It was February 1959 before Bill Boddy conducted a full road test, and after it he was to tell his readers that 'although the revised Austin A40 in Farina-styling is a refreshingly modern-looking small car, its original approach to finding additional luggage and rear passenger space is not so effective as it might be, while the car disappoints in matters of detail apparently because there has been a skimping on shillings in the costing department.'

He did relent a little by adding, '. . . to a large number of motorists this will not be apparent, and they will enthuse over an eye-catching little saloon which operates with a fuel economy of a pre-war Austin Seven, is easy to drive and possesses a brisk performance, its maximum speed being in excess of 70 mph.'

Then, he detailed the weak points, such as the intrusion of the wheel arches and spare wheel into the luggage space, the fact that the folded seat squab did not lie flat, as well as the difficulty of loading via a boot lid that was only supported by a rather feeble strap. He was happy with the excellent visibility, light interior and ample headroom for the rear-seat passengers, but he disliked the narrowness of the back seat between the wheel arches.

You could hardly argue with his criticism that 'in a car with such emphasis on the rear compartment and luggage-carrying arrangements, it is surprising to find the only interior lamp in the form of a tiny exposed bulb up under the fascia on the offside, which is ideal for telling the driver whether his shoes need polishing but is quite inadequate for illuminating the rear of the car.'

He found it 'astonishing in 1958' that neither the screen wipers nor direction indicators were self-cancelling, but all in all it was granted that 'the small shortcomings of the new Austin are forgotten to some extent, because the little car performs so willingly. The good roadholding of the A35, from which the A40 borrows its coil spring and wishbone i.f.s., is enhanced by a 4 in. longer wheelbase and a $2\frac{1}{4}$ in. wider track and the car is a delight round fast bends . . . . Whether you are an expert driver in a hurry or merely a family motorist, the new Austin A40 will be found pleasant to drive . . . the high compression engine making no complaint at pulling away from 20 mph in the 4.55:1 top gear. On the other hand,

by using the indirect gears 50 mph can be reached from rest in $21\frac{1}{2}$ seconds, 60 mph in 36 seconds.'

Bill Boddy finished his account by anticipating a few modifications 'which could well put this new Austin A40 at the top of its class.'

It would be some time before all the criticisms were dealt with, but an early start was made by adding an extra strap to help support the boot lid at about car 2000, a modification which had been decided upon before the car was launched. Another pre-launch decision, that early cars missed out on, was the fitting of an 'Austin' script to the left of the boot handle and an 'A40' script to the right.

In December 1958, the instruction was given to delete the 'Flying A' bonnet motif to satisfy the legal requirements of certain countries. In early 1959, a time-switch was employed to produce self-cancelling indicators.

It was routine procedure to test production cars as well as prototypes and, in the winter of 1958, an A40 was taken to Sweden with a prototype Mini. They were heading for the Arctic Circle, but had to give up the attempt about 400 miles north of Stockholm. The Mini's clutch had disintegrated. Like that A30 prototype, it had to be towed home, and as its engine could not even be run, it was a cold journey for the four occupants. When they reached Stockholm, the stricken Mini prototype was parked dis-

A40 Mk I saloon in October 1959. The 'Flying A' has disappeared. The lines of the car have dated much less than the dresses worn by these lovely ladies! *Courtesy Austin Rover*

Publicity shot of an A40 Countryman taken in late October 1959. *Courtesy Austin Rover*

creetly against a wall, partly hidden by the A40, its tow rope tucked underneath, but all to no avail. A week later, its picture appeared in the Swedish press.

Other winter-time testing took place in Switzerland, where the A40 was accompanied once again by a Mini. The main problem with the A40 was icing-up of the carburettor. Understandably, Charlie Griffin was pleased to see the SU carburettor of the Mini carrying on where the Zenith had failed, but it was not long before they had to drive the Mini on its ignition switch due to the throttle freezing open. One result of the trip was that an optional radiator blanking plate was made available for A40s to reduce the icing problem in severe conditions.

In the late summer of 1959, two A40 saloons (YOV 440 and YOV 441) were put through their paces for six weeks on the German autobahns. The party was based in Nuremberg and built up the miles by work-ing two shifts each day. At 7 am, the cars set out for Munich, where they turned round and made for Hof. After their return to Nuremberg, the cars would be taken over by the second shift, who repeated the procedure. A steady 65 mph was maintained all day. One car was fitted with a 4.55:1 rear-axle ratio, the other with a 4.22. The clearest result from the testing was that the lower engine rpm of the car with the higher gearing produced a substantial cut in oil consumption.

In February 1959, the body design department took a thorough look at the criticisms that had been made about noise levels. They produced a new schedule which increased the use of felt in the areas of the dashboard, gearbox cover and transmission tunnel, as well as the rear-seat pan and spare-wheel floor. They also called for the rubber-backed felt under the front and rear carpets to be replaced by needle-loom felt of a greater thickness, and for insulation board to be applied to the front bulkhead.

Many early A40s had to have their front and rear screens removed to be resealed. Leaks also occurred through the blanked holes in the body which allowed for alternative sighting of the wipers, or those allowing the brake and clutch cylinders to be repositioned for either right- or left-hand-drive cars. These often needed resealing, too. Almost all the early cars suffered water leaks through the poorly-blanked tooling holes in the floor. After a dust and water test in March 1959, the procedure for sealing these holes was tightened up, as were the instructions for sealing the rear window and boot lid. A new grommet with a wider lip was introduced for the petrol filler pipe to prevent dust entering the luggage compartment. Dust had also been entering by way of the drain slots in the bottoms of the doors. This was prevented by wedging a length of foam in each door in such a manner that it still allowed water to drain from the holes. The rear compartment was tidied up and made more practical, not only by the provision of a hinged boot floor, but also by the addition of rubber mats. The side panels had their trim extended to cover the sides of the rear compartment.

These and other improvements, like the addition of an interior roof light, were also to be found on the A40 Countryman when it made its first appearance in September 1959. The Countryman was an attempt to satisfy the demand for full estate-car versatility. This was achieved by providing a rear window that was hinged at the top. The boot lid was still lowered in its original manner, but was supported in the open position by two metal stays. The Countryman did not have the boot-area cover at waist level, so straps were used to hold the rear-seat squab in the lowered position. There had been suggestions that the earlier saloon should have been equipped with wing mirrors for when the back window was obscured by bulky loads. This was dealt with on the Countryman by providing a pair of wing mirrors, but no interior mirror. Further criticism soon led to its restoration.

Considering that the estate-cum-saloon shape of the body had been determined as early as 1956, it is surprising that a folding rear seat did not figure in the design until January 1958. When, eventually, the decision was made, it meant that a new rear floor panel was required. In the earlier prototypes, the spare wheel stood in a depression in the floor.

It is difficult to understand why the job was not finished properly there and then, with a floor over the now-horizontal spare wheel, but it seems to have

been a matter of timing rather than a total lack of foresight. The specification for a proposed ADO 8 Traveller version (admittedly with the word Traveller crossed out and amended to Countryman) was first made out as early as July 1958, and by August 1958 the amended specification included a hinged boot floor. Five days after the launch of the saloon, it was decided that it, too, should have the same boot floor. The early criticisms had reached top management during the Longbridge launch itself, and Fisher & Ludlow were asked immediately to quote for fitting a floor. It was stipulated that the floor should be designed for fitting by distributors in the event of complaints from customers (which, obviously, were expected) and that it should be possible to fit it without any welding which might damage the exterior paintwork. There had been a suggestion that time and money could be saved by making the panel from plywood, suitably treated 'to prevent attack by termites in foreign countries'. However, when Fisher & Ludlow's estimate for fitting a metal floor came to £2 3s 6d per body, with a tooling charge of £13,511 10s 0d, this was considered the best solution.

Producing the full Countryman conversion would be a more expensive business. It required 33 new panels or pressings and 29 additional fittings. The extra cost of the steel pressings came to £9 9s 8½d per car, while the tooling cost was £113,290.

The original drawings, from which these costings were made, included a depression in the tailboard for the rear number plate. The number plate was to be hinged so that long loads could be carried legally with the tailboard open. This idea was dropped because of the danger of exhaust fumes being drawn into the car through the open tail-gate.

The decision to produce the Countryman had been made well before the launch of the saloon. At first, it was proposed as an Australian version of the car. By September 1958, a prototype Countryman was actually on its way to Australia. However, reactions to the saloon in Britain made it clear that a Countryman version would be appreciated here, too, so by December 1958, Austin were asking Fisher & Ludlow how soon they could produce the new bodies. They replied that they could be in production by July 1959. The Countryman was announced in September 1959, but a month later, at Earls Court, the Horizon blue and Tartan red examples of the new model were overshadowed by the simultaneous appearance of the Mini, Triumph Herald and Ford 105E Anglia.

The A40 Countryman was still received well, but

as it was some 70 lb heavier than the saloon, its lack of briskness, compared to the A35, was more noticeable.

As the The Autocar of 8 July 1960 put it: 'One cannot deny that this lively little engine is a very willing performer which seems to thrive on hard work; yet at the same time the predominant impression is that the power available is not quite adequate for the car. At times on busy roads there is just not quite sufficient "steam" for overtaking even when the engine is taken well up in its rev range in third gear. The driver does not need to be in much of a hurry to find that he drives with the throttle wide open for much of the time, and there are frequent occasions when an unfavourable wind and slight gradient will hold the car's speed down to 60 mph.'

That extra sound deadening seems to have been appreciated, however, because they found that, 'When it is idling the engine is scarcely audible either from within the car or from outside, and it never becomes noisy even when the car is driven to the limit of performance on the open road.'

The fuel consumption figures were found to be very much the same as the lighter saloon, no doubt helped by the Countryman's 5.60 × 13 in. tyres.

On its introduction, the price of the Countryman was £659 17s 6d, including purchase tax. All in all, The Autocar was happy that the Countryman version of the A40 'would appeal to many'. The basic saloon was now on sale at £639.

The very first Countryman left the factory in CKD condition in a batch of 36 that was sent to Australia on 23 September 1959. The first to be assembled at Longbridge was produced five days later and went straight to the publicity department. The build-up to full production was rather slow. The first week of November saw only six Countryman models produced, and by the end of 1959 only about 300 examples had been completed, although that number would be built each week in the new year.

When production of the A40 Mk I ceased in September 1961, a total of 141,897 saloons and 27,715 Countryman versions had been built. The Countryman was more favoured abroad, the export market taking approximately 25 per cent of the saloons and 45 per cent of the Countryman models.

Norman Milne drove a Mk I saloon in the 1961 Mobil Economy Run and tells us, 'In preparation for the event, I drove the A40 to Evesham and back on several evenings to try and achieve optimum fuel economy. Cruising at a gentle 35–40 mph to average precisely 30 mph, I managed 60 to the gallon, eventually attaining 62 mpg after some fine adjust-ment, the most significant of which was to ensure that the car rolled freely. Not too bad, I thought. The A40 should manage 50 mpg on the event itself.

'Starting and finishing at Worthing, the 948 cc A40 performed well, with only a blocked Zenith carb bringing it to a halt on the Hirnant Pass in North Wales on the third day. Over the tough 1066 miles at 30 mph overall average—which meant 40–50 mph cruising speeds and bursts of up to 60–62 mph—we averaged a whisker under 48 mpg to come fifth in class. The carb blockage had lost us valuable time on the Welsh mountain stage, which called for 70 mph motoring to reach the checkpoint without incurring penalty.'

In Norway and Sweden, the car was known as the A40 Futura. No doubt, this name was chosen to signify a car of up-to-the-minute styling, but it also seems to have been to avoid confusion with the Norwegian word farin, meaning castor sugar.

BMC (Australia) were in close touch with Longbridge during the development period of the A40. They were determined to have cars that stood up well to Australian conditions. Their own testing of the Morris Major and Austin Lancer prototypes, the Australian variants of the Wolseley 1500, had shown up structural deficiencies. Vibration of the fascia and steering column, for example, had given much cause for concern. They were not happy with the dust-proofing either, and were most insistent that Austin should give the prototype ADO 8 'the works', as they put it, on dust sealing. The excellent performance of the Volkswagen in Australia was making them a little jittery, and the great popularity of the six-cylinder Holden (produced by General Motors in Australia) was seen as an even bigger threat. By early 1958, Holden already had their own proving ground in Australia with facilities that BMC (Australia) could not hope to match. To help counter this threat, a Holden had been sent to Longbridge, with the suggestion that it should undergo testing alongside the English prototypes to see how it compared.

Before the A40 was launched in Australia, there had been a period of some 18 months without any small Austin on sale. The mid-1950s saw a reduction of more than 50 per cent in the value of BMC exports to Australia. Competition from Holden and Ford was increasing, and credit restrictions, a high Australian sales tax and ever-decreasing import quotas had all played their part. Australia was after the 100 per cent Australian car, and to comply with that desire, BMC had invested £5,000,000 in the factory at Victoria Park, Sydney, in which the A40 Farina was to be built alongside models such as the Austin Lancer

Mobil Economy Run 1961. Norman Milne and co-driver Mike Stevens with their Mk I saloon on the Hirnant Pass. *Courtesy Norman Milne*

Sun-visor and venetian blind complete the specification of this early A40 saloon built in Australia. Note the two-tone paintwork. Popular colour schemes were either a pale-pink or cream top with a light-grey body. *Courtesy Terry Jorgensen*

and Morris Major. The Austin Lancer did manage to attain something like 95 per cent Australian manufacture, and it was intended that the A40 should do the same. After the earliest Australian A40s were assembled from CKD packs supplied from Longbridge, the idea was to gradually increase the Australian content. The indigenous body panels would be produced by Fisher & Ludlow in their press shops on the Victoria Park site, but as the 1500 cc engined Lancers and Majors sold much better than the 948 cc A40, plans for the latter took a back seat. Only the A40 Mk I was built there.

The A40, of course, would have much more of an Italian connection than merely its illustrious stylist. It would also be built in Italy by Innocenti of Milan who, as important producers of press tools, supplied manufacturers like Ford, Fiat and Volkswagen but were probably better known for their Lambretta scooters. Their desire to add car manufacture to their range of activities suited BMC, who were just as keen to get a foothold in the developing Common Market, having found it impossible to compete in Italy due to the high duty on imported cars.

Negotiations took place during 1959, and a car was sent out for them to study in detail. In November of that year, Harry Williams, BMC's chief cost accountant, and his assistant Bill Rowkins made a nine-day visit to Innocenti. They took with them the A40 ledger and design schedule to calculate the cost of producing the car in Milan and to determine

whether or not it would be competitive with the likes of the Fiat 1100.

As liaison officer at Longbridge, Geoff Cooper remembers his involvement with Innocenti well: 'It was a marvellous plant, absolutely spotless. The car business and scooters were only a sideline. They were big machine-tool people, making enormous machine tools—bigger than anything we ever saw. All the drawings that went out there were in English and, of course, a great deal of the drawing wasn't on the paper. I mean, it was "understood" by the people who used them.'

Recalling his meetings with Signor Cheni of Innocenti, Geoff Cooper continues, 'I used to dread his visits. A very dry, factual and meticulous chap, he'd sit on the other side of my desk and put his briefcase on the floor. "Well, what is it this time?" I'd ask. "Ah, yes," he'd say, in extremely broken English— you had to listen carefully, "What is this skidpan?" He'd found a reference to it somewhere, but didn't know how to translate it. He could sit for a week, firing them at you—colloquialisms that weren't translatable—on every drawing you could usually find a dozen or more—big-end, gudgeon pin, things like that. He'd come over every week or two and pull out his briefcase. You'd think he'd finished and then he'd pull out another batch. There had to be a lot of clarification of our "understood intentions". If I referred a problem to the works, they would just tell me, "We make it to the drawings." When you take a crank you have all the different limits—all clearances are specified—but all the inspection and production people slowly arrive at a set of tolerances that gives them what they want. This never gets on the drawings. All that information is kept in the shop. We are only talking of minute amounts but this shop practice is of great importance. Innocenti produced their own drawings at the finish and made a damn good job of them.'

Harry Wall remembers Innocenti insisting from the outset on having wind-down windows, which would later be adopted on the Longbridge versions, too. The Mk I door panels were drilled with additional holes so that they could accept either sort of window mechanism.

George Coates is another who saw something of how Innocenti aimed to ensure that their first attempt at car production would be successful. On one visit to the factory, he found them stripping down all the engines as they arrived from Longbridge and checking them over before installing them. He managed to persuade Innocenti that it was quite unnecessary, as the engines had all been run at Longbridge on the rotary stand. He was very impressed with their standard of trim and paintwork, but on some of the prototypes they were having difficulty in getting the 'high spot' on the steering in the right position. As George describes it: 'Just a fraction out and the cars would wander—the high spot had to be in the centre with the wheels perfectly lined up. That's where the adjustable drag-link came in. I took one out with me and it cured it. You could use it on the steering-box side of the car and adjust it. They said, "Well, that's what we've been waiting for all the time." Of course, I got into trouble for taking it out, but they introduced the same thing on our own A40 Mk II, didn't they? Oh yes, that's the way it goes.'

The directors of Innocenti were running round in the first five cars they had built prior to the launch. They had not noticed that one of them was a bit cockeyed and could not understand why George was so bothered about it. He explains, 'I knew it was definitely crabbing. I got them to spray water on the test track and drove across it, holding the steering wheel exactly where it was, resting my arm on the window and aiming for spots on the track. You could see by the tyre marks it was about half a tyre track out. They had the proper tracking tools and long straight-edges. We even tried the wheels without the tyres on and eventually faced off the brake drums, but it was still out. All the distances seemed to check. There were no signs of any cracks

or anything because we had the car on a fork-lift truck—got underneath and checked it all. We couldn't find the trouble, it was just that one rogue car.'

The initial agreement was to assemble CKD vehicles sent from Longbridge, with Innocenti supplying the tyres. Then, they would see what they could produce themselves, working up from the simpler panels to the more complicated pressings. It was not too long before they were producing many of the parts themselves and paying royalties on each car. There was even a stage where some of the A40s built at Longbridge were being turned out with Innocenti rear axles.

Officially launched in Turin at the 1960 Salone dell'Automobile, the Innocenti cars started rolling off the production lines in Milan at the end of the year. The plan had been to build 500 cars a week, but shortage of skilled labour was given as the reason for only managing some 320 per week over the first two years of production. Between November 1960 and January 1962, Innocenti turned out 6444 of their Countryman version, the A40 Innocenti Combinata, and 10,213 of their Berlina saloon version. The Series 1 Innocenti A40 was the cheapest in its class in Italy and looked like being quite a success story.

A reception was held in London to mark Innocenti's entry into car production. Pat Moss (now Carlsson), seated on scooter, and Ann Wisdom (now Riley) had already done great things with their A40 (see Chapter 12). At the reception, Innocenti presented both with Lambretta scooters. *Courtesy Pat Moss-Carlsson*

8

THE A40 MK II SALOON AND COUNTRYMAN

The A40 Mk II was introduced in September 1961, with Austin declaring that the A40 had 'grown without putting on an inch', which explains rather nicely what they had been trying to achieve—more space in the same car without increasing the overall dimensions.

Previously, the publicity department had done their best to get good mileage out of the association with Pininfarina; now they were to stress the advantages of the car's shape with copy such as: 'Some cars are rounded off at the corners. The Austin A40 is elegantly *squared off* at the corners—square cars carry more than round cars.' Another advert challenged, 'If you can find a car that encloses more space for your money than the Austin A40 (and carries it more elegantly), let us know.'

The new model certainly looked wider and more impressive from the front, its full-width grille blending well with the original styling. The major change, however, was an increase of 3½ in. in the wheelbase. At first glance, the side view of the car appeared unchanged, but the increase in the wheelbase had entailed considerable alterations to the floorpan, wheel arches and side panels, and the rear springs had to be increased in length.

The idea was to provide more room for the rear-seat passengers by moving the seat further back. The luggage-carrying arrangements were also improved by hinging the rear-seat cushion so that it folded forward into the footwell. This provided a perfectly flat luggage platform when the squab itself was folded down.

A black crackle finish set off the smart new fascia, which had a much improved layout and more stylish speedometer. The indicators were operated from the steering column and cancelled on the return of the wheel; the wipers were self-parking. Providing the wind-up windows, which the Italians had had all along, silenced the quibbles of some. They could now be lowered into the doors completely, making it much more comfortable to lean an elbow out of the window.

Trim panels and seats were in a two-tone arrangement of Damask silver and a colour to suit the

ADO 44 in May 1961, four months prior to its launch as the A40 Mk II in September 1961. The full-width grille now incorporates the side lights/indicators and sports its new 'Austin' badge. To the left of the car is the Longbridge styling studio. To the right is the 'Kremlin' garage, where Len Lord would park his car each morning before looking in at the styling studio. *Courtesy Austin Rover*

Mk II interior, October 1961. The carpeting, black crackle fascia, and Damask silver two-tone upholstery and trim help to produce a more luxurious appearance. The 'Flying A' plate in the centre of the fascia covers the space provided for an optional radio. The heater controls are now built into the fascia, their old position being taken by the central ashtray. The edge of the parcel shelf and the lower edge of the fascia are both padded. *Courtesy Austin Rover*

A40 Mk II Countryman, October 1961. The rear-seat cushion now folds forward to allow the squab to lie completely flat. The bulkhead formed by the metal base of the cushion protects the back of the front seats. The Mk II Countryman had the same 5.20 × 13 in. tyres as the saloon. *Courtesy Austin Rover*

exterior body finish. Basic models were turned out in a single exterior colour, but there were new and brighter two-tone colour combinations, Cumulus grey and Snowberry white roofs being added to the range. A black roof could still be specified, but only on cars in Horizon blue or Agate red.

The A40 had already had considerable success in competition work, and the roadholding of the Mk II benefited from the experience thus gained. An anti-roll bar at the front and telescopic dampers at the rear made the car more amenable to hard driving. The brakes became fully hydraulic by replacing the rear frame cylinder with a cylinder at each rear wheel.

The new car was over 1 cwt heavier than the Mk I, so a little more power had to be found from somewhere. It was provided by replacing the Zenith carburettor with the SU version from the Minor. Use of the Minor's manifold and air cleaner meant that carburettor icing in cold weather could be avoided by positioning the air intake over the exhaust manifold. As a result of the changes, 37 bhp was available at 5000 rpm, as opposed to the previous 34 bhp at 4750 rpm. This relatively small increase in power gave an increase of at least 3 mph in top speed and, more importantly, an improvement in performance throughout the whole range of road and engine speeds. If the extra performance was used fully, the car was a little thirstier than its predecessor, although under normal driving there was little to choose between them in terms of economy.

At a steady 50 mph, one could still achieve a full 40 mpg. A new 7-gallon fuel tank increased the car's range between fill-ups, and an SU electric fuel pump replaced the earlier mechanical type.

The de luxe version continued to offer stainless window surrounds, opening rear quarter windows, overriders and passenger's sun-visor. In addition, there was a water-temperature gauge and windscreen washer, together with the luxury of fitted carpets instead of the rubber mats of the basic saloon.

The seats could still be criticized for their discomfort on long journeys, and more thought could have been given to this aspect, particularly the lack of side support for the driver and front-seat passenger. Many found the rake of the seats uncomfortable, too. An attempt to produce a universal seat for the whole range of small BMC cars was probably to blame. There are many who consider the front seats of the early A30s and the Series MM Minors much more comfortable than the seats in later models.

This aspect apart, the car received praise as a lively, reliable family car with a well-above-average load-carrying ability. The Countryman incorporated all the modifications of the Mk II saloon.

The first Mk II saloon to leave the factory, in Horizon blue with a black roof and white-wall tyres, went to the Paris Show. A week later, in mid-October 1961, two saloons and one Countryman were the next to be dispatched, going to Earls Court in combinations of Cumulus grey and Snowberry white, all with Cardinal red trim.

THE A40 MK II SALOON AND COUNTRYMAN

New Zealand, Holland, Belgium and Eire continued to take the A40 in CKD form, while Longbridge-built cars were still being exported worldwide, with Sweden proving to be a particularly good market. Many cars going there were fitted with steering locks and dash-pot heaters, the latter consisting of a distance piece between the carburettor and manifold which incorporated a thermostatically-controlled heater. Carpets were soon ruined by snow, so the Swedes favoured the optional rubber mats.

The two-tone interiors had only a short run. In the following spring, the seats were redesigned with horizontal stripes replacing the Damask silver panels. Seats and trim were in a single colour, which either matched or contrasted with the body colour.

Additional modifications were still to be made to the A40 during its production run, by far the most important being the fitting of the 1098 cc engine. This had been developed to provide a suitable power unit for ADO 16, which was launched as the Morris 1100 in 1962. The use of the A-series engine for the proposed 1100 was certainly not taken as a foregone conclusion. Much work had been done in the research department on a completely new, narrow-angle, aluminium V4 engine that was based on the 1090 cc Lancia V4. Six or eight engines were built, half of 1100 cc and half of two litres. The larger engines were tested in the Farina-bodied A60, and the smaller ones in A40 Farinas. These rather fine little engines developed around 55 bhp, but the cost of introducing and building them was considered too great. Even in those days, it would have been necessary to lay out something like £2,500,000 for a transfer machining line to handle the new cylinder block, and the total outlay would have been something like £10,000,000.

While work on the V4 engine had been going on, the feasibility of uprating the A-series unit had also been considered. The designers were asked to produce an 1100 cc engine, using a cylinder block the length of which had been determined for an 803 cc unit. It was asking a lot, but they came up with a proposal that achieved its aim by employing 2.54 in. (64.58 mm) bores and a 3.30 in. (83.72 mm) stroke, while retaining the same cylinder centres as the 950 cc unit. This only left $\frac{1}{4}$ in. (6.5 mm) of metal between the bores, but rigorous testing proved it to be perfectly satisfactory. The decision to stick with the A-series meant that transverse or in-line units could be produced on the same machinery, according to demand.

The 1098 cc A-series engine, as used in the A40

A 1098 cc Mk II saloon. The boot opens with a push-button in the centre of a grip, and the 'Austin A40' script is at the lower left-hand corner of the boot lid. The bumper-mounted number-plate light is now a little obtrusive but does contain two bulbs for better illumination. The side pieces of the rear bumper are now shorter to match the new position of the wheel arch in the rear quarter-panel.
Courtesy Tim Hinton

Farina, had a compression ratio of 8.5:1 and developed 48 bhp at 5100 rpm. It was installed in the A40 from September 1962 onwards and, at the same time, the opportunity was taken to employ a 4.22:1 (9/38) differential in place of the earlier 4.55:1 unit. The car was improved further by a new gearbox that employed baulk-ring synchromesh. This made gearchanging much easier and quicker. Although the earlier gearbox had been well liked, apart from its rather weak synchromesh, the new baulk-ring box was to rank as one of the best gearboxes of any small car of the period. The extra power was transmitted by a clutch that had been increased in diameter from $6\frac{1}{4}$ in. to $7\frac{1}{4}$ in. The king-pins were beefed up a little by increasing the diameter of the lower end, which necessitated small changes to the stub axle and lower bush.

With its higher rear-axle ratio, in top gear, the car did 15.3 mph per 1000 rpm, making for quieter cruising. Although this meant that top-gear acceleration and hillclimbing ability were not as good as before, top speed was increased to something like 78 mph, and the fuel consumption was much improved. At a constant 50 mph, the car could return over 44 mpg. Of course, Farina's clean lines had produced a car that slipped through the air better than most of its day. Even in 1965, tests in the MIRA wind tunnel showed that it was still one of the most aerodynamically-shaped family saloons around.

Norman Milne had driven a 948 cc Mk II A40 in the 1962 Mobil Economy Run and failed to attain the magic 50 mpg by only 0.4 mpg. For 1963, he entered in a 1098 cc A40 saloon and, as he put it: 'Surely a bigger engine must use more fuel. That was the theory once upon a time, but A35 versus A30 had soundly disproved that. Would 1098 versus 948 continue the trend? The 1963 test runs gave us 60 mpg with ease, but quite a bit of adjustment (within standard settings) was needed to coax 62, 63 and finally 64 to the gallon, using the windscreen-mounted glass measuring tank. In the event itself, we managed 51 mpg, which just goes to show—well, steady, disciplined development pays dividends; that the SU was a better bet than the fixed-jet Zenith; and that a bigger engine coupled with some advantage on final-drive gearing must work easier than a small one under most conditions.'

The press treated the 1098 cc engined car quite well. *The Motor* of 13 March 1963 summed up their report thus: 'In its fifth year, the Austin A40 remains practical and attractive to the family or business motorist. It has never had very good steering or very comfortable seats which makes it all the more surprising that no one has even yet put matters right. Apart from this, the car is difficult to fault. It is smart and well finished, economical, quite fast and has a most useful layout for family and luggage. Its heavy steering and inadequate turning circle make it less useful as a shopping car than other small saloons but its safety, good brakes, and splendid gearbox will appeal to drivers of both sexes.'

The only other major changes to take place during production were those made to the trim and fascia in October 1964, when the black crackle finish was replaced by a twin-cowled fascia with a simulated wood-grain finish. The vertical lines on the trim and the horizontal lines on the seats were both more closely spaced and were heat-formed instead of stitched.

On New Year's Day in 1962, an A40 Mk II had the distinction of being the 4,000,000th Austin produced. The Mk II remained in production until November 1967, and during its six-year run some 172,568 examples were built. Almost the same number of Mk I versions had been built in half that number of years but, of course, the Mk II faced much stiffer competition. Not only was it competing with the evergreen Minor, the Triumph Herald and new Ford Anglia, but it also had to contend with the introduction of the Ford Cortina, Vauxhall Viva, Mini and BMC 1100. Very competitive days indeed.

Motoring Which of January 1963 undertook the task of comparing the A40 Mk II Countryman with the Mini Traveller, Anglia Estate, Minor 1000 Traveller and Renault 4L. They felt it behaved much better than the Mk I version. Its handling was the least affected by a full load, but the most affected by side-winds. The A40 required the most effort to park and had the poorest turning circle. For long loads, the Renault 4L and Anglia came out best, the A40 worst. As for luggage carrying, they found the A40 held the least, and took particularly little with the back seat in place. They noted that, 'The bottom half of the Austin A40's door had to be closed by releasing two stays, which was awkward.' About a third of their drivers wanted more adjustment to the seats than was available. They found no natural place to rest the left foot, and the seat squab did not give adequate support to the small of the back. A

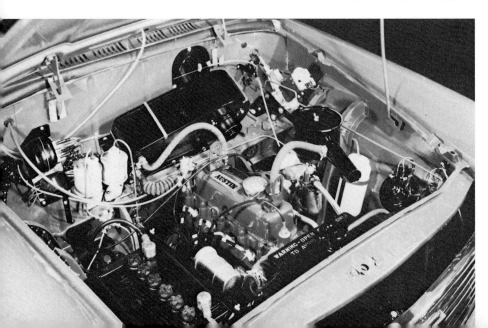

ABOVE RIGHT A simulated-wood-grain fascia was introduced in October 1964. The twin cowls house the speedometer and glove box. The heater controls now operate vertically. *Courtesy Tim Hinton*

LEFT Engine-bay of 948 cc Mk II A40 showing the SU carburettor. Most items, apart from the distributor, are very accessible, especially the battery. *Courtesy Austin Rover*

third of their drivers reported various aches and pains, 'mostly cramped stomachs and backache'. Even in this Mk II version, they found the rear seat rather firm and narrow, with very little room for the knees or feet. All of the cars were classed as noisy but, except for a rattle from the back door, the A40 was one of the best in that respect. Along with the Mini, its heater was considered very efficient.

They summed up: 'The Austin A40, costing £617, came out of our tests much better than the Mk I version . . . but it was the least useful as an estate car. We would think that for people who really need the carrying capacity of an estate car, one of the other cars would be better. But if you basically want a saloon car with the ability to carry a somewhat more than conventional load, the Austin A40 Countryman is a best buy.'

The Series 2 or Mk II Innocenti A40s were introduced in February 1962, almost six months after their introduction in England. Although basically the same as the Longbridge Mk II, they had several alterations to suit Italian regulations and tastes. The full-width grille was there, but the front indicators were oblong in shape. A white-painted dashboard housed the metric equivalent of the Longbridge speedometer, which was marked in the maximum speeds for each gear. Their duo-tone upholstery had the seat faces in one colour, the edges and backs in another.

An Innocenti A40 saloon was tested by the Italian motor magazine *Quattroruote* in June 1962. They had read in the British press that the Mk II A40 'behaved much better on the road' and, having tested the Innocenti version, declared, 'We have to agree that

BELOW AND BELOW LEFT The front views of these Mk II A40s show why many an A40 owner is not aware that the Mk II grille was altered in 1963. The earlier chrome-plated grille on 519 RHU has eight bars, one of which passes between the headlights and side lights. On the other hand, BFA 856C illustrates the later grille of seven slightly-thicker bars, which allowed for its production in aluminium. The lack of a bar between the lights is the easiest way to identify these later grilles. *Courtesy Tim Hinton*

519 RHU

BFA 856C

INNOCENTI AUSTIN *A40 S*

our colleagues beyond the Channel are right. . . the general behaviour of the car is improved greatly— better braking and roadholding, and more grip at the rear wheels with less lateral sliding on curves.' Acceleration was said to be improved, and the top speed of 130 km/h was thought notably good. However, they believed that comfort had deteriorated because of more noise from the transmission—the suspension seemed harder, too. The car's hillclimbing ability was said to be good, but was impeded by the stiffness of the gearchange. Fuel consumption was thought to be 'more than good', even at high speed.

They found the general design was still pleasing and felt that the internal and external finish had been improved. Something of a black mark was put against the pedals, which were too close, and they were not very pleased with the round accelerator pedal, 'which was devoid of a rubber covering'.

Surprisingly, the seating was said to be in the comfortable English style, low and restful, with plenty of legroom, but they did criticize the lack of width in the car. Access to the rear seats was classed as poor. Luggage capacity was considered 'sufficient for two people but scarcely so for four'.

On the whole, it was an excellent report, and the car gained good marks for ease of maintenance, except for the 'badly placed distributor'.

Over 16,800 of the 948 cc engined Series 2 Innocenti A40 were produced before the 1098 cc versions were introduced in December 1962. The new models were to be known as the A40S Berlina and A40S Combinata.

In April 1963, *Quattroruote* tested the A40S Combinata and gave all praise to the manufacturers for not altering the appearance of 'this pleasing car'. A new one-piece rear door, hinged at the top, was said to facilitate loading and unloading of luggage. The car earned much the same comments as before (there was obviously plenty of room for Italian legs, because they kept saying so), and they thought it 'generally pleasing for a semi station wagon which offered the advantages of good use of space'. They noted an 'increase in petrol consumption which even the makers admit' and, although they still did not like the closeness of the pedals, they were pleased to find that the accelerator with its 'disc' had been replaced by one with a square, rubber-covered pad.

The Innocenti A40 Combinata was always more popular than the saloon version. In all, 6861 examples of the A40S Berlina had been built when it went out of production in April 1965. The Combinata carried on until February 1967, by which time

INNOCENTI AUSTIN *A40 S*

LEFT A40 Futura Mk II. The 'Futura' script was in a pink anodized aluminium. Richard Younie of Leicester owns this example which he purchased in Sweden in 1966

TOP A 1098 cc Innocenti A40S saloon. Note the larger light to illuminate the rear number plate

CENTRE The Innocenti A40S Combinata featured a full lift-up tail-gate. With hindsight, we know that this is how things should have been from the beginning. Note the ash-trays in the rear trim panels, the white fascia, chrome horn ring, pivoting door-pulls and side repeater flashers

27,381 had been turned out. The peak year for the Innocenti A40 was 1963, when weekly production was only 50 short of the 500 target figure, but the same year saw the introduction of their version of

ABOVE **The Motor Show 1963. The A40 is still in the limelight, but just look at the competition from its stablemates!** *Courtesy Austin Rover*

CENTRE **This photograph is sometimes taken as evidence that the A40 Farina was being considered for badge-engineering. However, this was ADO 56, an Issigonis idea on which Barry Kelkin did much work. He recalls: 'It used a somewhat stretched Mini underframe with 12 in. wheels. It was front-wheel-driven from a transverse Mini-Cooper engine and was referred to as an MG Sport. It went like a bomb. We almost got it to production release before it was killed off.'** *Courtesy Austin Rover*

TOP **An A40 Panda car in service with Birmingham Police at Erdington in June 1967. During April, May and June of that year, the force bought 110 Mk II saloons in Police blue and white with Horizon blue trim. They were purchased through Bryant's of Bromsgrove.** *Courtesy Austin Rover*

9

VAN, COUNTRYMAN AND PICK-UP

The A30 (AV4) van was announced in August 1954. Its frontal appearance was almost identical to that of the saloon, only the flare to the front wheel arches having been altered slightly to accommodate 5.90 × 13 in. tyres. (The tyres of the saloon were 5.20 × 13 in.) From the front screen rearward, the van used all-new panels. To increase their rigidity, the side panels employed sunken pressings, and to give the whole van a unified appearance, the rear and side doors were given the same treatment. The single rear door was hinged on the offside and held open at 90 degrees. The flat-floored load area, with a capacity of some 60 cu ft, could be aired via a simple roof vent. Only export models had a passenger seat as standard equipment.

Heavier rear springs and a rear-axle ratio of 5.375:1 were the only other changes required to adapt the vehicle to its new payload of 5 cwt.

When put to the test by *Commercial Motor* in May 1955, the van was found to be: 'Smart and snappy . . . . Nimble in congested streets, easy to load and comfortable to drive.' They suggested, 'this little van has all the attributes required for local delivery work.'

In 600 miles, all covered within a 30-mile radius of London, they returned an average fuel consumption of 36 mpg. The new differential allowed for lively acceleration with a maximum speed well in excess of 60 mph. The ride at high speed was smooth and stable, whether the van was laden or empty, and the brakes were extremely efficient. The major criticism was that of poor rear vision, although it should be pointed out that the same criticism was made of almost every small van tested in that era.

The road tester went to considerable trouble in assessing the ease of servicing by actually doing the jobs himself. He accomplished everything 'without meeting any snags', but he suggested that the inspection holes for the rear dampers could have been larger and the distributor more accessible.

Some lively and enterprising advertising extolled the van's virtues, picturing it with either the greengrocer who 'knows his onions' or the baker who 'uses his loaf'. In those pre-supermarket days, such businesses constituted an important sector of the light-van market, since it was almost essential for them to offer a delivery service to a largely unmotorized public.

The A30 van certainly proved a favourite with many small businesses, but there were national concerns to aim at as well. Morris were so well established as suppliers of mail and telephone vans that there was little hope in that direction, but the A30 did have considerable successes with customers as diverse as the Co-op, the police and the Royal Automobile Club.

In October 1956, the introduction of the A35 (AV5) van coincided with the launch of the A35 saloon. The main change was the use of the new engine and gearbox from the saloon. In the van, the engine had a compression ratio of 7.2:1, but the high-compression version was also available if required. The low-compression engine developed 32 bhp at 4600 rpm. The rear-axle ratio was the same as the saloon (4.55:1), and the tyres were now 5.60 × 13 in., giving a road speed of 14.72 mph/1000 rpm in top gear. Overall fuel consumption was about 42 mpg. Although this first version of the A35 van had the painted grille and chromed horseshoe surround of the A35 saloon, it retained the trafficators and rubber side-light bases of the A30. A passenger seat, radio and recirculating heater were optional extras.

With its much-improved engine and transmission, the A35 van was suited to the needs of many more customers. Robinson TV Rentals of Bedford was a typical customer—they had over 100 vans which covered more than 1,000,000 miles a year. The RAC bought them for the officers who supervised their road patrols. Each van would cover about 25,000 miles a year, with petrol consumption approaching 40 mpg. Other vans were used by the road patrols

A30 (AV4) 5-cwt van at Longbridge on 9 August 1954. The side-panel detail is matched in the door skins. *Courtesy Austin Rover*

An A30 van engaged in temporary road signing for the RAC in 1955. *Courtesy RAC*

An A30 van being put to appropriate use in Austin livery. *Courtesy Austin Rover*

AUSTIN A35
5 CWT
PROTOTYPE
ENGINEERING VAN

themselves and seem to have given good service.

A35 vans were used in large numbers by water, electricity and gas authorities. The Scottish Gas Board used some 60 A35 vans at any one time, each sporting a pair of gas water heaters on the roof. Some of these vans were kept spick and span, being used by a regular driver in his job as a meter reader or installation inspector. Maintenance records have shown quite a few to have covered 130,000 miles and more on the original clutch and without any major replacements whatsoever. Vans involved in heavy on-site work, however, were hammered by a multitude of different drivers. Nevertheless, they gained a reputation for standing up well to such treatment, although the bodywork—mainly the doors—did give trouble when these hard-worked vans got a bit long in the tooth. The driver's door tended to droop, and the hinges of the rear door were prone to breaking.

The A35 van saw service in most parts of the world. Bangkok, in particular, had a great liking for them. From late 1956 onwards, they took many shipments, virtually all in Tweed grey with Cherry red trim, exterior sun-visors and white-wall tyres.

After the A35 saloon was discontinued in July 1959, the vans remained in production. In April 1962, the Mk II version was introduced as the A35 (AV6) 5-cwt van. The side doors no longer had sunken panels, and a plated strip ran along the waistline. Flashing indicators were introduced, and the radiator grille and wheels were painted white.

ABOVE **Rear view of 939 EXU. They certainly made a neat and thorough job of kitting it out.** *Courtesy British Telecom*

TOP **Prototype A35 Post Office Telephones van. It was one of only two A35s purchased by the GPO. Its companion, 940 EXU, was a post van and was, therefore, in Royal Mail red livery. The numbers over the wheel arches give the required tyre pressures.** *Courtesy British Telecom*

Prior to this, black had been the standard wheel colour for the A30 and A35 light commercials. The AV6 was only in production for six months. Of the 13,000 or so produced, only 155 were exported.

The Mk III A35 (A-AV8) 6-cwt van was introduced in October 1962. It employed the 1098 cc engine and SU carburettor, but it retained the mechanical fuel pump. With a compression ratio of 7.5:1, it developed 45 bhp at 5100 rpm. It was fitted with the larger $7\frac{1}{4}$ in. clutch and the new gearbox with baulk-ring synchromesh. A rear-axle ratio of 4.22:1 (9/38) and 5.60 × 13 in. tyres gave a road speed of 15.94 mph/1000 rpm in top gear. Windscreen washers and a rooflight were fitted as standard, and 5.90 × 13 in. tyres were offered as an optional extra.

Commercial Motor tested the Mk III van in December 1962 and found it an 'unusual mixture of the excellent and ordinary'. They credited it with a remarkable performance, better than any van of its type they had tested, but were worried by what they considered to be poor forward visibility. Of course, the van had been in production for some eight years and was getting a little dated when compared to more recent introductions that sported curved screens. They summed up the van by suggesting, 'As a lively, robust, economical and not unattractive small delivery vehicle, it is undoubtedly a good proposition at its current basic price of £388 (including painting).'

The opinions of Norman Milne, one-time editor of Austin's *Payload* magazine, can hardly be considered as unbiased, but he did do a good job in championing the van. In 1963, the 1098 cc van made the front cover of the September/October issue of *Payload*, and the caption inside proclaimed, 'Boasting one of the highest power-to-weight ratios of any goods vehicle built today, the famous Austin A35 van . . . in its latest 1100 cc form . . . offers an overall performance which is remarkable even by current private car standards! Our cover photograph shows the A35 van on test, travelling at 80 miles per hour along the M5 motorway—the corrected two-way maximum speed having been timed at 77 mph. Supplementing a laden power-to-weight ratio of 42 bhp per ton (or some 60 bhp per ton with only the driver aboard), sensible final drive gearing gives 16 mph for every 1000 rpm and provides an effortless and astonishingly economical performance.'

Norman's editorial in the same issue of *Payload* went under the heading of 'Something for Nothing'. He pointed out how the steady development of the A-series engine and the gradual improvement of the

A-AV8 1098 cc A35 van outside the styling studio on 29 April 1963. Note the white wheels and white grille that were introduced from the start of AV6 production. Twin wing mirrors were fitted from May 1959 onwards. *Courtesy Austin Rover*

power-to-weight ratio of the A30/35 van had resulted in a 20 per cent increase in both maximum and cruising speeds. He concluded that perhaps it was possible 'to have your cake and eat it', because even though the engine capacity had been increased by almost 40 per cent and the power output had gone up by some 60 per cent, it had all taken place without detriment to economy. Indeed, if anything, users would now find the van consuming rather less petrol than before.

The passenger's seat and recirculating heater were the only optional extras offered for the 1098 cc van, but export customers could stipulate a four-blade fan, km/h speedometer, right- or left-hand steering, and lighting and flasher equipment to suit any export requirement, all at no extra cost. Export customers were also offered the extra-cost options of heater, laminated windscreen, sun-visors, radio, overriders, locking petrol cap, ashtrays and wheel trims. By now, twin wing mirrors were standard on all the vans.

The final A-AV8 A35 van had an 848 cc engine which was an in-line version of that used in the Mini. With a compression ratio of 8.3:1, it produced 34 bhp at 5500 rpm. A rear-axle ratio of 4.875:1 (8/39) meant that the road speed per 1000 rpm in top gear was only 13.8 mph. This was rather a backward step; it produced an economical van for local deliveries, but one which was much less pleasant on the open road. It had the same gearbox, clutch and flywheel as the 1098 cc version.

The first 850 cc van was built in a batch of ten in October 1963, but the 1098 cc version remained in production until May 1966. General Universal Stores showed considerable interest in the 848 cc

Two A30 van bodies accompany two A30 Countryman bodies on their journey from Fisher & Ludlow to the assembly lines at Longbridge. *Courtesy Austin Rover*

vans and, eventually, both they and the RAC bought large numbers. This smaller-engined van continued in production until February 1968, just managing to outlive the A40 Farina.

The A30/35 van was a great favourite with private motorists of limited means. Exempt from purchase tax, it carried them about just as well as the saloon and had the added advantage of being a very useful load carrier.

In the RAC magazine, *Road and Car*, of summer 1985, readers were told that, 'A humble Austin A35 van started David Bellamy on his drive to conserve our countryside.' David was quoted: 'Of all the vehicles I have owned, I owe the A35 a great debt. When I was carrying out research on peat bogs, which gave me my basic knowledge of ecology, that van took me all over Europe—up to the borders of Russia, and from the south of France to the west of Ireland. I could never at the time have been able to visit all those sites any other way. And eventually it helped me get my PhD and become a world authority on peat bogs and peat lands.'

Several firms catered for those wanting to add rear seats and side windows to their vans, but if you succumbed to the luxury of windows, you were liable to pay tax.

To give some idea of the economics involved, let us consider a van that was purchased for £368 10s 0d in April 1960. A passenger's seat, heater, delivery charge, licence duty and number plates brought the total price to £401 19s 11d. Side windows and a rear-seat conversion, added later, cost £6 15s 0d and £19 respectively. The grand total stood at £427 15s 11d.

With the addition of the windows, the Customs & Excise collector took a new interest in the vehicle, sending the owner a demand for £43. An accompanying note, explaining that the money had to be paid within seven days, could hardly have endeared him to the van's owner. There was not much else to do but pay up—the penalties for evasion were heavy. Still, having fitted the windows and paid the excise duty, the owner could relax more while driving. Prior to that, it would have been a question of taking great care not to be caught exceeding the 40 mph speed limit that was in force in those days for even light commercial vehicles.

Of course, if you had the money, you could have bought the Countryman version in the first place and saved yourself all the bother.

The A30/35 Countryman

In Fisher & Ludlow's records, the A30 Countryman was often referred to as the passenger van. The production history of the Countryman runs parallel with the vans of the same period. The A30 (AP4) Countryman was introduced at the same time as the van, in September 1954, and was replaced by the A35 (AP5) Countryman in October 1956. The Mk II version of the A35 (AP6) Countryman was introduced in April 1962, but was only produced until September of the same year, when production of the A35 Countryman ceased altogether. This version of the Countryman is the rarest vehicle in the A30/35 range. Only 74 were built, and 13 of these were exported. With a weight of 14¾ cwt, the Countryman was the heaviest vehicle in the A30/35 range.

The mechanical specification of the Countryman, including the rear-axle ratios, was the same as the equivalent van, except that the A35 Countryman had the high-compression engine as standard, with the low-compression version available on request. The only external difference to the bodywork, apart from the side windows, was the lack of a roof ventilator on the Countryman versions. The A30 Countryman was produced with 5.90 × 13 in. tyres but, like the A35 van, the A35 Countryman had 5.60 × 13 in. tyres.

Other differences between van and Countryman lay almost entirely in the trimming of the rear portion of the body and in the rear seating and luggage compartment. Trim panels were added to the van sides and rear door. These, together with a full-

length headlining, made things less van-like and somewhat quieter. One half of each long side window could be slid open. Even with the rear seat in use, there was a reasonable luggage space. To accommodate bulky loads, the two separate cushions from the rear seat were placed behind the front seats. Then, the rear-seat backrest was folded forward to make a continuous flat floor. The advert ran: 'See the Austin A30 Countryman—it's two cars for the price of one! . . . For Work—rear seat folds forward to give 47 cu ft of space for a 5-cwt load. For Pleasure—roomy rear seat comfort, and you still have 19 cu ft of luggage space.' As in the van, the spare wheel and tools were conveniently accessible from below the flat floor, without having to disturb the load.

BELOW A30 Countryman at Longbridge on 4 October 1954. *The Autocar* later used the same photograph along with the following words: 'The lines of the model are neat, and indented panels, painted in a different colour from the rest of the car, take away any van effect. This is a clever way of keeping something of the particularly attractive appearance of the old-style timber bodies.' It may just be possible to make out the timber-graining effect that had been used on the darker panels. *Courtesy Austin Rover*

ABOVE This AP5 A35 Countryman provided mobility for an early Crypton testing machine. With an oscilloscope added to the meters and gauges of older testing equipment, it produced the UK's first all-in-one tester. Advanced for its day, it also incorporated an exhaust-gas analyser. *Courtesy TI Crypton*

LEFT Prototype AP4 A30 Countryman at Longbridge on 30 April 1954, four months before the launch of the Countryman and van in the following September. That could well be Spanish dust on the bumper and wheels because this vehicle was tested in Spain. The chrome trim of prototypes was often painted over in order to attract less attention. *Courtesy Austin Rover*

With the seating in place, the Countryman will carry four
people with generous luggage space behind the rear seat.
Courtesy Austin Rover

On its introduction, the A30 Countryman was
priced at £560 14s 2d (£395 basic plus £165 14s 2d
purchase tax). It was the only estate-type vehicle on
the market with a basic price of less than £400. Its
appeal lay not only in this fact, but also in its ability
to offer a surprising carrying capacity for such a neat
and manoeuvrable vehicle. Over the years, the price
fluctuations were mainly due to the changes in the
rate of purchase tax. In 1956, the basic price was
the same as on the day it had been launched, but
purchase tax was £198 17s 0d. Worse was to come.
By 1957, the basic price had risen to £425 and the
purchase tax was a massive £213 17s 0d, a full 50
per cent. The highest asking price for the Countryman was £648 14s 9d in January 1962.

In 1960, the Countryman would have cost you
£444 plus £186 2s 6d tax, making a total of
£630 2s 6d. If we add on the cost of a heater, delivery
charges, licence duty and number plates (to put the
Countryman on the road in a similar condition to
the converted van considered previously), we get a
total of £656 17s 5d, compared to £470 15s 11d for
the converted van. It is clear that the practical owner
could save something in the region of £170, or about
25 per cent of the cost.

The A35 pick-up—commercial or two-seater coupé?

Advertising for the pick-up billed it as 'everyman's
utility car'. In the event, this was to prove rather
ironic, as less than 500 examples were built. Usually
one does not regard pick-ups as having style, but
in this case Dick Burzi had produced something that
was very pleasing to the eye. There cannot be many
vehicles which attract such favourable comment
from the casual passer-by.

Why, then, should such a pleasant little vehicle
have great difficulty in finding even 500 buyers?
The idea had been to market what was really a two-
seater coupé that would avoid purchase tax by
masquerading as a commercial vehicle. This addition
to the Austin range was announced in *The Motor* of
5 December 1956, where it was suggested that the
main idea was to cater for the needs of builders and
the like, taking people and materials to the site of
work. The sales brochure showed how the rear compartment's hinged floor could form a temporary seat
for two people, providing 'an ideal arrangement for
switching labour quickly from one spot to another'.

People were sat in the back for the press-release
photographs to emphasize the open nature of the
rear, but some thought this unwise because it
stressed its role as a passenger carrier. They suggested that it would have been better to have thrown
a couple of pigs in the back, but the absence of a
tail-gate would still have made it difficult to argue
that the vehicle was a genuine workhorse. As it
turned out, the Customs & Excise folk were not
interested in such debates. They simply pointed to
the 'Vehicle Construction and Use' regulations,
which stipulated that the rear platform of a pick-up
had to be at least two-thirds of the vehicle's overall
length. Tax would have to be paid.

When it was apparent that there were problems
ahead, it was decided to produce a cheap sales
brochure in two colours only. Production had
started in November 1956, but no selling price had
been agreed upon by the time of the December press
announcement. In *Commercial Motor* of 11 January
1957, the extent of the problem was revealed. The
inclusive price of the pick-up would be nearly £130
more than expected. It had been hoped that the
vehicle would be assessed as a special case, with a
purchase tax of approximately £50. Instead, its
assessment as a passenger vehicle attracted £180 in
tax on top of the basic price of £360.

A short production run was inevitable. It was
going to be very difficult to sell a two-seater vehicle
of limited carrying capacity, which had lost the
advantage of tax avoidance. Many dealers had the
vehicles on their hands for so long that they threw
in the towel and used them as garage runabouts. The
production records show that the dates of production and registration of a large number of pick-ups
were many months apart.

Some 475 pick-ups were completed, but it seems
that at least 491 production bodies were built. There
are strong rumours of three pick-up bodies still in
the famous underground tunnels at Longbridge.

ABOVE A period showroom photograph of an A35
Countryman amidst other Austin LCVs in 1958–59. *Courtesy
Ken Jee*

RIGHT A35 AP5 Countryman, 10 December 1956. It still has
the A30's semaphore direction indicators and black wheels.
The side lights sit on the rubber bases used for all A30s
rather than on the chromed slippers of the A35 saloon.
Courtesy Austin Rover

BELOW RIGHT 'A30-type' pick-up, photographs of which were
used in publicity shots. By the time the photographs were
seen in the brochure, the trafficators, continuous grab rail
and chrome door strip had been carefully airbrushed out
of the picture and a flashing indicator had been added to
the rear wing. This vehicle had a bench seat in the cab, and
very likely an A30 engine and gearbox. The photo was
taken outside the Longbridge styling studio on 28 June
1956. The lad nearest the camera is John Chasemore, who
can still be found in the Longbridge photographic
department, which is within a few yards of where this
photograph was taken. Note the pre-production step on the
rear bumper and the rimbellishers on the wheels. *Courtesy
Austin Rover*

LEFT An A35 (AK5) pick-up at Longbridge on 10 December
1956. Note that this vehicle has the flashing indicators, step
and separate grab rails of the production vehicles. As the
spare wheel was out in the open, it was provided with a
lock. On this example, it is on the uppermost wheel nut.
Courtesy Austin Rover

Such rumours are not uncommon, but this one could just be true. There are also yarns of a pick-up that was still running around inside the Longbridge works in the mid-1970s. Could this have been the pick-up (chassis no. 13,386, body no. P.U.372) that was allocated to Alec Issigonis and Jack Daniels in the engineering design department and which was still in the works at the 1965 stocktaking?

Anyone reading the September 1954 edition of *British Automobiles Overseas* could be forgiven for thinking that there was such a thing as an A30 pick-up. The magazine proclaimed, 'Another new Austin exhibit [at Earls Court] is an A30 pick-up.' In the October issue, however, they corrected themselves: 'A late introduction at the commercial show was the Austin A30 Countryman, and not a pick-up truck on the A30 as said in our last issue.' Strangely enough, the pick-up was designated as an A30 on all the original drawings and parts lists at Fisher & Ludlow, where the bodies were built, although it always appeared as the 'A30 Pick-up AK5', rather than AK4, which would have been more logical had the intention been to produce it as an A30. In any case, it was not put on the market until the A35 was in full production, so no A30 pick-ups were sold. At least one prototype had semaphore trafficators and rear quarter panels which conformed to the A30's rear-light arrangement. It also had a bench seat, which would seem to indicate that it was powered by an A30 engine and gearbox. Surely, it would have been impossible to accommodate the A35's remote gearchange with such a seating arrangement. It is strange that the photographs used to announce the pick-up in *The Motor* of 5 December 1956 should show this A30-type pick-up prototype, while two days later *The Autocar* carried a photo of a pick-up with flashing indicators and all the correct details of the production vehicle.

The cab of the production version was fitted out in a similar manner to the A35 saloon, although the floor covering was in a vinyl-coated felt. Most pick-ups were trimmed in Cherry red, the floor covering, tonneau cover and spare-wheel cover having white edging, and the seats white piping.

The hinged boards of the pick-up bed were purchased by Fisher & Ludlow ready-primed and then finished in the body colour. They had Budget locks, which were operated by a T-shaped key that was stowed in a loop sewn into the scuttle side carpet. The area below the bed floorboards served as a tool locker.

Mechanically, the pick-up was the same as the 948 cc A35 van. Its engine had a compression ratio

of 7.2:1, with the option of the 8.3:1 ratio. The same rear-axle ratio of 4.55:1 (common to the 948 cc saloon, van and pick-up) gave a road speed of 14.72 mph per 1000 rpm. Norman Milne spoke of time spent behind the wheel of an A35 pick-up as follows: 'I used the press demonstrator pick-up for some time and thoroughly enjoyed driving it at speed. With standard A35 final-drive gearing and 5.60 × 13 in. van tyres, it easily exceeded 75 mph and would cruise at 60–65 all day, with 60 mph available in third. Acceleration was decidedly brisk due to its light weight, but its rear end would unstick itself all too readily in the wet—much more dramatically than that of a standard A35.' Undoubtedly, what Norman says is correct. On a wet roundabout, or in snow, you can certainly have some fun. To get satisfactory traction in the snow, it is essential to carry some ballast, but it is interesting to note that the manufacturer put the weight of the van, pick-up and two-door car all at 13½ cwt.

Generally, it is thought that all A35 pick-ups were turned out in Tweed grey with Cherry red trim, and it is not surprising that this should be so. Although the first pick-up was in green with beige trim, and the last was in County cream, there were 381 Tweed grey examples in between. The green one was the only non-grey example to be sold on the home market. It seems to have been the final prototype, with no body number allotted to it, and was built on 17 October 1956, some three weeks before normal production began. It was sold in the usual way, but not until 28 May 1957, when it was dispatched to Barretts of Canterbury.

Of the 475 pick-ups, 248 were sold on the home market and 227 were sent overseas, 91 of the latter being in left-hand-drive form. We have to turn to the export versions if we wish to investigate the total range of colours used. Many of those exported were in Tweed grey, of course, but others were as follows: County cream (33)—all with Cherry red trim, except one with brown trim; Island blue (10), Streamline blue (7), Speedwell blue (6)—all blue cars having blue trim, except one with dark-blue trim; Spruce green (10), all with green trim. In addition, 27 pick-ups were supplied in primer to overseas markets, so heaven knows what colours they became.

Production proper started in November 1956 and continued until 25 January 1957. During these 11 weeks, 414 pick-ups were completed, with production at its peak in December, when about 50 per week were turned out. A further group of 15 cars were made in February 1957, and the remainder were built in very small batches. More often than

Bob Koto photographed in the
Longbridge experimental department
with his full-sized clay model and
alternative frontal treatment

A close-up of the front of the full-sized
model. When put under a microscope
the badge was found to read 'Austin 25'
rather than A30

In Chapter 1 we saw one side of the full-
sized model. Here we see the alternative
styling offered on the other side of the
same model

A30 prototype used in the special 'Pre-release Edition' of a brochure given to Austin employees. The pretty girl, Yvonne Coates (now Hodson), is the daughter of George Coates. Yvonne worked in the publicity department at Longbridge. Her lovely red hair made her a favourite with the Austin photographer, Ron Beach. *Courtesy Austin Rover*

The photograph on the left and those on the following pages were used in contemporary sales brochures and advertising and are reproduced with the kind permission of Austin Rover

It's Speedy!

and so stimulating to drive

Buyable! Eyeable! Reliable! The slickest little car that ever
set wheels on the road and the best means of travel for the motorist
of modest means. Yes, it's the Austin A30 Seven, the
small car that is setting the pace for extra-economical
family motoring.

It's *Simplicity* itself to handle

Driving the A35 is a happy experience. Controls are sensibly positioned and the attractive, centrally placed instruments can be read at a glance from either left- or right-hand steering positions.

ABOVE With the advent of the A40 Farina, 'the latest expression of the Austin line', Austin advertising stepped out of the world of half-timbered cottages into the age of the motorway

RIGHT This picture of the main mechanical components of the Mk I A40 Farina could almost have come straight from an A35 brochure, the only visible difference being the front brake drums. Farina's styling had certainly transformed the 'package'

Austin line

OVERLEAF TOP The full-width grille of the Mk II A40 resulted in a more impressive and wider-looking car, yet blended well with the original styling

OVERLEAF BOTTOM The Italian job—built by Innocenti and launched in 1960—differed in details, such as wind-down windows, which were later adopted by Longbridge. Here we see their Series 2 version. *Courtesy Archivio Quattroruote*

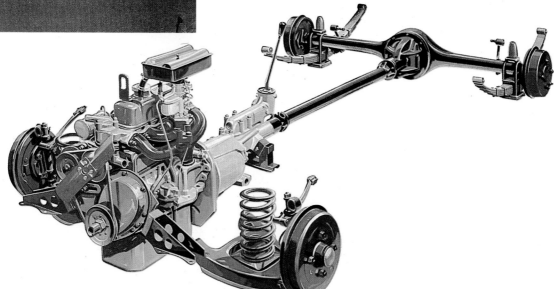

Way out in front—the **AUSTIN** A 40 MkII

A club publicity drive managed to bring together nine examples of this very rare vehicle for the Austin A30–A35 Owners Club National Rally, held at Knebworth House in

May 1983. Inset: Kjell Edding, who had driven his pick-up to the rally from Spanga in Sweden

not, only a single pick-up came off the lines in any one day. The last pick-up was built on 23 December 1957 and was dispatched to the island of Guam, in the Pacific, to join three others that had been sent there in the previous January.

It is probably as well to record the destinations of the exported pick-ups, since the information may well create interest that leads to more of these rare vehicles being unearthed. It also gives a good indication of the countries to which the other models surveyed in this book were dispatched.

A total of 48 pick-ups went to Chile, where they seem to have liked variety, because among those 48 we find all the colours that were produced. Bangkok had 23, while Penang, Singapore, Kuala Lumpur, Rarotonga and Suva all took one or two each. Single pick-ups were dispatched to Caracas, El Salvador and Bolivia, as well as to Dar es Salaam, Tonga and Lourenço Marques, while a brace of pick-ups went

to Beira. Three went to Lobito in Angola and seven to the Philippines. New Zealand took 17 pick-ups, four of which had exterior sun-visors, and five were sent in primer to Montreal. Zimbabwe had 31, four of them in primer, and four went to neighbouring Malawi, eight to Uganda and eight to Kenya. Norway took seven pick-ups, and Sweden four, while Denmark took only one. Single pick-ups also went to Zurich, Paris and Amsterdam. The Amsterdam car, in Island blue, was displayed at their 1957 Motor Show. Belgium took two pick-ups, as did Greece and Portugal, while one went to Gibraltar. Two went to India, nine to Sudan, three to Kuwait and one to Aden, while 11 went to the West Indies (two to Jamaica, two to Bermuda, three to Barbados and four to the Bahamas).

Recently, pick-ups have come to light in Norway, Sweden, South Africa, Zimbabwe and Canada, and although it is not known if the Tweed grey pick-up that went to Zurich in 1956 still exists, we do know what happened to it originally. For three or four years, it was used by Emil Frey, the Swiss distributor. In 1985, he recounted how he drove it everywhere and found it very handy for his regular shooting and fishing expeditions. Emil's son, Walter, who now heads their splendid organization, learnt to drive in this pick-up when he was only nine years old. As his father worked his way along a river, young Walter would keep the pick-up abreast of his father's position. At the age of 11, he drove it home some 20 miles on the road. Finding it difficult to reach the pedals, he sat on the front edge of the seat, a box of fishing tackle behind him for support.

In recent years, the production records have been used to verify over 50 A35 pick-ups that are still in existence. The relative ease with which they have been found would suggest that there may well be more than twice that number worldwide.

The A35 pick-up is a vehicle which warrants restoration from even a very dilapidated state. Although a rare vehicle, the pick-up is still perfectly suitable for daily use as a lively and economical means of transport. A restored version creates a remarkable amount of interest at shows and rallies. It may not be quite as practical as the van or Countryman, but its appeal and its rarity make it an undoubted classic, which a person of even modest means may aspire to without much fear of breaking the bank.

The A40 Farina van

The Countryman version of the A40 Farina was dealt with alongside the saloon, but this chapter on light commercial vehicles would not be complete without a mention of the A40 Farina van. Produced in both Mk I and Mk II forms, nearly all ended up in Finland and Portugal. These so-called vans were actually fully-trimmed Countryman models which had steel panels added to their rear quarter-light apertures.

Over 420 of the Mk I version were dispatched to Helsinki, and more than 40 to Portugal. Most were in Farina grey with Tartan red trim, but there were a few in Horizon blue with blue trim and one in Tartan red with black trim. Two of the Mk I vans went to South America in Sutherland green.

Both Portugal and Finland imported the 948 cc Mk II version. Portugal seems to have carried on longer than Finland, with at least 156 of the 1098 cc version heading for Lisbon in 1966–67. It is impossible to be more accurate, because the production records sometimes describe them as 'van', sometimes

An A35 pick-up in appropriate use. The author's pick-up graces the front cover of an issue of *Spotlight*, during his six-year stint as editor of that magazine. *Courtesy Anne Sharratt*

as 'metal type', sometimes as 'body-type van', but other unmarked Countryman models that were exported to Finland and Portugal may well have been A40 vans.

Export sales executive Stan Woodgate muses, 'We shipped them as vans, but you can bet your boots they ended up as plush little Countrymen. Oh yes, that was a fiddle—about six little spot welds that could be levered out—we had to do all sorts of things for different territories.'

Of course, there were more than six spot welds, but it would be a shame to spoil Stan's turn of phrase. In any case, the result would certainly be as he said. It was simply a question of overcoming import restrictions on private cars.

A-AW8 948 cc A40 van in November 1961. Steel panels took the place of the Countryman's side windows. This version was for export only and went almost entirely to Finland and Portugal. *Courtesy Austin Rover*

10
THE SHOP-FLOOR STORY

During the 1950s and 1960s, one area at Longbridge was transformed beyond recognition. At the end of the war, this elevated portion of land, known as the 'Flying Ground', was largely deserted. It was definitely the 'back door' of the factory. All you would find up there were a few piles of platform chassis destined for Austin Eights and Tens.

After the war, buildings rose thick and fast to produce a new 'front door', through which thousands of visitors from home and overseas were welcomed in fine style. You knew that you had arrived at 'Austin of England' by the impressive script high above the imposing curved frontage. On your right, you could not fail to notice the massive 'Flying A' on the end of the car assembly building—the remainder of the building disappearing into the distance. It all gave the impression that management and workers alike were proud to belong to 'The Austin'.

Having entered the reception area, no doubt casting a quick glance over the silver models depicting Austins through the years, you would pass into the vast exhibition hall. You might find a special display for the launch of a particular model, or a display of the complete range of Austin and BMC cars: 'A Motor Show in itself,' they used to say. The A40 Farina was launched in this exhibition hall. The old showroom that had seen the unveiling of the A30 had been demolished, and a new production planning department had taken its place.

After a tour of car assembly, you could enjoy a rest and a meal in the visitors' dining room or, if you were considered important, you would be taken across the bowling-green-like lawns to the privacy of the 'Kremlin'. A favoured few—very few—might get a peep into Dick Burzi's styling studio, and see the stylists and modellers padding around the highly-polished parquet floor in either soft shoes or galoshes. A glimpse at some of the futuristic styling sketches and the sheeted-over, top-secret new models would increase your awareness of being in a privileged position.

In the mid-1950s, when credit squeezes left new cars stockpiled everywhere, Leonard Lord was speaking of his plans for expansion, remarking, 'Wearisome tales are going the rounds of the

The car assembly building (CAB 1) in May 1953. Even at its original length, it was virtually impossible to take a photograph which showed the scale of the building. After extensions were added, it stretched from one side of the 'Flying Ground' to the other. *Courtesy Austin Rover*

imminent decline of the British motor industry, tales sometimes not disinterested, but in any event more often based on fancy rather than fact. These plans speak for themselves, we do not share this fashionable defeatism. They show—we want them to show forcefully—that we look forward to the future with every confidence.'

In his determination that the post-war, Longbridge-built car would be fully competitive in world markets, Lord had invested a great deal of money in a new car assembly building. It was very impressive, both in terms of its expansive façade and its clean, efficient-looking interior. The new building not only speeded up assembly, but also allowed for very efficient stock control. It was felt that the ability to keep reserve stocks to a minimum was crucial, the late 1940s having seen much greater rises in material costs than labour costs. Intricate sequencing arrangements meant that any combination of different models could flow down each track. The system did, of course, require quite different disciplines from those employed in the old erecting shed. Chief works engineer Duncan Brown was responsible for planning the new building, but the task of installing the vast range of new equipment and conveyor systems fell to Bill Davis, the superintendent engineer of the day.

A Hollerith punched-card unit controlled the sequencing operations. For everything to run smoothly, each part of the car had to arrive at the right place at exactly the right time. If parts got out of sequence, everything came to a standstill. In the early days of the new building, this happened quite frequently. Len Lord had the answer. Let the blighter who installed this complicated set-up make it work properly. Thus, Bill Davis the engineer became Bill Davis the production manager, with a vested interest in ensuring that all ran smoothly. Very soon, it did. Indeed, it was Bill's part in the planning of CAB 1 that changed the course of this ex-apprentice's career from that of an engineer to a production manager. Later, he would hold several directorships within BMC and British Leyland.

Although the new building was opened officially in 1951, for some months prior to that, it had seen the assembly of A40 Devons and Dorsets on line one, and A70s on line two. It was already common knowledge inside the works that the third track was being held in readiness for a new Austin Seven that would be announced shortly.

Longbridge was no mere assembler of bought-in parts. It possessed some of the finest engineering shops and body shops anywhere in the world, and it was particularly proud of its tool and press shops.

In designing a press tool, it is not simply a question of producing a male and female shape of the panel concerned. Obtaining the required shape is relatively easy; the real skill lies in designing a suitable beading to surround each tool. This grips the sheet of metal in such a way that it is drawn in at the correct rate in each area, ensuring that the finished panel is devoid of stretches, tears or creases. The final shape of the beading is usually a result of much trial and error.

The A30, with its chassisless construction, set quite a few problems for even some very skilled press-tool makers. Deep drawing of metal is always difficult, but that A30 bonnet surround was very tricky indeed. Wrinkles would form around the headlamp openings, and it took some time to produce an acceptable tool. Even during the production run, a fair amount of metal ended up as scrap at the foot of the press. Most panels require several clipping and punching operations to produce the finished product—the bonnet surround required something like 12 operations in all.

In early 1954, when press-tool capacity was stretched to the limit and the rows of presses pounded away ceaselessly, many of the door panels for the A30 were made at A. V. Roe in Manchester. Fred Craven, who worked on the Longbridge presses for the best part of 40 years, remembers being sent to Roe's with the four tools that produced the inner door panels, each tool weighing something like ten tons. At that time, A. V. Roe were producing the Avro Vulcan, a massive delta-wing bomber. A contemporary advert of theirs proudly proclaimed this fact. It showed their 750-ton British Clearing Press supposedly producing a panel for the bomber when, in actual fact, it was forming an inner door panel for an A30.

The majority of A30, A35 and A40 Farina bodies were built either in the West Works at Longbridge or by Fisher & Ludlow. With the A30/35, it was the van, Countryman and pick-up that were produced by Fisher & Ludlow, the saloon bodies being built at Longbridge, while Countryman and saloon bodies for the A40 were produced in both works.

The first 6000 or so A30 van and Countryman bodies were built by Briggs at their Doncaster plant—perhaps a little surprising, since the Briggs name in the UK is virtually synonymous with Ford. Briggs, with their main plant at Dagenham, had been bought out by Ford in 1953, but as the production of Jowett Javelins declined, the Doncaster plant took on the Austin contract to keep things ticking over

RIGHT January 1955. Just look at that one-piece bonnet surround and the complicated beading required for it to draw satisfactorily. Note the shape of the upper press tool. *Courtesy Austin Rover*

FAR RIGHT Fred Craven (left) and Joe Knight, tool setter, supposedly producing panels for the Avro Vulcan bomber. It is surprising what a little airbrushing can do—this untouched photograph clearly shows the tool for producing an A30 inner door panel. *Courtesy Fred Craven*

RIGHT An A35 van body in white has been marked up by body inspection for scaling and mopping at Fisher & Ludlow, June 1958. The mop was first dabbed in glue and then in abrasive powder. *Courtesy Austin Rover*

FAR RIGHT A35 van body in white undergoing a spot of grinding at Fisher & Ludlow in June 1958. The tool marks indicate they had had bother in mating the offside front wing with the bonnet surround. Those who have replaced a front wing will know the frustrations involved! *Courtesy Austin Rover*

RIGHT A rather artistic arrangement of A35 front wings in the panel store at Fisher & Ludlow, June 1958. It would be nice to come across a haul like that nowadays! *Courtesy Austin Rover*

FAR RIGHT A30 bodies being assembled in the West Works. If you are wondering how the roof managed to support all that welding equipment, you might be interested to know that that is exactly what the operators were wondering. It would seem that crossing one's fingers can work! *Courtesy Austin Rover*

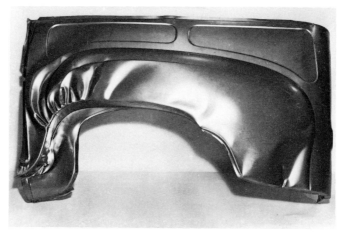

Whether it was Cadbury of Bournville or Fisher & Ludlow of Castle Bromwich, you could still get misshapes! *Courtesy Austin Rover*

ABOVE **AS3 (A30) bodyshells being prepared for the Rotodip in the West Works, November 1952. Isn't that flat cap a beauty?** *Courtesy Austin Rover*

TOP **One of a series of shots taken to illustrate the assembly of an A40 Mk I from a CKD kit.** *Courtesy Austin Rover*

until Ford were ready to allocate them the production of 103E Populars and 100E Squire and Escort estate cars in August 1955.

Trevor Page, who was a chargehand torch solderer at the Doncaster factory, spoke of building A30 van and Countryman bodies: 'The first bodies were stuck together any old how—it must have cost a fortune in time and body solder.' Apparently, much of the tooling had been produced in Sweden and a variety of errors led to roofs that were too short for the bodies, as well as problems with the door gaps and the small 'half-moon' gap where the top of the front wing meets the windscreen surround.

Arthur Ellis was foreman of A30 van assembly at Briggs of Doncaster and remembers that for about a month before normal production commenced, they sent the same van down the line several times—after being fully assembled, it was dismantled and sent down again and again until they were happy with procedures.

Not that everyone was ever entirely happy.

Stanley Edwards was involved in assembly and can remember that the chap receiving the vans out of the paint-drying tunnel really had his work cut out. Apparently, one man had to bolt on the steering box, steering idler and front dampers—each component having three bolts that had to be tightened up using a normal $\frac{1}{2}$ in. drive ratchet. With 50 vans a day to cope with, this meant him handling and fastening 100 dampers, 50 steering boxes and 50 idlers in an eight-hour day—600 bolts to tighten in all. No one wanted that job—however hard you worked, the vans just kept on pouring out of the tunnel to begin piling up. In no time at all, the painters would be round to see why the job was being stopped at their end. Stanley had the slightly easier job of fitting the front and rear bumpers, petrol tank and brake pipes, but says that, 'When you walked out of that factory at night you were absolutely buggered—you didn't want to go out or anything.' The vans left Doncaster fully painted and trimmed and only required 'motorizing' at Longbridge.

Between 1960 and 1962, an unknown number of A35 vans had their bodies built at the Morris bodies factory in Coventry, alongside MG sports cars and Morris Minor Travellers. The records are vague and classify such vans as having either 'Morris body', 'Morris paint' or 'Morris body and paint'. In the spring of 1961, about 25 to 30 per cent of A35 vans were recorded as having 'Morris paint'.

All A30, A35 and A40 bodies built at Longbridge went through a Rotodip process that was unique in Britain, even up to the time of the A40 Farina. Each body was attached to a giant spit and revolved during submersion in a series of tanks. The first contained a degreasing agent, the second a phosphate anti-rust coating and the third a primer. The system worked well, provided there was adequate penetration into the box sections and provided the liquids drained rapidly as the body left each tank. Slight modifications had to be made to the drainage holes in the sills of both the A30 and A40 to achieve the desired results.

There were further complications with the A40. All the floor panels were produced on the presses at Fisher & Ludlow, and some of the completed bodies were to go through their own slipper-dip plant, while others would go on the Rotodip at Longbridge. The slipper-dip method required an extra six drainage holes in the centre floor assembly and a further four holes in the rear floor assembly. Fisher & Ludlow wanted to add these extra holes to all the floor panels to simplify the pressing process.

Harry Wall, then chief designer of bodies at Longbridge, was not happy with that suggestion. Already, they were having trouble with water entering A40 bodies through the holes made for the attachment of jigging brackets. Why magnify the problem by having ten extra holes in the floor? They would all require plugging and be a further possible source of water leaks. In the arguments that took place, Fisher & Ludlow pointed out that holes for a similar purpose had been incorporated in their Wolseley and Riley bodies and that the coming ADO 15 (Mini) would require drain holes in the floor, as it was planned to put this through the Longbridge slipper-dip. However, Harry Wall carried the day, and it is fortunate that he did, because those extra holes in the slipper-dipped A40s did give trouble.

After the Rotodip process, the bodies were fed into a drying tunnel. Then, they received two coats of primer/surfacer and were rubbed down by hand before being rinsed off and oven dried. Sound-deadening and sealing compounds were applied to various parts of the body before it was sprayed in undercoat. After stoving and cooling, the body was smoothed off with very fine abrasive paper before the final two coats of synthetic enamel. This enamel had been used since the introduction of the Rotodip process in 1949. It was claimed to give a more durable finish than traditional cellulose and required less looking after.

The painted bodies were conveyed to a trim track, where they met up with the required bits and pieces. The badges were among the first items to be added, together with the side finishing strips for the A40, after which came the door locks and handles. Then, the wiring loom, brake pipes and petrol pipe were routed around the car. Next, the pedals, master cylinders and most of the accessories to be found under the bonnet would be fixed into position. The fully-kitted-out fascia was put in place temporarily, but not tightened up until after the windscreen had been fitted.

With the electrical system completed, the battery was connected up. By that time, the door trims and headlining would have been added. After treating the windscreen aperture with sealer, the glass and its rubber surround were offered up to the car. The lip of the rubber was persuaded over the edge of the aperture by the simple ploy of pulling on the ends of a piece of string that previously had been inserted in the groove of the rubber.

Brakes, springs, steering boxes, brightwork and electrical components were bought in from outside suppliers, but all the major mechanical components were produced at Longbridge.

ABOVE An A30 body leaves the drying oven of the paint shop in October 1954. The picture is the right way up, but that chalked 986 is no help in proving it! *Courtesy Austin Rover*

CENTRE AS3 (A30) bodies being hand-sprayed with their final coat of enamel at Longbridge, August 1953. *Courtesy Austin Rover*

TOP A40 saloon bodies undergoing Rotodip treatment in January 1960. Most A30 and A35 bodies were thus mounted, but earlier A30s were supported above the spit. Temporary holes were cut in bulkheads to accommodate the spit. *Courtesy Austin Rover*

ABOVE HRH The Duke of Edinburgh, accompanied by George Harriman, sees A30 bodies being rubbed down during his visit to Longbridge in 1956. *Courtesy Joe Edwards*

TOP A40 paint inspection, January 1960. The marks indicate that someone is in for a spot of rubbing down. *Courtesy Austin Rover*

Engine and gearbox production was down to a fine art. The rough casting for a cylinder block or cylinder head was transformed into the finished product by a series of multi-station, in-line, transfer machines. These accepted the lump of metal and automatically milled any required smooth surfaces, drilled, reamed and tapped as many holes as were necessary, and blew out any swarf between each stage. The cylinder block, for example, was handled by a transfer machine that was over 100 ft long and which performed 160 operations at its 32 stations. Only two operators were required: one to set a rough casting on its way and another to unload the finished block 64 seconds later.

Trip-operated micro-switches controlled the automatic cycles. Most of the machine heads were designed and built at Longbridge, so looking down

the row upon row of machines, one saw the 'Flying A' proudly affixed to each. Austin were transfer-machining a much wider range of components than other British manufacturers, and had even applied the process to crankshafts.

Assembly of the engines was equally impressive. Each man performed several operations, the parts slipping easily into place as the developing engine made its way down the line. Each completed engine was driven mechanically while filtered oil was pumped through it. This removed any manufacturing deposits and provided a certain amount of running in.

Final assembly was the most dramatic part of the entire process, with several different models rolling down the lines at once. We can see just how advanced things were at Longbridge in 1951 by the fact that you could stand in the same building 35 years later and watch virtually the same process being used to produce Minis and Metros. The coming of the Metro and its robotic body-assemblers did mean that the body panels were welded together in a much less laborious fashion but, that apart, the sequencing of the final assembly was very similar.

The component parts arrived in the car assembly building by various routes, including a system of underground conveyors. The fully-trimmed bodies were carried in cradles hanging from a conveyor, a series of studs on the cradle opening up the correct route automatically to ensure that each body arrived on the desired track. Power units on one conveyor, front suspension and rear axles on another, and the completed bodies on a third converged in an 1100 ft long tunnel. Other components arrived by trailer from elsewhere in the factory or from outside suppliers.

The conveyors were loaded in sequence from a master production plan. The start of body painting was taken as the reference point for any particular car. At that point, over 18 hours before the car would be completed, it was known where every other component should be if the sequencing was to be correct.

The fully-trimmed body was carried to a point above the assembly line which had already received the power unit, front suspension, propshaft and rear axle, as well as the complete exhaust system. These major units were dropped automatically on to jigs on the moving line which held them in the correct position for fitting to the approaching body. Before the arrival of the body, the exhaust system was mated to its manifold and the propshaft was connected up.

The track was kept on the move, but most men

CAB 1, 10 May 1953. A cradle bearing a fully-trimmed A30
body is about to meet up with the mechanical components
and begin its journey down the finishing track. Those white
overalls were specially issued for photographic purposes!
Courtesy Austin Rover

could 'beat the job'. Each man preferred to be able to do his own job and move quickly to the next ahead of the line, eventually gaining enough time for a breather. Problems could arise with slower men on joint operations. The worst job on the A30/35 was the joint operation of fitting the handbrake. One man fed the quadrant through from below and each put in a bolt, one from below and one from above. Another joint operation on the A30/35 and A40 was fitting the springs to the rear axle before the arrival of the body. The springs were put on with the axle upside down, one man working on each side of the track. After the U-bolts were tightened, the axle was turned over. If one man was slower than the other, the faster of the two had to wait for him to finish. It might only have been a matter of seconds, but it could cause a fair amount of tension over a working day.

As soon as the body was dropped over the mechanical units, men delved into it, under it and on either side of it until everything was attached. Even in the 1950s, much use was made of pneumatic tools for tightening nuts and screws. The nuts of each wheel were tightened in one operation by just

such a tool, which had a pre-set torque. After the car was dropped on to its wheels, it was still carried along by the track.

Most of the remaining jobs consisted of completing the plumbing-in of brakes (and clutch in the A40), fuel supply and cooling system before running the engine for a couple of minutes to check the settings. Then, the car was passed to final inspection.

Inspection procedures were tightened up in the 1950s, and attempts were made to bring home to the workforce the need for a quality product. A character called 'Particular Pete' was created in 1953. He was supposed to represent 'an ordinary working chap who thinks for himself. . . . He knows Austin products must be sold at home and overseas against fierce competition and that quality will help in keeping Austins in the forefront, apart from ensuring full-time work for him and his mates.' Posters, on which Particular Pete conveyed his thoughts in rhyme, were to be seen around the works. Workers were offered a £5 prize to encourage their own poetic skills for use on future posters.

By 1957, CAB 1 had been extended to allow installation of the latest inspection equipment at the end

Mini vans are seen on the adjoining track as an A40 Mk I leaves the finishing line of CAB 1 in June 1961. Note the tape-protected bumpers. *Courtesy Austin Rover*

of the final assembly line. Each car could be put on a rolling road and taken through the gears to check the brakes and transmission. All cars went over an inspection pit for checking the security of the suspension mountings and making any necessary adjustments. Any faults still outstanding were put right in the rectification bay.

Harvey Williams could be found in that bay in the 1950s, rectifying A30s, A35s and A40s; he could still be found there in the 1980s, carrying out roughly the same operations on Minis and Metros. At the time of the A30, he would get 8s 0d for changing a gearbox and 12s 0d for an engine. For a back-axle change, he only got 3s 0d, while a water pump came out at 3s 4d, and a radiator at 1s 4d. The chap who fixed the rates worked on the basis of one old penny per minute.

If the exhaust was blowing on the downpipe, they would get 1s 3d to rectify it. The job was known as 'R & R Clip' (remove and refit clip), but when the rate-fixer found out that the lads often managed to cure it by simply tapping the clip round or knocking each side upwards, he dropped the rate by a penny. For a 'BAB' (bleed and adjust brakes), they received 1s 10d. One man could do this job on his own, using a 1 qt can of fluid feeding into the reservoir while he dived underneath and opened each bleed nipple as he operated the brake pedal by hand.

ABOVE **Final inspection in CAB 1, January 1957. The rearmost A35 van stands next to the tracking equipment, while the saloon in the foreground goes through its paces on the rolling-road.** *Courtesy Austin Rover*

A strobe lamp being used to time the engine of an A35 in the final inspection pit of CAB 1 in March 1957. *Courtesy Austin Rover*

After its extension, CAB 1 was a third of a mile in length. Albert Green saw the building through its first 25 years and was made superintendent in 1960. After a lifetime in the job, he cannot even approach your car without automatically assessing the quality of the paintwork or whether the doors want setting, a job they did by inserting a 'totem pole' behind the door and then applying a skilled knee to the exterior. Two seconds under the bonnet and he might be telling you that the clips on the radiator hoses are bottoming and would never have passed his inspection, or he might point out the dash of red paint on the steering idler which, 30 years ago, would have reassured him that it had been filled with oil. Today, it would signify that the car still had its original idler.

Obviously, Albert found it a pleasure to go to work. He tends to disagree with those who dwell on the idea of assembly-line boredom. Of course, his own job was a very varied one; nevertheless, he found that when the line never stopped, the men went home satisfied with their efforts. Both he and Harvey would tell you that when the track kept going, they produced better cars with fewer faults, and it appears that the same holds true today. Certainly, there were gloomy periods of unrest and dissent, but in the main there was usually enough friendly banter to remove boredom from the tracks. There were black days, too. Through no fault of his own, Albert found himself in front of Birmingham's coroner four times after fatal accidents.

When the A30 came into full production, at the end of 1952, the cars were built on lines three and four. They experimented with track speeds of up to 33 cars an hour, but found that the best speed for maintaining efficiency was 25 cars an hour from

LEFT CAB 1 in June 1962. An A40 followed by a Wolseley 1500, a Riley followed by an A40 van, a Mini van followed by a Mini Traveller, and the building coped admirably. *Courtesy Austin Rover*

RIGHT An A40 Mk II has the honour of being the first car to leave the newly-completed CAB 2 on 7 September 1962. Third from the right is Dick Perry, then the assistant production manager and, at the time of writing, now the chief executive of the car division of Rolls-Royce Motors. *Courtesy Austin Rover*

each track. In total, they usually managed to turn out 40–45 cars an hour. On one particular Saturday, they started at 8 am with one track running, and the men were told that they could finish early if they made 95 vehicles. By 11.45 am, the 95 saloons and vans had been completed. It was a record that stood for many a year.

Cars for export had their carpets, windscreen wipers and hub caps packed in the boot. Their bumpers were always taped up, but in 1954 Wilmot & Breeden were asked to tape all bumpers before dispatch to Longbridge, because too many were being scratched between delivery and final assembly. All extras, such as the exterior metal sun-visors, were put on by the OVDS (Overseas Delivery Service). The exteriors of all export cars were given a coat of wax and their engine bays were sprayed with lanolin.

The expansion seen at Longbridge in the 1950s continued into the 1960s. By the end of 1961, a further huge car assembly building (CAB 2) was being constructed on land used previously to store completed cars. This created the need for a massive multi-storey car park with a capacity for some 3300 vehicles, which was the biggest of its type anywhere in the world.

Those who worked on the A30/35 and A40 remember the cars in a kindly light. Once they got them set up, they were 'little beauties to build'. After the track had been running for a while, it seemed to warm up and gain speed. Then, Albert would be accused of putting up the track speed: 'Hey up, Albert's put it up another notch.' He claimed that this was untrue, but then, with a twinkle in his eye, went on to say, 'Mind you, I don't say that I have *never* done it!'

11

FRESH-AIR MOTORING

The pre-war Seven was conceived as an open tourer; not so the A30. Times had changed. There were still a few fresh-air fiends, but now it was saloons that sold in any numbers. In any case, a saloon was considered a safer bet for what was, after all, Austin's first chassisless car. However, the idea of a convertible A30 had been toyed with, and they had even got as far as building a running prototype, the story of which only came to light quite recently and almost by chance.

In the summer of 1980, Malcolm Gardner of Zimbabwe called in on Anders Clausager, archivist at BMIHT. They got chatting about old cars and old times, including the period in the 1950s when Malcolm was apprenticed at Longbridge. He was soon telling enthusiastic stories of bowling along at 90 mph in A30 prototypes before they were detuned for production. He talked of testing and overturning an A30 in Wales, and then described how some of the best fun was had with the two-seater A30 convertible. Knowing that this would amuse me, Anders gave Malcolm my address. A photograph of this little convertible soon arrived, together with Malcolm's recollections: at speed, the car let in wind and rain through the loose-fitting side screens, and it was only a two-seater because the hood, when folded down, took up most of the space behind the front seats.

Enquiries at Longbridge resulted in a memo being sent to several departments. John Wheatley, of transmission design, recalled having seen at least one example of an A30 convertible. The company had sold it to Joe Edwards (director of manufacture for BMC at the time), who had bought it for his son, Michael. The news was not all good. John remembered it had been involved in a quite severe accident, and there was some doubt as to whether it had been repaired.

A visit to Michael Edwards proved intriguing. The first photograph he produced posed the question: was this the same convertible? In its crashed

TOP Malcolm Gardner testing the A30 convertible in 1952. Note the extra depth of the sills. *Courtesy Malcolm Gardner*

ABOVE The damaged convertible after its accident in 1956. The additional air vents can be seen on each side of the grille. *Courtesy Michael Edwards*

state, the car clearly showed air vents on each side of the grille and to the rear of the front wings. Malcolm Gardner's version had been devoid of these. Perhaps this experimental car had been fitted with an air-cooled engine at one time or another. Michael Edwards had vague memories of such goings on.

In 1955–56, Michael clocked up about 12,000 miles in the convertible before being deprived of its use rather suddenly. At the end of an all-night rally, run by Coventry Motor Apprentices, an Austin Atlantic hit them amidships. The convertible had always felt taut without any evidence of scuttle shake, and the accident gave further proof that this one-off vehicle had been constructed soundly—the Atlantic, which had been travelling quite fast, had its nose put well and truly out of joint. Michael Edwards and his friend Robert Le Sueur, who happened to be driving at the time, were more than a little fortunate, although Robert's arm was broken in five places and he remained unconscious for the first month of a six-month stay in hospital.

The car was recovered by the works tow-truck, but then the trail went cold. There were vague rumours of it having been seen in Bristol, but it seemed more likely that the convertible would have been scrapped, like the majority of Austin prototypes.

The story was published in *Spotlight*, in the hope that it would lead to further information. It did, too. A call from Chris Viljoen, a club member who lived near Bristol, told of how he had been chatting to the owner of a Morris Minor that was parked next to his A35. When the Minor owner remarked that he also had an A30, but that it was the sports model, Chris pricked up his ears. 'Not ROB 430?' The owner was a little surprised that Chris could quote him the registration number of a car that had not seen the light of day for 15 years, but ROB 430 had stuck in Chris' mind since receiving his copy of *Spotlight*.

A hastily-arranged visit to Bristol confirmed the story—the long-lost convertible had been found. Tony Cummings, the present owner, had purchased the car in April 1957 from OK Autos of Bristol. He only used it for one summer, but found it to be pretty nippy, holding the corners well. In 1960, he had tried to sell it, but people were not interested in a car without a chassis number; they felt it must have been a home-made conversion. There were thoughts of scrapping it, but the car was saved by its gradual burial in the garage under all manner of junk. On rediscovery, the driver's door showed signs of having been repaired rather poorly, but otherwise the car was all present and correct, still in its original primrose-yellow paintwork.

The boot of the car is quite extensive, because it goes right through to where the rear seats would have been. The hood folds down on to the platform formed by the forward end of the boot. With the hood erected, two extra people could just manage

December 1981. The convertible re-emerges from its 15-year burial. *Courtesy Tony Cummings*

to sit on top of this platform. Michael Edwards speaks of having done so, and Dan Clayton remembers sleeping on this shelf during night-time testing in Wales. The only identification on the car is its engine number, 2A 17,593, which is beyond midway in the production run of the earliest A30 (AS3) model. The car itself pre-dates that engine number considerably. Obviously, there was much more to be learnt about it.

The Diamond Jubilee Rally for the Austin Seven, held at Longbridge in the summer of 1982, seemed an excellent place to give the convertible its first airing for 16 years. What a day to break cover—with 700 other baby Austins in attendance and within a few yards of where they had all been built.

A notice on the windscreen asked if anyone could add to its history. This paid off. Godfrey Coates, who had worked on the convertible, was able to confirm that it was a very early car indeed. A friend of his had been demobbed in 1951, which was when they had started work on it. He remembered fitting the wing piping and bumpers, and pointed out the die-cast grille—the production version was in pressed steel. Running his hand over the car, he verified that most of the panels were hand-beaten, although the front wings had come 'off the press'. Godfrey, who has completed over 40 years in the experimental department at Longbridge, was fascinated to see the car again after so many years. If that name Coates sounds familiar, it should. Godfrey's father, George Coates, tested the A30 prototypes, and his sister, Yvonne, was the girl in the 'New Seven' brochure. As yet, the convertible is unrestored, but its even-

RIGHT The earliest A30 known to exist, shown among the windmills of Kinderdijk in 1982. The car was converted to drophead form some time prior to 1964

BELOW A remarkable reunion. The Longbridge multi-storey car park forms the backdrop as the present owner of the convertible, Tony Cummings, and previous owner, Michael Edwards, swap yarns about the car. The occasion was a rally to celebrate the Diamond Jubilee of the original Austin Seven in 1982

tual re-emergence will surely add interest to the classic-car scene.

Rumours of other A30 or A35 convertibles are heard from time to time, but when checked out, generally the trail runs cold or leads to one or other of the A35s which have been turned into open cars in more recent times by enthusiasts. On a club trip to Holland, I had the pleasure of driving an A30 convertible of particular interest. Its history is a little vague, but it was imported into Holland from Germany in 1964. The vehicle started life as a four-door AS3 saloon, but had been converted to an open car before it left Germany. It only had the shallow production sills of the saloon, but it felt quite taut, even when driven at speed on a fairly twisty road. At present, an A35 engine is installed, but the original engine (2A 292) has been traced. This car (chassis no. AS3L 246, body no. 252) is of particular interest, having been built on 20 June 1952. Apart from the prototype just discussed, it is the earliest A30 known to survive.

There were other Longbridge attempts to go top-less with a post-war Seven. In early 1953, Dick Burzi produced several clay models for a proposed 7 hp two-seater sports tourer. The idea was to use A30 mechanical parts in a totally new body. It began as a styling exercise, but later that year went ahead in the form of a running prototype. Eric Bailey did many of the drawings for the car, which was built in Howard Clare's shop. It was something quite different from the usual run of Austin prototypes, a fibreglass body clothing a tubular space-frame.

LEFT A clay model, produced
by Dick Burzi in May 1953,
for an A30 sports version.
Courtesy Austin Rover

RIGHT October 1953. Front and
rear views of the 7 hp
fibreglass two-seater. Howard
Clare is in the driving seat.
Courtesy Eric Bailey

Barry Wood welded up the frame from 1 in.
diameter tubular steel and made the bulkhead structures from $1\frac{1}{2}$ in. square tube that he had produced
by welding two angles together. On pulling the completed frame out of the jig, he found that the welding
had caused a shrinkage of $\frac{3}{8}$ in. in length, so extension brackets were added at the rear to make up the
difference.

A sports car had been chosen for this fibreglass
exercise, because by dispensing with doors, the
outer shell could be made in one piece in a single
mould. It only required the addition of a bonnet and
boot lid. Howard Clare made a model of the body
in wood, from which a female fibreglass mould was
taken. This, in turn, was used to produce the body
itself. Other parts of the car produced in fibreglass

LEFT A neat A35 drophead,
professionally built by
A30/35 enthusiast Dave
Whittington of Bedworth
Car Valet Services. The
photograph was taken at
Longleat during the 1985
National Rally of the Austin
A30–A35 Owners Club. Note
the attractive use of the pick-
up rear bumpers

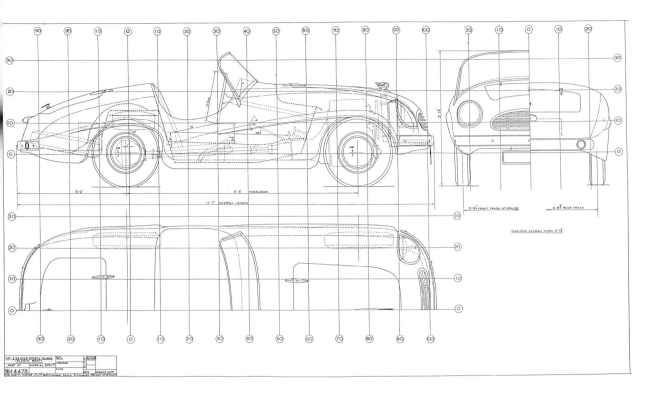

Layout drawing of 7 hp Sports. Space-frame and fibreglass body house A30 mechanical parts. Even the torpedo-shaped side lights could still be found under the faired-in headlights. *Courtesy Eric Bailey*

included the boot floor, dash panel, interior trim casings and the radiator bulkhead. The cockpit floor was in mild steel, and the front and rear bulkheads were in a combination of mild steel for the lower portions and hardboard for the upper portions. Aluminium bumpers set off the bright red paintwork. Len Lord had taken quite an interest in it. 'How's the red devil today?' he would ask.

It is amusing to see that the A30's torpedo-shaped side lights were still to be found, tucked away behind the perspex headlamp fairings. The hood was an awkward affair, being stowed in the boot. To erect it, the frame was slotted into sockets that were situated just forward of the boot lid. Had the car been intended for production, it would have required considerable alteration, because once the hood was erected, you could neither get in nor out.

George Coates and Max Oliver were given the task of assembling the car and running it in. Although it did quite a few miles, for most of the time the car

stood about in the experimental department, being pushed here and there whenever it was in the way. Eventually, it just disappeared.

Austin may not have wished to dabble in fibreglass bodies, but the possibility of A30 mechanical parts mated with a lightweight frame and plastic body certainly caught the imagination of Jack Turner. In the early 1950s, he had produced several cars that utilized a variety of mechanical parts, but by 1955, he had settled on his new recipe. The main frame was to consist of two 3 in. diameter longitudinal members, to which were added cross-tubes and outriggers. The chassis proper terminated ahead of the rear axle, reminiscent of a similar arrangement on the pre-war Austin Seven. In this case, though, the A30 axle was located by trailing arms and a Panhard rod, and it employed either torsion-bar or coil-spring suspension. The telescopic rear dampers were supported on outriggers. The front suspension was standard A30, except that lighter springs were fitted to match the car's very low kerb weight of about 11 cwt. Jack Turner was a racing driver and enthusiast whose cars were always built with the possibility of competition in mind, so the rack-and-pinion steering of the Minor was preferred to the A30's setup. Twin SU's were added to a virtually standard

ABOVE **The first production model of the 803 cc Turner A30 in 1956.** *Courtesy Jack Turner*

A left-hand-drive 950 cc Turner Mk I of 1960. The majority of Turners were exported to the USA, but a few also went to South Africa and Australia. *Courtesy Jack Turner*

A30 engine and gearbox, but 15 in. wheels raised the gear ratios considerably.

In Jack Turner's own words, 'The fibreglass moulding for the body was made in one piece, the only separate pieces being the bonnet, boot lid and

doors. The main shell was bolted to the steel inner structure through suitable steel reinforcements bonded to the inside of the moulding. I had a number of meetings with George Harriman at Longbridge with the aim of either a joint operation or, failing that, a direct supply of components at a manufacturer's price. This was not to be, and it was very annoying to find that three years after, he made a deal with Healey to produce the Sprite, which was a replica in many respects. We were forced to obtain our supplies through Austin dealers, and this increased the price considerably.'

You could buy a Turner A30, or 803 as it was known, either fully assembled at £525 plus £264 purchase tax (a total of £789), or you could purchase it as a kit of parts, in which case it was exempt from tax. The car had a claimed top speed of about 80 mph in standard form, and at cruising speeds it could return 40–50 mpg.

The 803 had a fairly short production run, because with the arrival of the A35, Turner took advantage of the new engine, gearbox and 4.55:1 rear-axle ratio. From 1956–59, the car became the Turner 950. About 270 of these 803 and 950 cars were built before the Mk I Sports was introduced. This would do 0–60 mph in 12 seconds and carry on to reach some 95 mph. It had a completely new fibreglass body, but was only in production for one season. As well as the 948 cc version, which used BMC components, the car was offered with a Coventry Climax engine. The Turner had always been competitive, but by now, it was becoming quite a potent machine. An Alexander version of the Mk I had the 948 cc engine with 9.4:1 compression ratio and crossflow alloy head. From 1962 onwards, the BMC engine was only offered as an option to Ford units.

By offering the mechanical parts of the A30 and A35 in a cleverly-designed, lightweight package, Jack Turner had brought very pleasurable motoring and, in many cases, much fun and success on the racetrack to quite a few enthusiasts who could not have afforded it otherwise. Turner 950s came first and second in the Autosport Championship of 1958, and a flip through the motor-racing press of 1955–65 leaves one in no doubt that the Turner was a very competitive car. Unfortunately, without the co-operation of Longbridge, it was impossible to appeal to a mass market. The Turner A30 (and the later 950) were definitely cars for the enthusiast.

The Austin Healey Sprite, however, was a different kettle of fish. In his entertaining book, *More Healeys*, Geoffrey Healey shows that the idea of a small, mass-produced sports car was one of Len

Lord's interests: 'The Sprite was first conceived in the winter of 1956, the result of a meeting between DMH [Donald Healey] and Leonard Lord. We always maintained a close relationship with BMC at various levels and DMH attended fairly frequent policy meetings . . . both men agreed that sports cars were becoming expensive, and that the market was contracting as the price went up. In his blunt, down-to-earth manner, Len Lord then commented that what we needed was a small, low-cost sports car to fill the gap left by the disappearance of the Austin Seven Nippy and Ulster models of pre-war fame. What he would really like to see, he said, was a bug. It is impossible to tell whether he was simply thinking aloud, or deliberately giving DMH a broad hint of what we should do, but this conversation certainly set DMH thinking as he drove back from Longbridge. When he arrived back at Warwick, DMH called me in and told me the gist of his discussion, then proceeded to outline his own ideas about a small, low-priced sports car.'

There is little doubt that Jack Turner's approaches had been partly responsible for rousing Len Lord's interest in a low-cost sports car, but Lord always played his cards very close to his chest. Geoffrey Healey wrote, 'What we did not then know was that Austin had already drawn up a car to this sort of specification—the 7 hp two-seater Sports Tourer, designed in 1953. This car was neither very sporting nor much of a tourer. It had a tubular frame chassis, expensive in mass production, with no doors and a number of costly features. Although it in no way fitted the bill, we were to hear continuing rumours about it as the Sprite developed.'

As early as 1952, the Healeys had given some thought to the possibility of producing a small sports car powered by the new ohv 803 cc A30 engine. Pressure of work meant that the proposal only got as far as preliminary sketches. Perhaps that was as well, because the Sprite was conceived at just the right time to benefit from the vast improvement of the 948 cc engine and gearbox. Although the mechanical parts of the A35 were to make a great contribution to the Sprite's success, it was designed independently of Longbridge at the Austin Healey works.

The styling was done by Healey's chief body designer, Gerry Coker. From the USA, where Gerry now lives, he wrote, 'I remember DMH suggesting common front and rear fenders [wings] for the first Sprite sketches, but it must have looked so horrible that over the years it has been purged from my failing old memory. DMH wanted a small simple sports car that a chap could store in his bike shed, and to keep the cost down, it would have a minimum of shapes and curves. These stipulations did not permit much latitude in styling with character. Of course, sometimes no character is character enough. The original design did have retractable headlights, but these were scrapped due to their cost, which was out of all proportion for the market we were after.'

Barry Bilbie, Healey's chief chassis designer, produced the platform chassis, and Geoffrey Healey, in his position as chief engineer, worked on the basic layout. In his book, he tells us, 'I had decided that we should use the A35 front suspension, and the basic case and track of its rear axle, with a 4.22:1 ratio. I had rejected the mechanically-operated rear brakes of the A35, however, as these were not completely trouble-free, and the installation would have

LEFT This photograph appeared in *Motor Sport* of June 1958, with the caption: 'Happy Smiling Sprite. The new Austin Healey poor-man's sports two-seater poses beside an Austin A35 saloon, many of whose components it incorporates. The headlamps, like two large eyes, are high-set to comply with American lighting regulations.' *Courtesy LAT Photographic*

RIGHT 'This picture gives an excellent idea of the compact construction of the Austin Healey Sprite,' said *Motor Sport. Courtesy LAT Photographic*

presented some ground-clearance problems. Instead, I decided to go for all-hydraulic brakes.'

Morris Minor brakes provided the answer at the rear of the car. The advantage of being able to call upon Morris bits, where preferable, was seen again in the steering. In *More Healeys*, Geoffrey put it thus: 'Before long we were assembling the Austin units into the first frame, which was to be built up as a running chassis. . . . We attempted to use the A35 steering gear, but it quickly became obvious that little of the Austin stuff would suit. We would have been back with the old problem of six ball joints, an idler and steering box all adding up to indirect and vague steering. Instead, we took the Morris Minor rack and pinion and laid this in position. It was soon apparent that this set-up would be superior, probably at not much extra cost.'

The intention had been to build the Sprite at Longbridge on the same production line as the A35, but it was realized that the car's construction did not suit the CAB 1 arrangement, where bodies were lowered on to the engine and transmission. The Sprite ended up at Abingdon.

It was powered by a twin-carburettor version of the 948 cc engine, which developed 42.5 bhp at 5000 rpm. In a car weighing less than 12 cwt, this provided a maximum top speed of around 80 mph and fuel consumption in the region of 30–40 mpg, depending on how hard the car was driven.

At the launch of the Sprite, in the spring of 1958, there was much amusement over the 'frog-eye' appearance (now regarded as one of the car's particularly attractive features), but the way the car handled and performed far outweighed any criticisms. Tommy Wisdom, one of the many motoring writers

who were taken with the car, dubbed it 'The first-ever people's sports car', and professed he had 'never driven a safer, faster car'.

At £668 17s 0d, including purchase tax, the Sprite was responsible for introducing many to the joys of fresh-air motoring. In all, some 50,000 examples of this version were produced and, although eventually it had to yield to the pressures for a more conventional front-end look, these early beginnings led to the production of over 300,000 Austin Healey Sprite and MG Midget derivatives. For a sports car, that is a large number. It reflects great credit on the Healey design, as well as on the A-series engine and transmission, which inspired the project in the first place.

As for the A40 Farina, one would hardly think of it as a car crying out to be converted into a soft top. Its virtue was as an economical, yet roomy, family saloon with above-average adaptability to luggage carrying. It was also unusual in being able to offer these features in such a small and stylish package. However, there are always those who are determined to remove the roof of almost any car.

Barry Kelkin remembers many instances where firms such as Weathershields, Webasto and others sent converted cars back to Longbridge to determine whether or not their alterations would invalidate the car's warranty. Just who it was that produced an A40 with a roof that slid off the car entirely, seems to have been forgotten long ago. With this roof used in the optional manner of sliding it backwards to overhang at the rear, there could well have been the problem of exhaust fumes affecting the rear-seat passengers. Flow tests, done on this and other A40s, indicated that this would be so. In October 1958, the research department investigated the possibility of adding a ventilation grille to the underside of the rear window's overhanging peak. Tests in the wind tunnel failed to find any position at the rear from which exhaust fumes would not enter the car if the grille was open. Road tests confirmed that even if a small strip of the boot-lid seal was removed, dust and exhaust fumes entered the car as soon as any window was opened. That sliding roof would have caused the same problem.

There were at least two other more conventional fresh-air A40 Farinas. One was a Farina grey Mk I saloon (chassis no. 11,453) that was built in January 1959. On loan to Vanden Plas, it was fitted with a Webasto sunshine roof.

Although Jensen Cars of today cannot confirm it, it would seem that Jensen produced the most complete and orthodox convertible version of the A40 Farina. They had taken an early Mk I saloon and mounted an electric motor and hydraulic pump in the boot, allowing hydraulic cylinders on either side of the rear seat to be used to operate a power hood. After folding the front section of the hood into the optional 'de-ville' position, it was simply a question of flicking the fascia-mounted switch for the hood to lower itself completely. Then, it could be hidden with a red tonneau cover.

This unusual car, quite striking in its white paintwork, black hood and red trim, caught the eye of John Aston of Bromsgrove while it was still being run by a Longbridge salesman. John managed to buy the car when it was less than two years old and sold it two years later to Bert Pendross, a well-known motor trader of Kidderminster. Bert sold the car to Saunders of Worcester, but there the trail runs cold. Or does it? Remember, the A30 convertible did turn up eventually.

ABOVE The A40 drophead believed to have been converted by Jensen. Rain would sometimes drive its way in if the hood had not seated properly on the cant rails. *Courtesy John Aston*

LEFT Fresh-air A40 motoring: for the cautious . . . and the carefree

12

RACING AND RALLYING – DIDN'T THEY DO WELL?

Those who are unaware that the A30, A35 and A40 had considerable success in both racing and rallying may be forgiven for their ignorance. The cars hardly exude a sporting image.

The action really began with the introduction of the A35 and carried on with the A40, but we must not forget those keen souls who drove even the A30 to its limits. In both hillclimbs and local rallies, the A30 could more than hold its own in its class, but its greatest sporting success resulted in an appearance on the front cover of *Autosport* in May 1956. Quite justifiably, too. The feature inside was headed 'Bravo the Brookes', and described how Raymond Brookes, with his father Ted as co-driver, had performed a giant-killing feat in the Tulip Rally.

The Brookes had always fancied the excellent power-to-weight ratio of the A30, and on receiving the regulations for the 1956 Tulip Rally, they were so convinced that the A30 stood an excellent chance that they went out and bought one. The plan was to increase the car's advantage, particularly in the hillclimbs, by travelling extremely light. They set out from London with the other British starters, travelling via Dunkirk and Reims to Champagnole on the edge of the Jura, where competitors from all the different starting points converged. From the start of the special sections, the A30 took a lead which it never lost throughout the rally. On reaching Monte Carlo, the cars headed north again by way of Grasse, Digne and Uriage, before a ten-mile hillclimb stage to Chamrousse. It was on this climb that the Brookes had the pleasure of overtaking Hengst's Morris Minor that had set out well ahead of them.

The rally continued through Luxembourg and Germany and on into Holland, where the final tests took place on the Zandvoort track. The A30 won the rally outright, performing far better in the special tests and hillclimbs than the handicappers had envisaged—as had the Standard Eights. As *Autosport* reported, 'The organizers were so astonished at the performance of these little machines that the Technical Jury advised a complete examination, easily the most painstaking and searching that has ever occurred in a rally. Even such components as valve springs were weighed and measured, the number of spirals being checked with normal stock parts. All four leading cars were found to be completely standard, to dumbfound the experts.'

When the scutineering and inspections were over, the Brookes were satisfied that they had backed a worthy horse. Not only had they come in ahead of the Standards and Morris Minors, but they had also beaten 200 or so other cars, including Aston Martins, Jaguars and Mercedes.

A30s were also having fun on the racetrack. Peter Brock, generally accepted as Australia's most exciting and consistent driver of racing saloons, came to fame at the wheel of his A30. Admittedly, it had been modified by stuffing a Holden engine into it. The character of the car is best described by motoring writer, Rob Luck. After trying out the car, he declared it to be 'savagely powerful, totally unpredictable, bordering on the unstable and dangerous', but he went on to say that 'Brocky drove it consistently under the chequered flag as if he was wheeling round a luxury limo; he was silk smooth even then.' It seems that the crowd would be 'standing on its ear' during any race in which the A30 competed, and it was not long before any Australian kid with a fast car was said to 'do a Brocky' if they drove with daring and exuberance.

Speaking of exuberance brings to mind the way Dave Brodie has driven over the last 25–30 years. He, too, began in an A30. Describing his first drive after fitting an 1100 cc block with a 584 camshaft, Formula Junior crankshaft, con-rods and pistons, and twin Amal carburettors, he wrote, 'I remember I was in fourth gear when I decided to give it full throttle, so it was a blip and down to second, out with the clutch and up to 8000 rpm, then third to 8000 and then top—oops, I'm running out of road—well, no A30, even to this day, ever went through

ABOVE Keith Fry (left) and Bruce Little, his navigator, broke the Brisbane-to-Melbourne record in this A30 in 1956. They covered the 1178 miles at an average speed of 49.8 mph. For their efforts, they were presented with a brand-new A30 by UK and Dominion Motors of Brisbane. *Courtesy Terry Jorgensen*

RIGHT Dan Clayton competes in an Austin Apprentices Rally at the Longbridge works. His father had an Austin dealership in the north of England—hence the appropriate number plate. *Courtesy Dan Clayton*

Stanmore High Street that quick. Wow! Was I impressed! We spent the whole weekend just blasting along everywhere at 8000 rpm, blowing anything that cared to resist into the weeds. 90–105 mph? I never did know how fast it went, as the speedo took a dive on that first blast in Stanmore—and I never ever fixed it again!'

Of his first race (at an Eight Clubs meeting at Silverstone), Dave Brodie recalled, 'I knew nothing about scrutineering or signing on. I thought the competition licence was enough of a bother without all these chaps poking the car and kicking the wheels—made me real cross. Meanwhile, my pals are changing the tyres from my road Michelin Xs to Dunlop R 6s, but halfway through, this chap says, "If you don't get out on the circuit now you have missed practice!" So, out I went with two racing tyres at the back and Xs still on the front! What did I know about tyres?

'I drive out of the pits, not having a clue which way the circuit goes, oops, a right turn, then all these cars start blasting by, then another right turn after what seemed ages [Becketts], then down a long straight. Wow, this really goes nice, seems a mile long and then another slow right turn. OK, not bad. Hey, there are my pals waving in the pits. I wave back. I'm hitting 8000 in third, just get top and then the first corner comes up again. I brake hard, turn in and get on the power coming out—Jesus, I'm hanging on for my life. It's as if the car has a mind of its own—all over the road—it's the same for the next two laps and by this time I'm looking for new pants—thank the Lord, the chequered flag!

'Drive back to the pits—"What's it like? What's it like?" "You must be joking," I said. "I'm not doing that again, no way." "What?" they all said. "What? You're the one that's had us working all night for a week. You're driving and that's that." Dad takes me to one side. "Look, son, you just can't go home and let the boys down. You must race."

'Out come the jacks again—put the R 6s on the front. Check the brakes. Something wrong with the rod-operated rears and no way to fix them. Where is the hack-saw? That'll do it. Wire the loose bit up, we'll only use the fronts.

'Then this bloke in a TR-engined thing called a Peerless says to me, "Are you really going to race that thing?" "Well," I said. "If I don't my pals will kill me." "It will surprise me if you can get it out of the paddock," he says. "B— sauce," I said. "You watch."

'Down came the flag and away I went—bit of wheelspin, second gear, third, just about to take top—hang on, I'm turning right into Copse Corner. What's this, the car is behaving OK—even got a little slide—hey, this may just be fun. Down to Becketts—wow, wheelspin, whack it into third and wang off down the long straight. Christ, this is quick. Went past two funny-looking specials, now for Woodcote. The car is diving about all over the place on the brakes, seems like I'm on them for ages, second gear, power out—cor, this is all right, third gear, wave at my pals—they are all falling about laughing.

'That's how it went for the next eight laps, kept passing all these odd-looking cars with blokes' heads sticking up in the wind, then the chequered flag. Glad it's all over, as I'm now having a job stopping the thing. Drove the slowing-down lap, all these flag marshals keep waving at me, nice chaps, guess they must get lonely out there all day.

'Slowly into the paddock and find all my pals going ape. My dad grabs hold of me. What did I do wrong now? "You bloody won, son, you bloody won!"'

With the introduction of the A35, its better power-to-weight ratio and much improved bearings and gearbox meant the action would centre around the racing of production saloons. On a tight track, they could run rings round much higher-powered cars. Many of the most famous names in British motor racing cut their teeth on A35s.

Jackie Stewart, three-times Formula 1 World Champion, was not one of those who raced A35s, but the first four cars he owned fit nicely within these pages. In *Road and Car* of autumn 1985, he described his A30 as 'a great wee car' and went on: 'It gave me freedom for the first time.... I think that this little car gave me the most pleasure of all the cars I have owned; maybe because it was the first.... I soon moved up to an A35; powder blue and just a little quicker.... I could reach Stirling from our garage in 39 minutes—that's about 39 miles.... I changed the A35 for a Farina-designed Austin A40. This was very stylish and the first-ever hatchback... mine was red with a black top. I ordered it with black upholstery with red piping, and tricked it up by painting the wheels red, with chrome trim.... After this... I bought a white Austin Healey Sprite... another great little car, although not very good for courting.... I fitted Speedwell tuning modifications. Graham Hill was working at Speedwell then, and I'll never forget phoning up to order two new SU carburettors and a special cylinder head and camshaft. It was a big deal speaking personally to Graham Hill, even then.... This was in his early days, in the late 1950s,

The directors of Speedwell Conversions were certainly not sleeping partners. From left to right: Len Adams, Graham Hill, George Hulbert and John Sprinzel. They formed the winning team in the 750 MC Relay Race at Silverstone in 1958. *Courtesy LAT Photographic*

before he became big time and long before I had even started.'

In his book, *Life at the Limit*, Graham Hill related how, in his early days as a driver for Lotus, Esso offered him a £1000 retainer in 1958: 'Such a large sum of money, it was unbelievable. I celebrated by going out and buying my first brand-new car, an Austin A35.' This car, 69 PMT, was to become very well known on the tracks. Writing in *Life at the Limit*, Graham recalled a race at Brands Hatch that had given him particular pleasure: 'I was in third place leading the 1000 cc class, while just ahead of me Les Leston and Ron Hutcheson were having a great dice in 1500 cc Rileys, battling door handle to door handle. On the last lap, I was right behind them up the hill into Druids, and they were so busy trying to out-fumble each other that I was able to slip through on the inside. The crowd went wild at the sight of this little A35 slipping through like a tiny minnow as the two Rileys battled with each other. I managed to hang on to my lead for the rest of the lap and won the race.'

In addition to racing the car, Graham used it as his personal transport. Not only did he drive it to all the British circuits, but also to Spa, Le Mans, Reims and Monza, as well as to the first Grand Prix event he ever competed in at Monaco in 1958.

The success that Graham Hill, John Sprinzel and Len Adams were having in racing their modified A35s led them, along with George Hulbert, to form Speedwell Conversions. They marketed tuning kits for a variety of family saloons, and built and sold Speedwell Supersport Austins—new A35s, Sprites, A40 Farinas, and even A55s, which had been modified to appeal to the driver who wanted a little more excitement and pleasure from his motoring. The cars cost a little over £100 more than standard production versions, but by all accounts, it was money well spent. Naturally, Graham Hill's own A35 had the full Speedwell treatment—lightened flywheel, balanced crankshaft, gas-flowed head with bigger valves and heavier springs, twin SU carbs, high-compression pistons and a special camshaft. It also had competition dampers, a front anti-roll bar and Ferodo VG 95 brake linings. In this trim, the car would sing along all day at 6000 rpm with complete reliability, never once letting Graham down. For the trip to Monaco, he fitted a 3.7:1 differential, which allowed 85 mph cruising at under 5000 rpm. It was the ability of his modified A35 to perform this dual role of racing saloon and long-distance hack that endeared it to him.

Writing in *Autosport* of 5 February 1960, after a class-winning drive at Silverstone, Graham described how, instead of braking, he would throw the car into the corners and keep his foot hard down:

'I found that I was going into Stowe Corner flat out at 6300 rpm—90 mph—and coming out at 4800 rpm—70 mph; all the momentum was lost in negotiating the corner. I found that the best technique for cornering the A35 was to put on a full half-turn of the wheel going into a bend—to set up the car in a drift—and then come back to a quarter-turn, after which there was generally no further need to move the wheel until the corner had been negotiated.' In the same article, he told of how they had used an A35 to help them learn the Nürburgring circuit prior to the German Grand Prix in 1958. He commented, '. . . although some of the corners seemed really sharp, the Austin always managed to get round them. It was extremely stable, whatever we did, and could always be got out of trouble by winding on more steering lock. From experience on the "Ring" and elsewhere, I would say that it must be an extremely difficult car to spin.'

A dip into the programme for the 1958 British Grand Prix reminds us how Graham drove the 17 laps of the touring car race in his A35, and then jumped into his Lotus for the next race, the 75-lap Formula 1 Grand Prix. The first event was a warm-up for the big race in more ways than one. The A35 was overheating, so Graham countered this by turning the heater on full.

In 1961, an A35 was the first racing car owned by Frank Williams, of Williams Grand Prix Engineering fame. From his present position at the very top of the Grand Prix world, Frank is still able to look back on 'some very enjoyable moments when racing my A35', although he did manage to destroy the car at Mallory Park. He replaced it with a quick A40, but reckons that he was never in the money with it, because he was always flying off the road.

John Barnard, designer of the three-times world championship-winning Marlboro McLaren MP4, was quoted in *Autosport* of 8 October 1981, as saying, 'I started with an A35 when I'd just turned seventeen. . . . My father point-blank refused to buy me some special I fancied, which would do a hundred miles an hour, so I bought an A35 instead, and looked around for a supercharger. . . . I found an Arnott blower and fitted it. Frog-eye Sprites were the thing at the time, but the A35 would blow the pants off them until you wanted to stop. It was a good introduction to what happens when you do it wrong. I think back now and say, "Gawd Almighty, how did I get away with it?"'

That reference to the Almighty reminds me of the tales the Reverend Rupert Jones tells of his Cambridge days, when he and other members of the Cam-

bridge University Automobile Club put together a team of A35s. They lacked money but not contacts, having helped previously with exploits like the A35's long-distance run at Montlhéry. Consequently, they managed a very smart turn-out of three brand-new A35s. Their trump-card was to procure the services of Don Moore, who prepared the cars. Don advised them to clear off and not come back until each car had done 5000 miles—only then, was he prepared to breathe on them. His tweaks and modifications paid off—in their 54 outings, the cars suffered no mechanical failures and, as *Autosport* put it in April 1959, 'relentlessly demolishing the opposition in the calmest possible way', they managed eight firsts, 11 seconds and five thirds.

The Cambridge undergraduates would have won even more races had they not been up against such tough opposition. These were the days when Graham Hill, John Sprinzel and others were setting the crowds alight with their antics in the Speedwell A35s, and Doc Shepherd was about to do great things in an A40 Farina that would also be prepared by Don Moore.

John Sprinzel's car was perhaps the most famous racing A35 of the period—certainly, it was the most written about—and not without reason. To see him nip past Jaguars by taking the inside line on a corner was stirring stuff. To him, taking the inside line was the obvious thing to do when driving an A35, 'in case you needed to lean on the car inside you in order to stay upright.'

During the 1957 season, Sprinzel's car provided much entertainment and took nine first and six second places. It was knocking up a considerable mileage between races, too, competing in hillclimbs and continental rallies, or acting as a test-bed for Speedwell developments and demonstrations. Originally Court grey in colour, it was later turned out in red. According to John, the colour change was 'in honour of a Communist cow' with which he had tangled in Yugoslavia during the 1957 Liège–Rome–Liège Rally.

At first sight, the car looked fairly standard. It had no hub caps or wing-mounted side lights and had acquired a pair of fog lights, but only the number plate, painted on the car above the radiator grille, suggested any sporting pretensions. A closer look revealed a redesigned dashboard that held an impressive array of instruments, including a Halda Speed Pilot for rally work. As a Speedwell A35, it had much the same mechanical modifications as that of Graham Hill.

John Bolster, testing the car for *Autosport* in

November 1957, found '. . . the performance is obviously equal to a 1½-litre machine. This is achieved by most painstaking work on the ports and head shape, coupled with special valves and springs. There are twin SU semi-downdraught carburettors on curved ramming pipes, and the exhaust, though improved in efficiency, is still commendably quiet . . . . The Speedwell A35 has outstanding low-speed torque and is far more flexible than a normal model. If desired, one can drive through town traffic and up considerable hills without changing from top gear. The engine also idles exceptionally slowly and quietly. If one really gives her the gun, things begin to happen. The engine appears to peak between 5500 and 5800 rpm, and there is a "hard" feel about it, but it is not objectionably rough. The excellent gear-change aids and abets the driver in making full use of this willing power unit, and the stop watch confirms that the performance is very much out of the ordinary.

'From standstill to 30 mph takes 5.2 seconds, 0–50 mph takes 10.2 seconds, and 0–60 mph occupies 15.6 seconds. Over 33 mph comes up on second gear, and the ultimate maximum on third gear is just 60 mph, which renders it a most useful overtaking and cornering ratio. The maximum speed of the car, as tested, is a highly creditable 83 mph.'

Bolster found the roadholding and cornering to be much better than standard, but was not too happy when cornering at speed. He was 'extremely enthusiastic' about the Speedwell conversion of the 948 cc engine and felt that, 'Above all, it emphasizes the excellent engineering embodied in these engines, for 100 per cent reliability has been a feature of the car during the whole of its extremely tough competition life. Finally, unlike most "conversions", this one actually improves the shopping manners of the little saloon, and "mum" will like that.'

When the same car, 119 KMH, was tested in December that year by *Motor Racing* magazine, it was obviously not in quite the same mechanical trim, because they produced some very different figures. A limit of 6000 rpm, suggested by Sprinzel, produced a genuine 90 mph top speed, and the car cruised comfortably at 82 mph and 5500 rpm. They found: 'The highly tuned engine ran without a falter at very low speeds and pulled smoothly from about 1500 rpm, while a quick drop into third was enough to take advantage of any gap for overtaking.' They were more enthusiastic about the car's cornering ability than John Bolster, remarking, 'The whole of the rear end is standard, in fact, which renders all the more amazing the roadholding which has been

demonstrated on British circuits. Modifications to the front end take most of the credit for this, the "Suspension Conversion" incorporating stiffening boxes and anti-roll bar. On fast corners it is only necessary to point the nose in the required direction—and the car follows round in complete obedience. Roll is so much diminished that the handling resembles that of a low-built sports car rather than a very upright little saloon.'

Under rather poor test conditions, they noted that, 'Wheelspin (and indeed, axle-tramp) limited "get away" revs and made 0–30 in six seconds less impressive than 0–50 in 12.8 seconds, 0–60 in 17.2 seconds . . . . By way of comparison, it is necessary only to note that the standard model required an extra ten seconds to reach 60 mph from standstill.'

Anyone wishing to tune the engine of their A35 to roughly the same standard as John Sprinzel's could have bought a Speedwell Stage Two engine conversion kit for about £75. If a single carburettor was acceptable, a Stage One conversion was available for under £50. The highly desirable anti-roll bar, together with the necessary strengthening plates, could be purchased for an extra £10 or so.

Another Speedwell A35 was tested by *Sports Cars Illustrated* in July 1958. Their feature, 'Potted Power', constituted a test of an over-the-counter Speedwell A35 that was already in the hands of a private purchaser. It began: 'In the last year or so, John Sprinzel has really put the Austin A35 on the map as a high-performance car, both in rallies and races. His lap speeds on British circuits have caused many raised eyebrows amongst users of machinery generally considered much more potent than the impudent little A35.' After remarking how standard the little car looked, they suggested, 'It is this innocent appearance which makes the Speedwell A35 such fun, for even if the prospective purchaser has no inclinations to competition motoring, he (or she) can play "Q cars", the expression on the faces of so many other drivers being well worth the extra cost, particularly those in charge of sports cars.'

The car under test had the standard compression ratio of 8.3:1, but produced some 50 bhp at 5100 rpm. They, too, approved of the car's flexibility and lack of fussiness, finding that it would 'trickle along happily at 10 mph in top gear, and accelerate away cleanly with no trace of pinking provided a light and progressive throttle opening was used . . . even with the high percentage of hard driving during the test the average fuel consumption worked out at 34 mpg—a very satisfactory figure for what is a high-performance machine by any standards. There is no doubt that if the car was driven in the customary "District Nurse" fashion it would record figures of around 45–50 mpg.'

They also remarked, '. . . the car can be hurled into roundabouts and corners with something approaching gay abandon . . . . There is only a trace of roll at high cornering speeds and virtually nothing at lower speeds . . . . It was not the maximum speed that made the Speedwell A35 such a fascinating machine, but its ability to out-accelerate so many cars and to effortlessly maintain a 70 mph cruising gait . . . . The wonderful handling contributed to its ability to put up excellent averages, and as a point-to-point car on British roads, the Speedwell A35 must be considered as very hard to beat.

'The price of £675 is absolutely all-in and includes those normally annoying extras, such as delivery charges, petrol in tank, number plates and tax. Even the seat belt is included. The fact that the company is selling five per week of these interesting little cars is proof of the soundness of the scheme.'

The performance figures they obtained were 0–30 in 5.5 seconds, 0–40 in 7.5 seconds, 0–50 in 10.5 seconds, 0–60 in 15.0 seconds, and 0–70 in 23.2 seconds. Maximum speed was in the region of 83 mph.

Bill Boddy, of *Motor Sport*, was quite taken by the Speedwell modifications, too. In February 1959, while reviewing his previous year's motoring, he wrote of the 'exceedingly nice little Speedwell modified Austin A35 which provided some of the jolliest motoring of the year . . . . Certainly this little Austin, best qualified by the adjective "brisk", suffered from none of the shortcomings often associated with souped-up "bread-and-butter" cars, and its floor gearchange, in conjunction with the more-than-usually eager engine, was a joy indeed.'

Mike Adlington is one who typified the keenness of the amateur's approach to saloon racing. As one of the last indentured apprentices at Armstrong Siddeley Motors, he found himself in a hotbed of enthusiasm. Of preparing to race a high-mileage A35 in 1958, he recalls, 'We bored out the block 0.060 in. and spent many hours balancing all the reciprocating parts. Because they were lighter and had fully-floating gudgeon pins, we fitted Standard Ten conrods. The cylinder head was polished and we managed to squeeze some Sapphire exhaust valves into the inlet side.

'The camshaft remained standard, but we fitted a $1\frac{1}{2}$ in. SU carburettor. A new exhaust system was fabricated, using an apple tree as a bending machine, and a TR2 silencer, used to finish the system off,

produced the most glorious note on the overrun. We set to work on the roadholding by lowering the car all round, removing the rear roll bar and fitting one from John Sprinzel to the front. Our first race was the Eight Clubs at Silverstone where we finished third but where, more importantly, I became absolutely bitten by the racing bug.

'We had our fair share of success and had some wonderful scraps with the A35 protagonists of the Cambridge racing team, especially Gerry Boxall, as well as Paddy Gaston, Geoff Hopkinson and various folk driving ohv Minors and Anglias. I remember a wonderful race at Goodwood, which was a real driver's circuit, setting up for a lovely drift through St Mary's and being horrified to see Paddy on two wheels just ahead of me. Later, someone showed us a photograph of four A35s with only eight wheels on the ground. Paddy pushed me across the finishing line with his bumper firmly wedged under the rear apron of my car.

'Oulton Park, on the original long circuit, was another great experience, the great challenge being not to brake for Knicker Brook—you just shut your eyes and prayed. Playing about with tyre pressures and roll bars meant the car could be set up with just a trace of understeer, which is the quickest way through a corner, provided one observes the golden rule of "slow in, fast out", not joining the late-brakers' club.

'Although the racing was very close, it was a friendly rivalry, and I cannot remember there being any serious incident in two years of competition. As more experience was gained with the A-series engine, so cars appeared with Weber carburettors and, in one case, four Amals. It became more difficult to stay at the front. My car was used for work and play, so I was reluctant to turn it into an outright racer. The cylinder head was always removed the night before a race to touch up the valves, but we still got to the boozer before closing time. It is extraordinary to relate that not one mechanical failure ever occurred. This speaks volumes for the built-in strength of the mechanical components.'

By May 1959, the A40 Farina was starting to enjoy itself on the tracks. The racing correspondent of *The Autocar*, reporting on a Silverstone meeting, remarked that, 'Dr Shepherd and his chunky Austin A40 seem to have everything their own way among the small saloon cars nowadays. He won his class by over half a minute, and enjoyed himself dealing with David Shale's Ford Zephyr in doing so. Bob Gerard (A35) managed a new class lap record at 77.48 mph before retiring on lap seven.'

Brands Hatch, September 1960. Doc Shepherd (A40) leads Powell's Jaguar into Druids. Shepherd came second to the 3.8 Jaguar of Jack Sears with whom he shared the fastest lap of 75.71 mph. *Courtesy LAT Photographic*

In June 1959, *Motor Sport* were writing of Shepherd's A40: 'Family Racer—Impressive at Goodwood and outstanding at Silverstone, George Shepherd's astonishing Austin A40—the new sort— is as steady as it is fast.' At Silverstone, he had taken the up-to-1000 cc class in the International Production Touring Car Race at an average speed of 75.65 mph.

Reporting on an Eastern Counties MC meeting which took place at Snetterton, *Motor Sport* of July 1959 congratulated him thus: 'Well driven!—Doc Shepherd (A40) and Len Adams (A35) kept much more powerful machinery at bay in the 37-lap (100 miles) saloon car marathon, finishing very creditably in fifth and sixth places and beating the entire 1500 cc entry.'

In his Seasonal Survey of 1959, which appeared in *Autosport*, David Pritchard showed that he had also taken note of Doc Shepherd: 'There were several newcomers to the circuits during 1959 which brought added interest to the categories affected. For instance, although there were still many A35s in circulation, such as Robin Bryant's Barwell machine and the beautifully presented Cambridge racing team cars, they found new opposition from the A40s,

those of George Shepherd and Geoff Williamson being prominent.'

The Autocar assessed the Doc's A40 in a feature on 30 December 1960, entitled 'Cambridge's Flying Doctor—the test of a remarkable A40.' It began: 'Anyone who in the last year has attended motor races, watched them on television or heard a commentary over the radio will probably recognize the name of Doctor George Shepherd. The racing exploits of this general practitioner from Cambridge and his Austin A40—UCE 13—have stirred spectators at racing circuits in the length and breadth of England. With their traditional love of the under-dog, British crowds have been delighted by the sight of this little black-roofed grey car mixing it with the larger and more powerful machinery—and on occasions even leading Jaguars home on moderately fast circuits.'

Doc Shepherd was fortunate to have Don Moore to prepare his car, and perhaps even more fortunate to have an engine that was specially developed by Harry Weslake. The modified 948 cc engine was still under 1000 cc, but when Weslake and Moore had finished their work, it was producing 65 bhp at 5000 rpm, and 84 bhp at 7500 rpm, using a compression ratio of 11.5:1 and a specially-cast cylinder head.

Describing the other mechanical details, *The Autocar* continued, 'On the suspension side, the rear leaf springs are standard Austin A40, but have been flattened, while the front coil springs have been shortened. Standard shock absorbers—with different valves—are retained at the front and a stiff anti-roll bar added. At the rear, Armstrong adjustable dampers are fitted and a Panhard rod has been found beneficial. Tyres are 5.25 × 13 in. Dunlop Racing. The gearbox is a prototype BMC close-ratio one with roller bearings. The crown wheel and pinion are Austin A30 type, giving a direct drive ratio of 4.875:1. It was not found necessary to change the ratio for different circuits. Front brakes are Austin A40 but the rear ones have been replaced by Nash Metropolitan brakes. . . . Considerable lightening of the body has been carried out. The interior is completely stripped and two bucket seats replace the normal seating. Doors, boot lid and bonnet are of glass fibre and aluminium. With the exception of the windscreen, all the glass has been replaced by lighter plastic.'

When tested by *The Autocar*, a new body, fitted after an accident at Brands Hatch, meant the car was not in as light a trim as that in which it had raced during the season. Even with the heavier body and 2 cwt of test equipment aboard, the car reached 30 mph in 3.5 seconds (about twice as fast as a standard A40) and 50 mph in 7.6 seconds (about three times as fast as a standard car). It could reach 100 mph in 40.8 seconds, and had a mean top speed of 105 mph. Upward changes through the gears were made at 7800 rpm.

During the 1960 season, the A40 competed in 13 events. It failed to finish twice; on one occasion, it had simply lost a wheel, but, as previously mentioned, it crashed on one outing when the Doc got a little too enthusiastic. Apart from these two occasions, the car was always first in its class and sometimes scored an outright win.

Alexander Engineering were among the several tuning firms offering conversions for the A40. A car they had modified was tested by *Motor Sport*, whose report appeared in their issue of November 1959. The modifications comprised a reshaped and polished cylinder head with modified ports. There were special valve springs, twin SU carburettors on a ribbed inlet manifold, and the compression ratio had been raised to 8.9:1. A full-flow, centre port adaptor had been provided on the exhaust manifold to replace the existing siamezed port. The conversion cost £37 10s 0d, with a further £2 10s 0d for modifying the exhaust manifold. The view of *Motor Sport* was that, 'The A40 was not only transformed in respect of greatly improved acceleration, and was

Don Moore (left) and George Shepherd, photographed with the Doc's A40 in 1960. Note the forward-opening fibreglass bonnet. *Courtesy Autocar and Quadrant Picture Library*

very fast, the speedometer needle going "off the clock" at over 80 mph on any reasonably straight road, but it was extremely docile, pulling away smoothly from 20 or even from 15 mph in top gear . . . . Petrol consumption worked out at 37 mpg on a cross-section of fast and moderate driving, but 100-octane fuel was used, although only a trace of pinking was discernible on normal premium grades.' During the test, *Motor Sport* obtained acceleration figures of 0–50 mph in 15.8 seconds and 0–60 mph in 22.6 seconds.

In 1959, an A40 was prepared by Mann Eggerton of Norwich for an attack on the Snetterton circuit's 24-hour record. The record was held by a Singer Gazelle that had averaged 58.04 mph in the previous year. Although the A40 was the smallest car ever to attempt this endurance record, and although night-long fog meant that it could not achieve its secondary target of covering 60 miles in every hour, it took the record by covering 1417 miles in the 24 hours at an average speed of 59.55 mph. It had been necessary to mark the trickiest parts of the track with improvised flares to keep the car circulating at a reduced speed during the night. This meant that it had to be driven flat out as soon as dawn arrived, and the record was only broken with about 15 minutes to spare.

It was not only on the racetrack that the A40 excelled. Pat Moss and Ann Wisdom, driving for the BMC rally team, gained themselves and their A40s

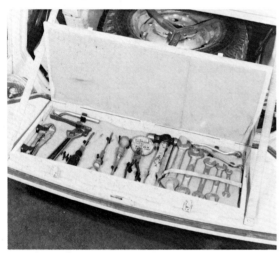

ABOVE The boot contained extra fuel cans, a spare Town & Country, a shovel and some readily accessible tools. *Courtesy Austin Rover*

TOP As Pat Moss put it, 'a very fancy car indeed . . . all the extra equipment made it a lot heavier than it might have been.' Extra instruments pack the fascia, and a Halda Speed Pilot sits over the gearbox. The headlamp flasher switch extends towards the steering wheel. *Courtesy Austin Rover*

a great deal of publicity with their excellent showings in the Monte Carlo and other rallies. A very early Mk I saloon (A-A2S6 2642), in Farina grey with a black roof, was their entry for the 1959 Monte. Known as 'Zoe', due to its registration number (XOE 778), it helped them gain four top awards—including the *Coupe des Dames* and the RAC Challenge Trophy. In *Motor Sport* of March 1959, these feats were acknowledged, and the ladies were offered 'Warmest congratulations on beating 106 male crews by bringing their new A40 home in tenth place.'

They had started from Paris, and all went well until a section was cancelled after deep snow had made it impassable. This should have given them $1\frac{1}{2}$ hours' leeway, but after clocking out of the control, their engine died. The weight of the Weber carburettor had caused the induction manifold to fracture. Then, it was a race against time to get the thing welded. They made it, but only just. Apart from that, the car ran well, and later Pat described it as one of the nicest cars she had ever driven. Although she also remembered it as 'slow, desperately slow', she found it handled beautifully.

To show their success was no fluke, Pat and Ann won the *Coupe des Dames* again in the following year. This time, they were in a black-roofed, Tartan red A40 (A-A2S6 56896), which had been christened 'Alf' from its registration number of 947 AOF. They started from Oslo, dreadful weather making it tough going. From a field of nearly 300, there were only 78 still going at the finish. Arriving at Monte Carlo, Pat and Ann were rather dejected to find themselves 64th overall. They decided that would never do and determined to go all-out on the timed stages over the mountain circuit. With 'Wiz' working the clocks and Pat driving for all she was worth, amidst the ice and the snow, the hairpins and sheer drops, they gradually climbed through the field to become the leading ladies and 17th overall. Now a much respected rally team, they had more than earned the right not to be referred to as simply Stirling Moss' sister and Tommy Wisdom's daughter.

In all, they drove four A40s. Apart from Zoe and Alf, there was an unchristened car in which they continued their winning ways by taking the *Coupe des Dames* in the Canadian Winter Rally of 1959. Zoe was Pat's favourite. It helped them to lift four ladies' cups and, apart from the manifold problem in the 1959 Monte, it never gave any trouble. Their efforts in 'Zokky', an A40 with the registration number XOK 195, were almost in vain. Pat described it as 'a horror, but very fast'. It was fast enough to win

ABOVE January 1959. Pat Moss, Ann Wisdom and 'Zoe' enjoy their first joint success in the sunshine of Monte Carlo, spending nearly two hours being interviewed and photographed. *Courtesy Pat Moss-Carlsson*

LEFT January 1960. At it again. Pat and Ann (this time in 'Alf') on their way to Monte Carlo to win the *Coupe des Dames* for the second year running. *Courtesy Pat Moss-Carlsson*

September 1985. Paul Skilleter and Paul Rosenthal demonstrate that, even in old age, Zoe can still show the opposition a clean pair of heels. *Courtesy Paul Skilleter*

them a bronze cup in the 1959 Alpine Rally as the fastest ladies on Monza, but it let them down mechanically. They lost a couple of gears, and after that it was not long before the clutch decided that it had had enough, too. That same year, they also had to retire from the Liège–Rome–Liège Rally when lighting problems left them overdue at controls. To add to their misery, a con-rod came through the side of the engine as they made their way home. In 1961, they set off for Monte Carlo in Alf for the second year running. A decision to modify the car further, so that it could compete in Group 3, turned out to be a considerable disadvantage. They were having to drive at speeds way beyond the limits of the car's roadholding. They had hoped to take the ladies' cup for the third year in succession, but this time they had to settle for second place.

Zoe, the Mk I A40 in which the women did so well in the 1959 Monte, was registered in November 1958. It was rediscovered a few years ago, minus engine and in such a sorry state that it was hardly worth rebuilding. It was fortunate that motoring historian Paul Skilleter should come across the car. As managing editor of *Practical Classics*, he was able to justify the full and expensive restoration of a car that otherwise might have been scrapped. The more work that was needed, the more his readers would benefit.

During the restoration, Paul was surprised to find that considerable interest was being shown in the project, even from 'owners of quite exotic machinery whom you wouldn't think would be in the least interested in the fate of an extremely run-down A40 Farina.' At every meeting or rally he or his staff attended, they would be asked what was happening to Zoe.

Immediately after its restoration, the car enjoyed a further spell of rallying. In their second attempt at the Coronation Rally—a rally for classic cars that was inaugurated in 1983 and takes its name from the rally held in Coronation Year, 1953—Paul Skilleter and Paul Rosenthal were ready to take on all comers. Zoe was once more on full song.

David Lewis in his A40, working hard to hold off a brace of 'those damned Lotus Cortinas'. *Courtesy David Lewis*

The 948 cc engine had been prepared to full race specification by Aldon Automotive and was mated to a close-ratio gearbox and 5.3:1 differential. Stopping power was provided by Midget discs with DS11 pads at the front, while the rear drums were of Morris Minor parentage with Ferodo VG 95 linings. The front suspension had shorter springs and Midget dampers. Alterations to the rear end involved removing a leaf from each spring, as well as fitting telescopic dampers and an anti-tramp bar. The wheels were from a frog-eye, as they had been in 1959, but they were modified to accept 175 × 13 in. Uniroyal Rallye 340 radial tyres.

The result was a very enjoyable rally. Zoe came first in the under-1200 cc, pre-1960 class and picked up the overall-winner award, as this was calculated on a performance index. How nice to see the car in action again and acquitting itself so well against the likes of the Mini-Cooper, Lotus Cortina, Jaguar XK 120, Porsche 911 and other quite rapid machinery.

There were two A35s taking part in the same rally, entered by keen A30–A35 Owners Club members Peter Simpson and Robert Rendell. Although Peter had to retire and Robert suffered from a shortage of brakes, they had both given it what Robert calls 'Beaucoup de Welly'; no doubt, they will return to fight another day. The rally had taken place on the Epynt ranges, a large mountainous area in mid-Wales that Robert describes as, 'The most ridiculously hostile and devious place to take your favourite classic.' He had tackled several Swiss mountain passes in the car during the previous week, when our A35s had been brought to a halt by an avalanche that blocked the Susten Pass completely for a while. To take part in the Coronation Rally, Robert simply set off home a few days earlier than the rest of us. Arriving on the day before the rally, he threw out his luggage, bolted down the seats, added a fire extinguisher and was on his way.

We have seen how A35s and A40s competed regularly in saloon racing events of the 1950s and very early 1960s, but mention must also be made of today's racing scene. It is well over ten years since these cars took to the track once more, in the guise of classic saloons. In the main, this type of racing has taken place under the auspices of the Classic Saloon Car Club, whose members have managed to delight the crowds at many a meeting with thrilling tussles that re-create those earlier days. Until recently, and the introduction of pre-1965 saloon racing, the A40 Farina was too young to take part, but is now adding further interest to the scene.

David Lewis, whose father was in the party that took the A30 prototypes to Spain in 1950, has forsaken his racing A35 to race a 1966 A40. His first outing in it was at Brands Hatch in the summer of 1985. The 1120 cc engine was based on a Midget block and had been built to race specification by John Beattie. In David's words: 'The A40 ran like a clockwork mouse and finished second in class, behind the quicker but similarly-engined Morris Minor of Pat McCloy. A second race at Silverstone, later in the year, saw her again second in class. This time the A40 beat McCloy's Minor, but not the more powerful Ford Anglia 1200 of Ian Claridge.'

At that Silverstone meeting, David was persuaded to race the A40 in a new series that was being introduced by the British Racing & Sports Car Club for the 1986 season. The new series allows more modifications to these 1960s saloon cars, being based on the Group 2 regulations that were in force during that period. As David put it: 'This meant the A40 could be fitted with the larger 1275 cc Midget engine, together with other mechanical modifications and fibreglass panels, all designed to improve performance, speed and handling. The car, with its new 1380 cc engine, was entered for the July meeting at the Castle Combe circuit in Wiltshire. This new power unit had been built for me by Austin Rover development engineer and former special saloon champion Charles Bernstein. Charles had previously been responsible for the engine in my racing A35. The A40 took fastest lap in its class together with the class lap record and came a commendable third overall, sandwiched between Lotus Cortinas. This was to be the pattern of events throughout the season. At both Brands Hatch and Mallory Park, fastest laps and class wins were again the order of the day. The car is extremely fast—the 1380 cc engine delivers 110 bhp at the wheels, so the Anglias and Cortina GTs are having great difficulty in keeping pace with it.'

David expects to improve his lap times by 'doing a Doc Shepherd' and fitting fibreglass bonnet, boot and doors. The side windows and rear screen will be replaced with perspex, giving a total weight saving in the region of 160 lb. The car is already attracting a great deal of interest and, as more A40s return to racing, we can expect some exciting moments. If the achievements of the A35 drivers are anything to go by, this will certainly be the case.

Phil Wight had a great season with his A35 in 1980, winning his class seven times and coming second twice in a total of ten races. Needless to say, he won the championship. More importantly, how-

ever, he had done it in style, delighting the crowds during some great duels with other A35 drivers, such as Tony Raine and Tom Hinds, and giving the Jaguar drivers quite a fright at times, too. I remember Phil telling me that it had been a case of, 'If you don't succeed at first, spend more money,' because in 1978 he spent nearly £2000 in blowing up engines. It was a case of learn as you go. He found, for example, that taking Druids at Brands Hatch without a baffled sump could be a case of, 'Whoops, another set of ends!'

It was no fluke for an A35 to take the Classic Saloon Car Championship. Robert Trevor proved that when he repeated Phil's triumph in 1983. Robert was fortunate in teaming up with Cedric Osbourne, who had been involved in racing development for over 25 years and was able to put

ABOVE Oulton Park, July 1982. Most of the Jaguars were racing elsewhere, so Henry Crowther's Mk VIII was under threat from a grid full of A35s at the start of the race. The result: Glen Maskell (A35) first, Henry Crowther (Jaguar) second, Tony Raine (A35) third

LEFT 1980—the year Phil Wight's A35 won the Classic Saloon Car Championship. Seen here at Lyddon, he clearly demonstrates why John Sprinzel would talk of taking an inside line on the corners in case there was need to 'lean' on the opposition. Believe it or not, it did not roll.
Courtesy Phil Wight

Robert Trevor, Classic Saloon Car Champion of 1983, brings his A35 through the chicane at Donington on the way to the title

his knowledge to good use in providing Robert with a competitive car. It had the usual modifications, such as Midget discs and front anti-roll bar. They were competing in the Road Going series, so had to use the standard 26 VME Zenith carburettor. After calculating the maximum carburettor through-put, they designed an inlet manifold to match it. They also carried out a great deal of test-bed running to design their own exhaust manifold. The best compromise seemed to be a long centre-branch manifold incorporating a pulse pipe fitted to the centre branch. The length of the pulse pipe matched the camshaft and head characteristics. This gave a good scavenging effect from the centre exhaust port, and in this trim the engine had excellent torque right down to 3500 rpm on a 648 camshaft. Apart from needing rebuilds to replace worn parts, the engine ran for two seasons without a fault.

What a bonus it is for any enthusiastic owner of an A30, A35 or A40 to be able to see the little vehicles still performing so happily on the track in today's classic saloon racing. Their owner/drivers are usually very ready to chat to other enthusiasts about how they prepare their cars, and this makes the whole business very enjoyable. Of course, it is very easy to get bitten by the racing bug, and it is surprising what even a casual visit to a motor-racing circuit can lead to—so be warned!

13
FROM TURBINES TO AUTOMATIC TRANSMISSIONS

The era of the A30, A35 and A40 Farina was one in which all manner of experiments were taking place in the research department at Longbridge. This department was under the direction of Dr John Weaving, a man who was described by colleague Roger Lewis as having 'knowledge pouring out of his ears'. He was an authority on two-stroke diesels and, in the mid-1940s, was working on a single-cylinder, two-stroke diesel with a view to its possible use in cars. At about that time, however, the motoring pundits were telling us that the turbine car was the thing of the future, so Doc Weaving was diverted to work in this field.

It was uncharted territory, so there were some exciting test runs, but by 1954, they had installed their turbine in an Austin Sheerline. Unacceptably high fuel consumption and problems with pick-up lag turned their attention to developing the turbines for more appropriate use as emergency power generators, producing some 250 bhp.

A diversion from the main programme occurred in 1953, when a contract was obtained from the Ministry of Supply, who were encouraging research into a 30 bhp vehicle turbine. A unit was developed successfully to the stage where it achieved its 30 bhp at the design speed of 56,000 rpm, but fuel consumption was well off target. With the knowledge gained in later research, it is probable that this small turbine would have met all its targets except one—that of cost. Very high tooling costs, and the need for expensive materials for the turbine blades and discs, meant that a miniature turbine could never compete financially with the normal petrol engine. Drawings had been produced showing the small turbine installed in an A35 as a test-bed, but that is as far as it got. Speaking of his gas-turbine research, Doc Weaving puts it rather nicely, although much too modestly, by saying, 'At least we had increased our knowledge of the problems.'

In the 1950s, a variety of other projects could be found going on in odd corners of Longbridge. In

1953, Norman Horwood joined the Austin Motor Company as personal assistant to Johnnie Rix, but soon discovered that he was only one of 11 such assistants. Anything left by the other ten seemed to come his way—he was being used as a general dogsbody. However, this meant that Norman could follow up all sorts of new ideas, one of which was an attempt to build an all-aluminium car. The suggestion that Austin should do some work in this field was being pushed at Leonard Lord's level by the Aluminium Development Association. In August 1953, the ADA and Austin agreed that their first joint project should centre on a two-door A30.

Although there were many at Longbridge who took an interest in the project, there were others who found it rather a nuisance. It is fairly obvious that the ADA held out greater hopes for its success than did the Longbridge management. The Association had seen their French counterpart, Aluminium Français, collaborate with Panhard to produce a car which suggested that aluminium might have a great future in the car industry. Widely acclaimed as one of the most interesting exhibits at the 1953 Paris Show, the small (but six-seater) Dyna Panhard was ultra-modern in conception, its aerodynamic aluminium bodywork being of integral construction. An 850 cc, air-cooled flat-twin engine could propel the car at over 80 mph and return 40 mpg.

The ADA sent a Panhard to Longbridge to see if the engine and front drive unit would fit into the A30 bodyshell, but the Dyna unit was much bulkier than that of the Austin. Fitting it would have entailed a complete redesign of the A30's front end but, more to the point, the weight of the Dyna Panhard front drive unit was greater than that of the A30's engine, gearbox, propshaft, and radiator (including the water). Had it been installed in an aluminium A30, there would have been a weight saving of only about 200 lb compared to the standard car. It was not enough.

It was decided to produce the A30's own engine

in aluminium. The casting of the aluminium blocks and heads was done by William Mills of Wednesbury, but all the machining was carried out with production tooling at Longbridge. Nothing special was done to allow for the change in material. In Norman Horwood's words: 'We just pressed on and kept our fingers crossed, tightened the whole thing up and pressed the starter button. To everyone's surprise, it went! The engine was fully tested on the East Works test-beds and performed to a higher standard than the equivalent production engine.'

In pre-war days, Bill Appleby had gained much practical experience of aluminium engines. He had produced the majority of the detail drawings for the all-aluminium, twin-cam, 750 cc engine used in Murray Jamieson's racing Seven. In correspondence with the author, he wrote, 'I remember well the all-aluminium A30 engine and confirm that it ran quite well. However, we could not afford to standardize it, as the cost approached twice as much as the standard cast-iron engine. Much of the extra cost was probably due to the fact that the cylinder block and cylinder head were made from sand-castings. Had the cylinder block been made as a die-casting, doubtless the cost would have been much less. However, at that period, no one had had any experience of making such a large die-casting as a cylinder block, and this change was never contemplated. . . . In addition, aluminium is much more resonant than cast-iron, so the engine was noisier than the standard engine.'

The difficulties of producing A30 body panels in aluminium, from dies designed for use with steel, did lead to some talk of the need to design a completely new car, using light alloys for all the major components. Smoother body lines, as in the Panhard, would have made it easier to produce the light-alloy pressings and would have improved both the performance and fuel consumption of a small-engined car.

After much trial and error, aluminium panels were produced for the A30 in a relatively trouble-free process, albeit with some variation in pressing quality. Sometimes, the surface finish of the dies had to be improved, and the edge-holding radii were altered on the more difficult panels to prevent the aluminium tearing as it was fed into the heavily-worked regions. Some panels required localized flame annealing to help the drawing of the metal, while others could be drawn with the aid of Russian tallow fat—normally used in the body shop for lead-loading.

In January 1955, an aluminium A30 began to take

ABOVE The East Works wind tunnel on 28 December 1953. A wind-cheating covering of clay has been applied to an A30 bodyshell. It would have been much easier to produce aluminium body panels for this smoothed-off version of the car. *Courtesy Austin Rover*

RIGHT Forming the aluminium panels was not easy. There was severe splitting in the outer rear wings, rear-seat pan and gearbox cover, while the roof panel (shown) was badly creased. Some panels, such as the petrol tank and radiator grille (which was anodized), were hand-made. *Courtesy Norman Horwood*

shape on jigs that had been used for the first A30 prototypes, but work was held up by the poor quality of the spot welds. A 200 kVa spot welder solved the problem, but it meant building a new electricity sub-station next to the assembly bay. Even with the new machine, it was still necessary to use gas welding and rivets where the spot welding was inadequate, or where aluminium had to be joined to steel. For a satisfactory spot weld, an aluminium flange needs to be at least $\frac{5}{8}$ in. deep to prevent the metal squeezing out at the free edge. Having been designed for steel, the flanges on the A30's panels were much less than that.

The original plan was to produce two cars: one as light as possible, with the minimum of steel components for light road work only; the other strong enough for strenuous road testing, using steel pressings for the front and rear suspension mountings and

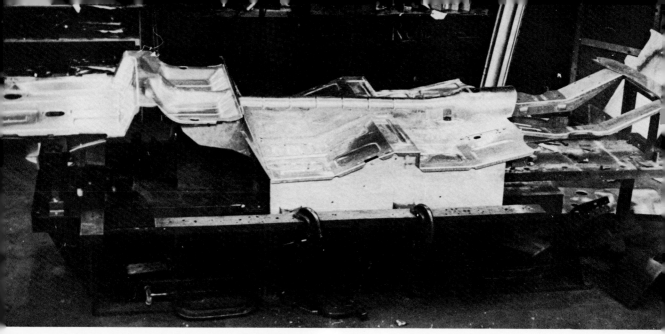

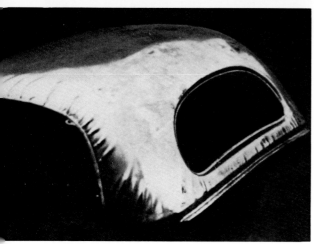

associated structures. Difficulties with the spot welding meant that both cars would have to be built to the stronger specification, but the second car was never completed.

The first car weighed a mere 10 cwt, compared to the $13\frac{1}{2}$ cwt of the standard saloon. It was said to handle and accelerate like a sports car. Overcooling produced a slight drop in power output, but this seems to have had a beneficial effect on the exhaust valves and their seats. When an engine was stripped down in May 1957, after completing 2000 miles in the aluminium car and a further 100 hours of endurance running on the test-bed, the valves and valve seats had the appearance of only having had some 20 hours of running. Indeed, the whole engine was found to be in excellent condition with only very slight indication of crankcase distortion. There had been no troubles with oil or water leaks, nor

ABOVE Aluminium everywhere with a few extra creases here and there, but otherwise satisfactory. The front inner wings and suspension mounts were the only parts to be produced in steel. *Courtesy Norman Horwood*

TOP Work begins on the assembly of the aluminium A30 in the experimental body shop, using the jigs that had been made for the first A30 prototypes. *Courtesy Norman Horwood*

was there any evidence of corrosion in the cooling system, other than on some of the steel components. The aluminium water pump and impeller were in perfect condition.

Norman Horwood ran this royal-blue A30 for some months, estimating that it must have done about 500 hours in all. Apparently, the car was a pleasure to drive, even on the *pavé* at MIRA, since the reduced weight had been compensated for by a reduction in suspension spring rate. In particular, Norman recalls a journey to London to show the car to the ADA: 'I had my wife and young son aboard. My driving was enthusiastic and the soft springing got to my son's tummy. He was starting to be ill in the car, so I stopped in a hurry and pushed him and my wife out fast, so that the inside could be saved. They landed on the grass verge in a heap, and a local resident ran over to see if they could help the poor beaten-up wife and child thrown on to the roadside! I had some explaining to do!'

By the autumn of 1957, the testing of this first aluminium A30 had been handed over to East Works, and the project was progressing so satisfactorily that the ADA became increasingly hopeful that their investment was about to pay off. They began pressing for the completion of the second car, but the Austin management felt it necessary to slow things down a little.

The ADA, on the other hand, had several ideas that they wanted to pursue with Austin. They hoped for more research into perfecting the aluminium engine and an all-aluminium water circuit. They suggested that a design study should be applied to a larger car and that the testing of the two aluminium A30s should continue in order to build up a complete case history. Austin were fairly interested in the knowledge being gained from the aluminium engine, but were not convinced that there was much to be gained from producing cars in aluminium. An aluminium car demanded styling appropriate to the metal, and the fullest benefits would only be reaped by utilizing front-wheel drive to eliminate the propshaft and lower the whole profile of the car. It would have taken much courage to initiate such radical departures in policy. Aluminium was already expensive, and its price was rising at an alarming 16 per cent a year, compared to nine per cent for steel. George Harriman did provide the ADA with confidential figures showing the likely requirements for aluminium should Austin decide to use the material on one or more vehicles, and the ADA obtained quotes from suppliers on that basis, but there the matter rested.

The great hopes for a large increase in the use of aluminium in the car industry, during the early 1950s, were not to be fulfilled. Even if a manufacturer had gone to the trouble and expense of producing a car designed for this metal, they would not necessarily have been on to a winner. Certainly, the Dyna Panhard was a well-designed and efficient essay in aluminium, but eventually even Panhard reverted to the use of steel for this model. It was not just a question of cost. The number of badly-dented Dynas requiring expensive repairs after the nudging methods employed in Parisian parking seemed to have played a part. Indeed, a minor accident, involving the aluminium A30, finally provided a reason to abandon the project. A Ford Consul had halted at a pedestrian crossing. In a lapse of concentration, the driver of the A30, coasting up behind, collided with it at no more than 4 or 5 mph. The damage to the light-alloy car was fairly extensive, but there was not a mark to be found on the Consul. By then, it was June 1959, and with the second of the aluminium A30s still only 90 per cent complete, it was decided that both cars should go under the hammer, and that did not mean at an auction sale. The Aluminium Development Association tried to persuade George Harriman to let them have the completed car for further evaluation, but did not succeed.

Another fascinating project was the small automatic transmission, which underwent considerable testing in A35s and A40 Farinas. As a result of approaches made to Longbridge, Dr Duncan Stuart, Doc Weaving's second-in-command, went to Stuttgart to inspect a transmission that had been designed by Heinrich Ebert. He was taken to the NSU works at Neckarsulm where, to his surprise, he was given a scooter to ride. The automatic transmission was in the swinging arm of this NSU Autoroller.

Fred White was also in on the early days of the story. He received a mid-week call to go to George Harriman's office, where he was handed a cylindrical object and asked what he thought it was. Fred suggested it was a type of swash-plate pump, and he was correct, in that it was the automatic transmission from the scooter's swinging arm which used a swash-plate pump to produce the hydrostatic drive. Harriman asked Fred to take it away and design an automobile transmission along the same lines, saying, 'You could bring me a scheme on Monday.'

Not to be outdone, Fred immediately enlisted the help of Dr Duncan Stuart. He needed to know how much fluid would have to be pumped, and at what

LEFT An early example of a crumple zone! The aluminium A30 after its 5 mph nudge. *Courtesy Norman Horwood*

BELOW March 1962. Noise analysis on the hydrostatic transmission in the East Works research department. The test facilities in use here would normally measure the efficiency of the transmission, the pump being driven by a dynamometer and the motor driving an electric brake. *Courtesy Austin Rover*

rate, to be able to decide how many pistons and of what size were required to do the job. While Duncan worked on his slide rule, Fred did his best at the drawing-board.

The project was taken over almost immediately by the research department because, in the words of Doc Weaving, 'It seemed the answer to a maiden's prayer. The design was such that a large part of the power would be transmitted mechanically, and so it had the possibility of being much more efficient than the average automatic transmission.'

The transmission consisted of a pump and motor arrangement with a porting block in between. The pump and motor units each consisted of a circular cylinder block containing pistons, rather as a revolver holds its bullets. The pistons were made to move back and forth in their cylinders as they bore against an angled, circular swash plate. An increase in the swash-plate angle would increase the stroke of the pistons. The movement of the pump pistons would force fluid through the porting block and thus push the motor pistons against their own angled swash plate. The consequent ramp action would cause the motor's cylindrical cylinder block to turn as well. It was only necessary to alter the swash-plate angles to vary the gear ratio—the transmission was infinitely variable. Nor was it limited to a 1:1 ratio, so, in effect, overdrive was also available.

The angles of the swash plates were altered by movement of a dustbin-like tube which encased the whole thing and slid backwards and forwards. With the pump swash plate vertical, no pumping occurred and everything locked up to transmit the drive mechanically in a 1:1 ratio. The top forward ratio (effectively about 15 per cent overdrive) was achieved at one extreme of the tube's movement, while reverse was achieved at the other extreme. Neutral was obtained by opening up a bypass between the two sides of the hydrostatic circuit so that no pressure differential existed and, therefore, no driving torque. Obtaining drive from rest was achieved by progressively closing the bypass valve (held open by a spring) with a simple engine-driven, centrifugal-weight device. The bypass would close fully at a relatively low engine speed of 1100 rpm. This gave it similar take-up characteristics to a fluid flywheel.

The complete transmission was only about 15 in. long and 8 in. in diameter, so it fitted easily in place of the conventional gearbox. There was some leakage from the system, so it was necessary to have an oil sump with a low-pressure pump to recirculate the oil. The sump was ribbed to aid cooling.

In theory, the transmission offered considerable advantages over conventional automatic gearboxes. In practice, the very high loads on the swash-plate bearings, and on the domes of the hardened steel pistons which rode against the swash plates, meant that bearing and lubricant technology were being stretched to the limits. Undaunted by early problems, they made good progress. The transmission was first used in an A35 in 1957.

Those undertaking the first road tests spoke of an impression of being in charge of a motor boat rather than a car. Under full throttle, acceleration took place at constant engine speed, so there was no way of sensing the acceleration by a change in engine note. Alterations to the ratio control valve and accelerator linkage produced a more conventional feel to the drive.

Among the party-pieces of vehicles fitted with hydrostatic transmission was their ability to go straight from forward to reverse with nothing more than a bit of wheelspin. George Harriman suggested that Len Lord should try out the car round the 'Kremlin' circuit. When Lord asked how to put it into reverse, Harriman pointed to the appropriate lever, telling him that it simply needed to be pulled back. He immediately did so, with the car travelling forwards at about 40 mph. The engine probably touched about 7500 rpm, but the changeover was remarkably smooth. In such circumstances, the bypass valve opens to act as a safety valve.

In early 1959, one car was doing 3500–4000 miles a week, and from September 1959, the testing was done at Cowley. By 1961, the transmission could be relied upon to be fault-free for 50,000 miles, and the target of 100,000 trouble-free miles was considered within sight. One transmission covered 90,000 miles in an A35 before its bearings collapsed. The cars had 948 cc engines which had been uprated to 40 bhp to compensate for the power losses in the transmission.

Gradual improvement resulted in an efficiency of 91 per cent at medium speeds in the 1:1 ratio, dropping to 87 per cent at high speeds. Acceleration and hillclimbing were improved at low speeds, but were slightly worse at anything over 45 mph.

Weighing 141 lb, the transmission (as used in the A35 and A40) was very heavy compared to the 51 lb of the standard clutch and gearbox. In 1957, it was estimated that it would cost about £43 to manufacture, against about £16 for the standard gearbox and clutch. Later improvements in design reduced the weight considerably. The estimated cost of equipping the Mini or 1100 with a hydrostatic unit

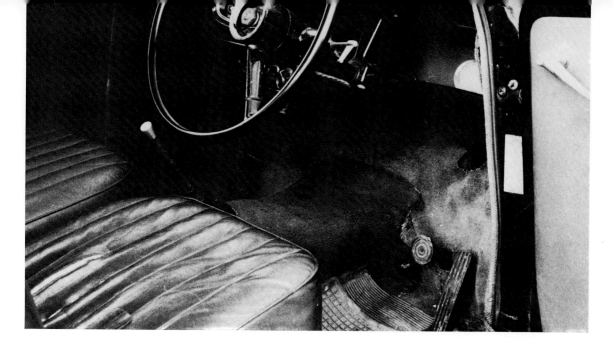

Two pedals, both operated by the right foot, make it easy
to adapt to this A35 with Hobbs automatic transmission

was only £2 more than the standard gearbox. George
Harriman liked it and stuck by it all through the
development stages. The remainder of the engineering hierarchy, including Sir Alec Issigonis, did not
show much interest. The fact that no hydrostatic
power was being transmitted at the 1:1 ratio made
it a particularly efficient transmission, but Dr
Duncan Stuart felt that this feature went largely
unrecognized by those making the decisions. The
coming of the Mini hampered the project somewhat,
because the design team had to do a complete rethink
to adapt the transmission to a transverse engine.

Duncan Stuart's wife, Ann, did many miles in an
A35 equipped with this transmission. It never let
her down, and the more Duncan recollected the
details related above, the more he regretted that it
had never been fully developed. It was in the forefront of technology at the time, and he firmly
believes that infinitely-variable transmissions have
not really caught up yet, not even with the passing
of 25 years.

There was another automatic A35. It was built by
Hobbs Automatic Transmissions, a firm set up in
1945 by Howard Hobbs in Leamington.

In 1955, BSA bought a controlling interest in the
company, and Sir Bernard Docker hoped to use a
Hobbs transmission for a 1.6-litre Lanchester Sprite
they were designing. Originally, they had hoped to
base the new Lanchester on the Dyna Panhard, but
the difficulty of producing the alloy panels seems
to have put them off the idea.

Some prototype Lanchester Sprites were fitted
with preselector gearboxes, but the only Sprite to
survive was fitted with the Hobbs automatic box.
After Sir Bernard Docker was ousted from BSA, the

Sprite was doomed, but Hobbs had been busy working on a similar box for 1-litre cars. The first of these
small transmissions was fitted to an Austin A35 in
1958. Prior to the formation of BMC, Hobbs had done
much work in conjunction with Morris. Nearly all
the first prototypes of their automatic transmissions
were tested in Morris Oxfords. The small transmission had been put in an A35 to try and interest
Austin. That little A35 had a very busy first year,
as it was tested by just about everyone—
manufacturers, motoring journalists and racing
drivers, they all had a go. Both Stirling Moss and
Graham Hill borrowed the car for a week. Rootes
did some very energetic testing—so energetic that
they blew the engine—but the gearbox took it all
in its stride.

In his approaches to Longbridge, John Hobbs, son
of the company founder, was given the impression
that they were not interested. Knowledge of the time
and money that Austin were devoting to the
development of their own hydrostatic transmission
makes this more understandable. After further
development, the small Hobbs transmission went
into a number of Ford Anglias and into several hundred Cortinas.

The Hobbs transmission did not incorporate a
torque converter. The drive was purely mechanical,
and although the absence of a torque converter made
providing smooth changes difficult, it did produce
a more efficient box. Two clutches were incorporated, the solid shaft of the first clutch passing
through the hollow shaft of the second. In top gear,

October 1986. John Hobbs with A2S5 HCS 66696, the only
A35 to be fitted with a Hobbs automatic transmission

both clutches were engaged, but the three indirect
gears used only the first clutch. Reverse gear used
only the second clutch. The ratios of the planetary
gears were selected with the aid of disc brakes rather
than bands—a novel idea in those days.

The only A35 ever fitted with a Hobbs transmission is not only still in existence, but is still in
the Hobbs family. It was pensioned off some years
ago, but is safely under cover. In 1986, with 58,000
miles showing on the clock, and having stood for
some considerable time, it was still prepared to
respond to a couple of jump leads applied by John
Hobbs. Priming the fuel pump brought the car back
to life. Without an MOT, a full road test was not
possible, but even a run on unmade roads showed
the transmission to be pleasant and controllable. The
gear lever can be left in automatic or can be moved
forward or backwards to select any gear. From rest,
the drive changes up to any preselected gear, and
a kick-down mechanism looks after the need for sudden acceleration. It is sad that the efforts of Hobbs
Transmissions were not rewarded better, but it is
pleasing to see this car preserved.

The petrol-stretching abilities of five-speed gearboxes has meant a sharp drop in the demand for
automatic transmissions. As John Hobbs put it: 'Producing automatic gearboxes has always been a good
way to lose money, but if you'd told me in 1959 that
in 1986 only three per cent of British cars would be
automatic, I'd have thought you were mad.'

14

AN ECONOMY CAR

When the A30 was launched in 1951, there were those who questioned whether it was a true economy car. A four-seater saloon with a very useful boot and the added luxuries of four doors, a four-cylinder overhead-valve engine and 12-volt electrics was hardly minimal motoring. It was Austin's aim, however, to compete with the austerity models of the continental manufacturers by offering the A30 as a 'large car in miniature', rather than as an out-and-out economy model. Advanced production techniques were expected to give the car a competitive edge over its more austere rivals.

Some argued that Austin policy had fallen between two stools, and it was not very long before the debate spread to the Longbridge board room. When Dr Josef Ehrlich arrived at Longbridge in 1952, he knew nothing of this debate. He was simply one of the many who regularly approached Austin and BMC with ideas or inventions. Most went home disappointed, but Joe Ehrlich managed to persuade George Harriman that he did have something to offer. Joe had brought along a papier-mâché model of a baby car, from which George Harriman could see that he had given much thought to the idea of minimal motoring. His plans for the engine were of particular interest.

Certainly, it was out of the ordinary, for although it operated on the two-stroke cycle, each cylinder had twin bores. The idea was new to Harriman, but a follower of motorcycle TT racing could have told you of the twin-piston 'Jerries', which screamed round the track with their own distinctive note, to very good effect. They would probably be assuming that Ehrlich's bikes contained the similar-sounding DKW engine, and although they would have been wrong, they would have been on the right track. Josef Ehrlich was from Vienna, and pre-war he held many of the patents for twin-piston two-strokes, notably those used in Puch motorcycles, from which the racing DKW seems to have developed. As early as 1935, Joe was racing his own designs suc-

cessfully in TT events. He left Germany in 1937 and established his own engineering business in London. Fifty years later, you could still find him putting his engines through their paces, striving, as ever, to keep abreast of the competition.

His arrival at Longbridge came at an opportune moment. George Harriman felt that they ought to know a little more about these unusual two-strokes. Not that other Longbridge men could be expected to think the same way. Surely two-strokes were noisy, smoky, smelly and rough, and definitely not suited to real motor cars. Realizing that Joe's ideas would not be received too readily in the main channels at Longbridge, George Harriman asked Johnnie Rix to get one of his personal assistants to look at what Joe had to offer. Thus, Fred White was introduced to Joe and, at first, he was not impressed with his ideas for an economy car. It was supposed to be driven by only one of the two rear wheels, and 'when they scaled up the model and tried to insert

A drawing of Joe Ehrlich's initial proposal for an economy car. Note the air intake for the air-cooled engine, the absence of doors, and the upholstery buttoned to the bench seat that formed part of the floorpan. *Courtesy Joe Ehrlich*

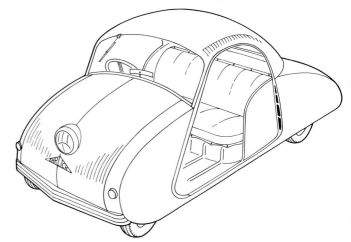

George [a little plastic man], the screen was just about up to his knee-caps.' The proposed engine, however, was worthy of further investigation.

With a two-stroke engine, it is difficult to evacuate the exhaust gases fully without losing some of the fresh charge as well. With the twin-piston two-stroke, the inlet and exhaust ports are operated by one of the pistons, and the transfer port is operated by the other. By this means, efficient removal, or scavenging, of the exhaust gases is much improved. The two pistons are joined to a common, Y-shaped con-rod and run side by side in their respective cylinders. The design of the con-rod depends on the characteristics desired of the engine, but it is arranged so that both pistons reach top dead centre at the same time and thus share a common combustion chamber.

As with a standard crankcase compression engine, it was expected that Ehrlich's engines would produce 50–60 bhp per litre at something like 4200 rpm, and that the torque figures would be some 20–30 per cent higher than those of a four-stroke engine. It was not desirable for car engines to be revving at anything like the 11,000 rpm of a racing motorcycle, so Joe and Fred set to work on designing a more sedate 500 cc twin with two pistons per cylinder.

This did not quite mean an end to the fun Joe had experienced on the racetrack. The Longbridge experimental department became interested in a high-revving two-stroke as a source of exhaust gases on which to run a turbine. Joe obliged by producing a split single which ran at something like 12,000 rpm. By all accounts, it provided plenty of turbo gas and plenty of power, but it also made plenty of noise. When it was under test in South Works, Don Hawley returned one afternoon swearing blind that he had heard its high-pitched scream as he left the centre of Birmingham. You could hardly blame the nuns in the convent opposite the works for complaining and you could hardly blame Joe for itching to see how it performed on the track. He asked George Harriman if he had any objections. He did not, but neither did he want to know about it officially, telling Joe, 'Don't forget, it's EMC not BMC.' EMC, of course, were the initials of Ehrlich Motor Cycles.

Joe did not have to go far to find someone to ride his experimental machine. Within spitting distance of where the engine was being developed, Harvey Williams was rectifying cars in the assembly building. Harvey, who had been competing in motorcycle trials since he was 16 years old, had come third in

the British championship on a bike he had built himself. As a result, he was sponsored to ride in the Isle of Man TT. He did well, being the first British machine and the first private entrant across the line. Apart from his obvious courage and riding ability, Harvey had another great asset: he weighed only $6\frac{1}{2}$ stone. He finished fourth in the world championship when riding for MV Agusta, before the Italians gave up racing. In 1953, his lack of a ride fitted in nicely with Joe Ehrlich's plans. Riding the machine was a little more exciting than Harvey had bargained for. He had considerable success in the 125 cc category, but had a serious accident on the Isle of Man in 1954. After crashing on a bend at 90 mph (flies having blocked the air scoops to his brakes), he spent eight weeks unconscious in hospital. Later, he was told that they had rescued him from a tree and that his tachometer had stuck at 9000!

In the meantime, progress had been made in the design of the 500 cc engine. It was not long before the schemes for the complete engine were ready, and Fred White was asked to take the drawings up to George Harriman. He seemed sold on it completely, telling Fred, 'This is the engine of the future,' and paying Joe Ehrlich £5000 in advance royalties. Joe, employed as an outside consultant, was only at Longbridge two days a week, but asked Fred, 'What are your initials?', intending to share the money. 'Not at all,' said Fred. 'I'm paid by Longbridge.' Mind you, at that stage, he did not know that £5000 was involved.

They went on to build the engine, the bores of which were chromed. After chroming, a cylindrical screen was inserted in the cylinders and acid sprayed in to etch an oil-retaining finish in the cylinder walls. The first engine was installed in the A30 convertible. (Michael Edwards was right; those air vents had been to aid cooling.) At first, it was run with two standard A30 fan blades, their tips being trimmed to produce a four-bladed fan of 10 in. diameter. The angle of twist on each blade was increased from the standard 24 degrees to approximately 30 degrees. Later, a VW arrangement was rigged up.

The convertible was only being used to road test the engine while a lightweight version of the A30 was being developed. In early 1954, Dick Burzi had ordered a special lightweight body from Fisher & Ludlow. It was produced in steel that was a couple of gauges lighter than normal, and many of the panels were altered to keep weight to a minimum. The opening boot was dispensed with, as was the rear bulkhead. The rear-seat back folded down to

ABOVE EMC, not BMC! Harvey Williams on the Ehrlich two-stroke, prior to his accident, in the 1954 Isle of Man TT. *Courtesy Harvey Williams*

LEFT The dismantled Ehrlich racing engine, showing the arrangement of connecting rod and cylinder barrel for the twin-piston set-up

The 500 cc twin-piston/cylinder, air-cooled Ehrlich engine. This engine was originally installed in the A30 convertible and later in the A20, but was tracked down to an enthusiast in Kent in 1985

MIRA, on the normal routes to Wales and on Austin's 200-mile Cotswold route. It did not bear any 'Austin of England' badges, and when out on the road, its 'Flying A' was taped up. That piece of tape did not hide the 'Flying A' and surely must have made the car more obvious. In February 1955, the A20 was put through some performance tests by Doc Weaving's development department. They changed the rear-axle ratio from 5.375:1 to 5.125:1 and, after much tuning and adjusting, managed to get a cross-country petrol consumption of 44.5 mpg. Because the engine was a two-stroke, running on a mixture of 24 parts petrol to one of oil, this could also be expressed as 46.3 mpg for petrol and 1110 mpg for oil. It was estimated that a standard AS3 saloon would have given a petrol consumption of approximately 49 to 50 mpg and an oil consumption of 4000 mpg under similar test conditions.

The maximum speed obtained was only 52.8 mph. It took 10.7 seconds to go from 10 to 30 mph in third gear, and 20.55 seconds to go from 20 to 40 mph in top gear. To accelerate from 30 to 50 mph in top gear took 32.9 seconds. At a steady 20 mph, the car returned 48.8 mpg. At 30, 40 and 50 mph, the respective figures were 63.8, 52.0 and 42.0 mpg

The car's hillclimbing ability was tested on Rose Hill, where an experienced Austin tester could tell you what he thought of a car within a few minutes of leaving the works. With the pre-war Sevens, for example, the tester would put his foot down from the Bilberry Tea Rooms at the foot of the hill, and if he was still in top gear as he passed the school gate on the right-hand side of the road, the car was up to standard. Then, it would be expected to be happy with second gear until it reached the telegraph pole at Lickey Church, where Sir Herbert Austin now lies buried. The earliest of the pre-war Sevens would have to drop right down into first gear to complete the climb, but later versions would get over in second. A standard A30 would take about 58 seconds to climb the hill in top gear, but the 500 cc two-stroke was put into second when the speed dropped to 20 mph, so it took 74.2 seconds to crest the hill. These figures showed that the car, as it stood, was not up to contemporary road conditions. Nor was it very pleasant to drive. The slow running was very erratic due to four-stroking, and the engine missed badly at speeds below 25 mph in top gear. It was also popping back through the carburettor. Even at higher speeds, there were problems. At anything above 45 mph, the engine would start to vibrate quite severely. George Coates remembers: 'You could feel it rumbling through your

allow access to the luggage space. Further weight had been saved in the design of seats and trim. In Fisher & Ludlow's records, the car was known as the Lightweight 7. Norman Horwood, who was working on the lightweight aluminium A30 at the same time, knew nothing of this alternative lightweight project. Eventually, he did learn about it when he was taken to task for overspending. When he checked, he found that £2750 had been pirated from the aluminium budget to pay for the lightweight steel version. Not quite cricket.

This version of the A30 weighted 11½ cwt, and as the 500 cc engine developed 20 bhp, it was known to Joe Ehrlich and others on the project as the 'A20'. In Tweed grey with a red interior, it was tested at

ABOVE AND LEFT The body which Fisher & Ludlow referred to as the 'Lightweight Austin 7' and which was also known as 'the two-stroke car' or the A20. Note the external spare wheel and bolt-on rear wings. Access to the luggage compartment was gained by folding forward the rear seat

ABOVE AND LEFT **More views of the Lightweight Austin 7,
which had a one-piece front. Spartan trim, lightweight seats
and fixed quarter-lights all helped to cut down weight**

stomach.' Obviously further development work was
required, but there were also moves afoot to design
a completely new economy car.

Preliminary discussions had begun in the summer
of 1954, when a meeting was called to consider proposals for an experimental mini-car. All those
present were given a chance to contribute their own
two-penn'orth. There was quite a divergence of
opinion. Joe Ehrlich wanted a well-styled vehicle
with characteristics of its own—in the true sense,
neither car nor motorcycle, but able to recruit customers from among those who owned motorcycles
or motorcycle combinations. He said it should have
independent suspension at each of the four wheels
and hold three people on one bench seat. To be inexpensive, it should be small, open, and without doors.
He favoured an air-cooled two-stroke engine sited
at the rear. Fred White agreed that it should be an
unconventional, three-seater vehicle, either without
doors or with very simple ones, as on the Austin
Champ.

Jim Stanfield, chief body designer, seemed quite
happy that one bench seat should provide the seating capacity, either for two adults or, perhaps, for
two adults and a child, but he wanted it to have the
appearance of a well-styled small car. It could be a
drop-head, but must have doors. A fixed top unit
could be available as an option.

Billy Ellcock, chief chassis designer, wanted a
modern, conventional appearance, including doors.
He suggested a 2 + 2 seating arrangement, but went
along with the suggestions for a rear engine and
independent suspension on all wheels.

Dr John Weaving wanted the car to have a
modern, streamlined body, and favoured a 2 + 2
arrangement to minimize the frontal area and keep
down fuel consumption. He plumped for a two-door
saloon body of stressed-skin construction, and felt
that a roof was required to give the necessary support for a very light structure. His proposal for an
open version entailed leaving the roof edging in
position to provide adequate structural strength and
simply using a roll-back canvas cover. He seems to
have been advocating something on the lines of that
French umbrella on wheels, the Deux Chevaux,
because he also suggested using tubular front seats
with simple deck-chair covering. He wanted the
propshaft eliminated, but felt more thought should
be given as to how this could be achieved—an
engine at the front, driving the front wheels, or an
engine at the back, driving the rear wheels.

The three established Austin men, Jim Stanfield,
Billy Ellcock and John Weaving, were convinced
that if the vehicle was too unconventional, it would
not have sufficient sales appeal. They recognized
they were aiming at a mini-car, but felt it should

not be too much of a utility vehicle. Perhaps it had been rather easier for Porsche when he designed the Volkswagen. He was told that it must be able to carry three soldiers and one machine-gun plus the necessary ammunition. It may or may not have paid to argue the toss with Len Lord, but it certainly did not pay to argue with Adolf Hitler.

It is hardly surprising that opinions differed. The design of any vehicle is a matter of compromise, and the smaller the vehicle gets, the more difficult it is to balance all the requirements. In Europe, there were examples of almost every possible combination of engines and transmissions, and an equal variety of seating arrangements, each having its strengths and weaknesses.

In any case, certain points had been agreed upon. The vehicle had to be capable of 60 mph and at least 60 mpg. It should have a modern, streamlined appearance and be of monocoque construction. A suggestion of Jim Stanfield's would be looked into— with a very low vehicle, it might be possible to arrange access by folding back the roof and side protection, allowing one to step in over very low sides. The seating arrangement would be considered again

after layouts had been examined. It was hoped to keep the weight down to not much more than 7 cwt. The independent suspension would use trailing links at the rear and leading links at the front. A rear engine seemed to offer a cost-saving which could not be ignored, so a modified Ehrlich two-stroke of 500 cc, and developing 20 bhp, would be tried first. Billy Ellcock was not alone in suggesting that other engines ought to be considered.

Over the next few months, several competitors' cars were seen at Longbridge. Renault, Panhard, Goliath, Fiat and Volkwagen were all scrutinized carefully. It was not the first time that the design of the VW had come under scrutiny at Longbridge. Just after the war, when the plans for the Volkswagen were being offered as part of war reparations, they were laid out in the Longbridge drawing office. A young Barry Kelkin found everyone pulling them to pieces, 'Laughing at them—Lord was laughing,

The completed A20 stands in the experimental department at Longbridge. The headlights and 'wire-mesh' grille have helped its looks a little. *Courtesy Ian Elliott*

and I suppose because he was laughing, we all joined in. There were scale drawings and full-sized drawings—everything—it seems barmy now—we could have said yes, and killed it.'

This reaction to the VW plans was not peculiar to Lord or Longbridge; throughout the British motor industry, it was felt that we could do better and had nothing to fear from it. By 1954, of course, the story was very different—the VW was having phenomenal success—perhaps it would pay to take a closer look. George Coates was asked to bring a VW Beetle back from Geneva and, after buying a set of metric spanners, he dismantled it in the 'Kremlin'.

The close scrutiny of continental cars did not really help, because no two designers seemed to have come to the same conclusion. However, it did move thoughts away from an unorthodox mini-car and back into the realms of more conventional economy cars. By October 1954, ideas were centred on an inexpensive, four-seater vehicle of roughly the same size as the Morris Minor or Volkswagen with a target weight of $12\frac{1}{2}$ cwt. It had been hoped to reduce the weight further but, as this could only be done by using aluminium, cost ruled it out. The Morris Minor wheelbase and track, 86 in. and 50 in. respectively, were used in the first calculations. By December, it was realized that the target weight would not be achieved unless the wheelbase was reduced to that of the A30. Dunlop recommended 4.80 × 13 in. tyres, and there was even a proposal to use tubeless tyres and do away with the spare wheel.

A maximum speed of 60 mph was still the goal, so it was decided to enlarge the Ehrlich two-stroke engine to 670 cc. A twin-cylinder, horizontally-opposed engine was also under serious consideration. There was still indecision on the engine's position, but a rear-mounted engine, with its gearbox in line with the axis of the car, seems to have been favourite. The main scheme was to have the gearbox,

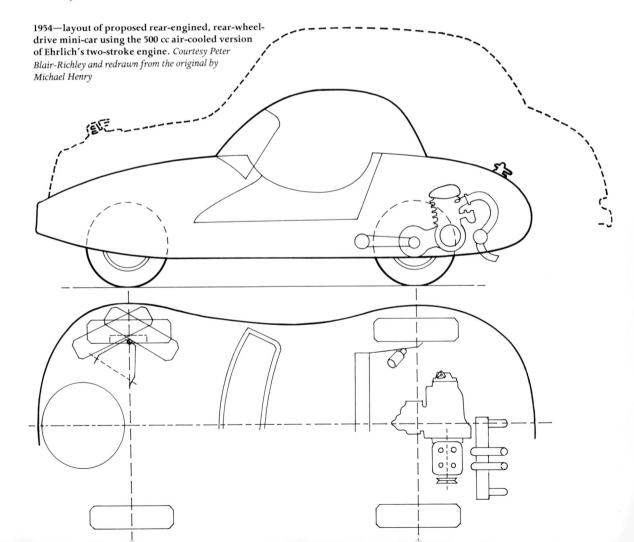

1954—layout of proposed rear-engined, rear-wheel-drive mini-car using the 500 cc air-cooled version of Ehrlich's two-stroke engine. *Courtesy Peter Blair-Richley and redrawn from the original by Michael Henry*

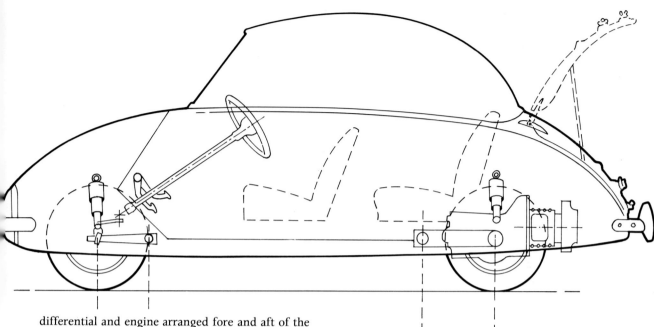

differential and engine arranged fore and aft of the rear axle, as in the Volkswagen, but with the 670 cc Ehrlich engine taking the place of the VW's flat four. Such a scheme meant that it would be possible to substitute a horizontally-opposed engine, should this prove desirable. The plan to use a VW-type transmission with the air-cooled, twin-piston two-stroke engine was similar to one of Porsche's earliest proposals for his people's car. He, too, had experimented with a twin-piston, two-cylinder two-stroke engine of the Puch arrangement. Indeed, a photograph of this *doppelkolben Motor*, as it was known, shows it to be almost identical to the Ehrlich engine. However, Porsche came up against the problem of the pistons overheating on the exhaust side of the engine which, allied with the other disadvantages of two-strokes, made him abandon the idea.

Almost every possibility was pursued at Longbridge. Schemes were drawn up for both transverse and longitudinal power trains for both front- and rear-wheel drive. For the longitudinal (in-line) arrangement, the VW-like transmission unit contained an A30 (AS4) differential carrier and bevel gears, designed so that the crown-wheel position could be altered to obtain the correct direction of rotation for either front- or rear-wheel drive. The transverse arrangement was designed around the twin-cylinder Ehrlich engine, mated to an A30-type gearbox to which a spur-gear final drive had been added. There was even talk of having a front-wheel-drive Morris and a rear-wheel-drive Austin. By mid-1955, it had been decided to use 4.80 × 12 in. tyres.

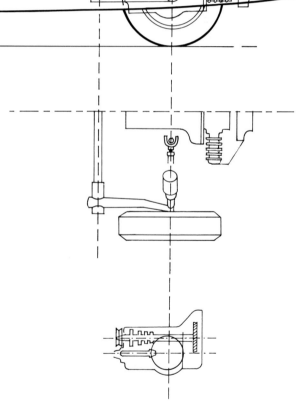

1954–55. A Longbridge Beetle—the economy car that was to be based on the Morris Minor and Volkswagen Beetle. Note the Beetle-like front. The rear end was pure Morris Minor except that when you opened the 'boot' you would have found a twin-cylinder, horizontally-opposed engine! The Ehrlich engine was another option with the same transaxle transmission. *Courtesy Peter Blair-Richley and redrawn from the original by Michael Henry*

A roll of drawings is still in existence which shows the different variations considered. A layout drawing of Ian Duncan's Dragonfly was found among them. His ideas were still food for thought.

As work proceeded, some began to favour a water-cooled two-stroke. Fumes likely to result from trying to heat a car from an air-cooled engine were giving cause for concern. Not only that, the pistons of the 670 cc engine were prone to seizing in their cast-iron cylinder liners, and it was thought that water-cooling would alleviate this problem, as well as reducing the noise level. A new 670 cc, two-cylinder engine was built, still a two-stroke, still in aluminium, but it was water-cooled and the idea of twin pistons per cylinder had been abandoned. It was felt that they had entailed too much reciprocating mass, which led to balancing difficulties and roughness. Petrol injection was under consideration as an aid to more economical running. The engine was still inclined to seize up when installed in the A20, but a plan to fit a water pump never came to fruition, because in 1956 the project was abandoned.

The entire two-stroke project had been regarded as an unnecessary saga by some, but it should be borne in mind that there were many calling for the British car industry to be more inventive and less conventional. The use of two-strokes had produced successful and well-liked cars in the front-wheel-drive DKWs and early Saabs. Established Austin men, however, did not see the need for an outsider to show them how to build engines, particularly after the two-strokes had smoked them out once or twice when under test. Satisfactory fuel consumption and silencing were proving difficult to obtain. It was not easy to silence a two-stroke adequately without increasing fuel consumption or losing power.

Simple though a two-stroke engine is, more than one cylinder necessitates a built-up crankshaft, which calls for a completely different engine-building technique. The number of press-fits did not endear such an engine to the Longbridge production engineers. They would have had to become versed in new tricks of the trade, all to produce what was, to them, an inferior engine. In any case, it was not to be. Leslie Farrar, the managing director of Villiers, remembers a visit from Joe Graves, George Harriman's deputy: 'Joe Graves knew me well and spent a day with me at Villiers, examining our methods of producing engine/gearbox units. At the time, we made a twin-cylinder unit of 325 cc capacity. He told me of the work done by Ehrlich, but expressed his own opinion that the probable manufacturing costs of the larger-capacity unit would be at least as much as for their smallest four-cylinder unit, and I remember that shortly afterwards the idea was dropped.'

The original air-cooled two-stroke engines, in the A30 convertible and in the A20, were in-line units mated to a standard A30 flywheel, clutch and gearbox. The water-cooled two-stroke engine was mated to an A35 remote-control box with a specially-produced casing. In the early days of two-stroke testing, Eric Bareham remembers the excitement when the flywheel came loose from the crankshaft. He did not like the idea of a flywheel whirring about on the loose near his nether regions, so after that it was located by a couple of stout dowels in addition to the bolts.

When Joe Ehrlich left Longbridge in 1958, the A20 went with him. It was never registered for normal road use, but in testing it had covered several thousand miles. Joe Ehrlich had often used it to travel to London for the weekend and found it quite pleasant. No petrol pump was required, because the tank was under the bonnet, as it had been in the original Seven, and as it would also appear in some of the early sketches for the Issigonis Mini. After several years of standing about, the A20 was scrapped in 1975, although its engine lives on, having been donated by Joe Ehrlich to the Austin A30–A35 Owners Club.

During the final stages of the two-stroke project, Issigonis was working at Longbridge on a prototype 1500 cc car of advanced design. He had returned to BMC early in 1956, after a period at Alvis, having left Cowley soon after the merger that created BMC. Leonard Lord enticed him back by offering him a free rein to develop new ideas. This was the start of an era in which each new car would be developed in a cell made up of a small number of people.

Within months, the 1956 Suez Crisis and the consequent petrol rationing told Leonard Lord that he needed an economy car in double-quick time. Issigonis was asked to concentrate his energies in that direction. The Mini was on its way.

Issigonis was not one to take note of what others were doing. He preferred to think everything out for himself, using myriad sketches and notes. He was brilliant—but fortunate. In Jack Daniels, he had a co-worker with the ability to bring his ideas to fruition. As Jack Daniels put it, modestly: 'Issi's was the inspiration and mine was the perspiration.' In Geoff Cooper's words: 'Issigonis threw out ideas like a dog throws off fleas—a lot were no good, but that's inevitable. People fell out with Issi because he didn't want to listen to anyone who would water down his

The water-cooled, twin-cylinder Ehrlich engine after being fitted with fuel-injection equipment in the late 1950s. Note the two large dowels to help locate the flywheel and reduce the danger of it working loose due to vibration. *Courtesy Joe Ehrlich*

ideas—his cars had to be unadulterated Issigonis.'

Of course, the work already done on the Long-bridge economy car saved Issigonis time. Most of the results, allied with the experience of the experimental front-wheel-drive Minor, convinced him that his hunch for a front-wheel-drive car was correct. Leonard Lord simplified the matter even further by declaring that he must make do with an existing engine—there was nothing for it but to use the A-series. Whether the two-stroke or flat-twin engines could provide an acceptable power unit no longer needed debating, and a twin-cylinder version of the A-series had proved unacceptably rough.

The engine apart, Lord had decided on his usual tactic of backing more than one horse. A further project for a mini-car was put under way at Cowley under Charles Griffin. The target for both Griffin and Issigonis was a car which could be built for £300. Charles Griffin's car was on target at £295. Alec Issigonis was off target at £325. Charles Griffin suggests, very generously, that Sir Alec's car was preferable by far: 'Ours was full of things that were unacceptable.' He explained that it had a canopy which slid back and allowed one to step in but which exposed the trim and occupants to the weather at the same time. It was to be driven at the rear wheels by either that rather rough twin-cylinder version of the A-series engine, or the twin-cylinder two-stroke. The price had been kept low by using what Charles Griffin described as 'bent rods and rubber bushings in the steering connections', adding, 'Len Lord came and had a look and compared it with the Mini—the Mini won and Lord was right.' When discussing the earlier debates about whether to plan an economy car with two, three or four seats, Charles Griffin suggested that, 'The market place itself has always said that if it hasn't four seats, it won't sell.'

In planning a baby car around a four-cylinder engine, most designers would probably have gone along with the prevailing continental configuration of a rear engine driving the rear wheels, but the handling characteristics of this arrangement would not have satisfied Issigonis. He was determined to go for front-wheel drive. The problem was to find a sufficiently compact set-up for the engine and transmission. As he saw it, the engine would have to be placed transversely; therefore, the transmission would have to go in the sump—there was

LEFT By the end of 1957, Mini prototypes were running round with the A35 grille as camouflage. *Courtesy Austin Rover*

BELOW Joe Ehrlich leans over the author's A35 pick-up in 1985 to check that all is present and correct with his water-cooled engine which, together with its gearbox, had just been unearthed from a shed at his works. The engine had been tested in the A20 but only ran for a short while before seizing up. Joe had intended fitting a water pump to the engine, but pressure of other work meant that the project was shelved

no other place for it—a solution that seems obvious now. Bill Appleby remembered the day he was called to Len Lord's office and asked to give his blessing to such an arrangement. Could the same oil lubricate the engine and gearbox satisfactorily? Appleby was given the impression that he had to decide, and that an immediate decision was necessary. Obviously, Issigonis was very pleased that Bill supported his idea, but it seems that, eventually, Issigonis would have got his own way in any case.

The development of Sir Alec's Mini is well chronicled elsewhere, but during that time arguments were raging in the motoring press. *Motor Sport* was being castigated for its continual championing of the Volkswagen and other foreign products. In January 1957, Bill Boddy was telling his readers how he had 'fallen in love' with the Renault Dauphine. He told them, 'The Dauphine seemed rather crudely finished but earned full marks during a 640-mile test for its combination of 65 mph cruising speed and better than 45 mpg consumption of petrol from its rear-placed 845 cc engine, which had no tendency to wag the tail of this beautifully proportioned saloon or to induce oversteer.'

In March 1957, the editorial in *Motor Sport* quibbled with a view from the other extreme. The *Sunday Express* had told its readers that 'British cars at the 1957 Show will be smoother, simpler and far ahead of any rivals.' *Motor Sport* felt that this was a sweeping statement to make about cars which had not been seen yet, let alone tested. The *Sunday Express* had also stated that independent rear suspension was being tried on some British prototypes. That they were correct in this has been shown in this very chapter, but *Motor Sport* rightly pointed out that it was already to be found on the VW, Fiat 600, baby Renaults, Citroën 2CVs, Saabs and Skodas, and even on the diminutive Goggomobile. They suggested that it was high time all British designers adopted independent rear suspension, and that makers who tried to get away with primitive cart springs and rigid back axles would only have themselves to blame for sales losses in both home and overseas markets. Once again, Bill Boddy declared himself in favour of rear engines and irs, but preferred the former to be air-cooled. He thought that although water 'is fine in the bath or with whisky, we have no wish for it in a low-powered engine.'

By April 1957, the arguments had reached the House of Commons, where British manufacturers were reprimanded by William Shepherd, MP for Cheadle, for lagging behind the continentals. He suggested that, 'The continental driver does not want to be told how to drive his motor car; he wants to buy a car in which he wants to go as near as possible to breaking his neck without actually breaking it. If he drives a British car on the bends and on the cobblestones as he would drive his own car, he faces certain death; and, naturally therefore, he does not want to buy our motor cars.' Commenting on the speech, *Motor Sport*, of March 1957, hoped 'that our technicians will be encouraged to experiment with front-wheel drive, when engines are at the front, or with rear engines with rear-wheel drive to eliminate the propshaft, and that air-cooling, the two-stroke cycle, petrol injection and gas suspension will not be overlooked.' They also suggested that it would be nice to see a miniature version of the Morris Minor, using a flat-four engine of about 500 cc. They thought that such a vehicle was needed to compete with 'the armies of new mini-cars which march along the autostrada, autobahn and autoroads better than some of the British mini-cars which, with primary chains and motorcycle engines, have rather too close an affinity with those cycle cars from the dim and distant past.'

In 1959, the launch of the Mini silenced most of the critics, although its teething troubles did give it a rather shaky start. Now, Bill Boddy was congratulating BMC for 'pulling their finger out'. He felt the Mini 'must surely undermine continental mini-car sales in this country and probably throughout the world.'

Certainly, it was a new concept in motoring in every way. During the design stage, after Issigonis had taken Barry Kelkin's suggestions of rounding a bit off here and there, he asked him, 'How about that, young blood? Is that any better?' 'It still looks like a shed on wheels,' joked Barry. Today, of course, he recognizes that Issigonis knew what he was doing. He simply had no time for stylists, claiming that they were employed to build in obsolescence: 'I made my cars so that they couldn't be obsolescent and so gave good value for money.' Perhaps this makes it fitting to leave the last word on BMC's economy car to A40-stylist Pininfarina. On being shown the Mini, he was asked if he could suggest ways of improving it. 'Leave it,' he said. 'It's unique.'

Once again, we had a new Austin Seven.

RIGHT This is roughly where we came in! The Longbridge version of the Mini was launched as the 'New Austin Seven', and the publicity shots still harked back to the pre-war car. Once again, 30 years separate the two cars, from 1929 to 1959. *Courtesy Austin Rover*

BELOW The author gets the Ehrlich engine running again at the national rally of the Austin A30–A35 Owners Club in May 1986. Most of the smoke is from oil poured down the bores to improve the compression, which was low due to sticking piston rings. *Courtesy Anne Sharratt*

RIGHT The early prototype Minis still had the A35's 948 cc engine and Zenith carburettor. Later the engine was turned round to overcome the problem of the carburettor icing up, and the capacity was reduced to 848 cc. The earlier cars were thought to be a little too lively for the general public. *Courtesy Austin Rover*

15

OWNING AND RUNNING THE CARS

Whether you prefer an A30, A35 or A40, excellent examples are regularly available at very reasonable prices. If you are patient, less than £1000, sometimes considerably less, will still buy a first-class car. If that is hard to believe, then just try selling one for more. Many try, but few succeed.

Prices suggested here can only be a rough guide in an ever-changing scene. For any of the A30, A35 or A40 variants, the price will vary much more with the condition of the car than with the actual model. Non-runners can still be found for £25–£50, and sometimes for the taking away. Sound cars with MOTs start in the region of £300–£400 and only rise towards £1000 if in first-class order. An original, low-mileage car may break the £1000 barrier and even reach £1500, but not too often. Generally speaking, A35s are slightly easier to sell than A30s, while A30/35s tend to make £200–£300 more than an A40 in equivalent condition. In the past, A30/35 vans have been worth £100–£200 less than an equivalent saloon, but original and unmodified vans are now starting to increase in value. A genuine A30/35 Countryman holds a small premium over the saloons. A35 pick-ups, though scarce, are still not particularly easy to sell, but when they do, a pick-up in A1 condition can realize £1800–£2500. Club publications and classic-car magazines will soon bring a prospective purchaser up to date with values.

Where the car is only intended as a hobby or second vehicle, the choice of model is of less importance than if it is expected to do regular and lengthy motorway trips. For the latter purpose, one could hardly recommend an A30. That is not to say that an A30 cannot handle such trips, but the A35 and A40 were designed to cope much more readily with the stresses and strains involved.

The A30 has more of the flavour of yesteryear,

with its traditional chromed grille of pre-'mouth-organ' days, its small rear window and the 'ker-chung' of the trafficators, the rarity of which makes the A30 quite exciting to drive in today's traffic!

The A35, more suited to modern conditions, still carries enough charm to earn many compliments for a caring owner. Being a much livelier car, yet possessing the same brakes and narrow track of the A30, it can offer its own brand of excitement, too.

The styling of the A40 Farina was so far ahead of its time that, even today, it may pass unnoticed in a line-up of modern cars. It is remarkable that it should be so unremarkable after nearly 30 years. Today, it might still be chosen for the extra room and versatility it offered its original owner, and for simplicity and neatness of line, it is hard to beat. On the current market, it offers unquestionable value for money.

Whatever the preferred model, the main aim of any purchaser must be to find a car without serious body rot. No car is impossible to rebuild, but the price of doing so may be quite uneconomic. Most of us tend not to keep a thorough check on exactly how much is spent on restoring a car. We remember the major expenses, but probably prefer to forget the many smaller items that can total up to several hundreds of pounds. Those brave enough to keep an exact check have proved that it is easy to spend £2000–£3000 on a baby Austin. Be warned, you will never recoup such expenditure. In the long run, it is always far cheaper to buy the best car available.

Small though the cars are, bills for welding can be large. With patience, it is possible to find examples that need little of the welder's skills, and these are the ones to seek out. From inside the car, check the condition of the floor and inner sills; in particular, the area of floor supporting the forward rear spring hangers. On the A30 and A35, the inner sill on the driver's side acts as part of the handbrake attachment, so give this a good going over. A check inside an A30/35 boot will show if it is rotting above the rear spring hangers. Underneath the car, priority

September 1984—the cars return to the Longbridge factory. An observer at this reunion could be in no doubt that those who own the cars today greatly appreciate the efforts of the Longbridge men and women who built them

must be given to inspecting the points of suspension attachment. In the main, this refers to the rear suspension, as the area at the front is usually well preserved by oil and grease. If in any doubt, it is best to get a second opinion from an experienced owner who knows the possible extent of what might be fairly harmless-looking rot.

Though younger, the A40 is more prone to rot than the A30 or A35. When we compare production with present-day figures, we can see that, of the three models, the A40 is disappearing the most rapidly. However, this must be due, in part, to the A40 Farina having had such advanced styling for its day. The cars are getting long in the tooth before they have become remarkable enough to warrant much money being spent on their restoration. Generally, it is accepted that the A40 Mk II rots much more readily than the Mk I, and that both Mk I and Mk II Countryman models have added problems due to water entering the poorly-sealed rear end. The main areas to check for rust on all the models have been mentioned already, but with the A40 Mk II there is often considerable rot around the trap formed under the headlamps at either side of the full-width grille. The rear wheel arches, boot floor and even rear spring hangers can become a bit of a nightmare, too, so check it all out carefully. With any of the cars, it would be unwise to do any serious checking with the car jacked up by the sills, although it might be a good way of proving to the seller that the vehicle is not as sound as claimed!

Assuming a sound car, or one that has been made so after purchase, the aim must be to keep it that way. A look under any old car should provide all the evidence that is needed to confirm the treatment required. Those parts which have been constantly covered in oil, escaping from the engine, gearbox or differential, will be as sound as the day the car was built. Reproducing these conditions under the whole car, by regular application of oil or grease, will ensure little further need of a welder.

Where new metal has been added, or where metal with a slight rust covering has been exposed, it will pay to derust before painting. In such cases, treatment with Jenolite has proved very effective. As a follow-up, there can be few paints more effective than Hammerite, but a good underseal should be applied as well. This not only protects the paint and the metal beneath, but also reduces noise. Most underseal benefits from a six-monthly (pre-winter and post-winter) application of Waxoyl. This keeps the underseal supple and seeps into any cracks that otherwise would allow the weather to penetrate.

Dutch, German and UK enthusiasts enjoying a holiday in the Netherlands during Easter 1983

Some may prefer to paint on a mixture of oil and grease, but a car coated in underseal and Waxoyl is less mucky to work on. Those who fall behind in their applications of oil should bear in mind that the really vulnerable parts of the car take very little time to treat. Do not make the excuse that there is not time to do it! It is easy to squirt oil into the sills and other double-skinned areas, such as the front apron, front wings, rear boot and rear-wing area. Apply plenty of oil to the inside of the rear-wings from each side of the boot. The double-skinned A40 boot lid could do with a couple of holes drilling at the top of the inner skin so that it can be injected thoroughly with Waxoyl. The inside of the doors are best treated with Waxoyl, too, as it is less likely than oil to find its way on to the clothes of those using the car.

Judicious soundproofing can make these vehicles much more pleasant to drive. A thick felt under the carpets works wonders, but it must be lifted regularly to ensure it is not causing rot by acting as a sponge and holding water that enters the car. If water is entering the car, every effort should be made to trace the source. The joins between panels may require additional sealing, as may the plugs in the A40 floor. The front and rear screen rubbers may need renewing. Replacing tired or missing grommets, particularly between the engine and passenger compartment, helps to prevent fumes entering the car, as well as reducing noise. The air intake below the A40's windscreen will also take in water. This is provided for by drain holes on the bulkhead beneath the bonnet. If these holes are not kept clear, rot will attack this area.

One of the great strengths of the A30/35 and A40 is their simplicity compared to their modern counterparts. However, it must be stressed that to prevent expensive repairs to the steering and front suspension, it is essential to oil and grease the components regularly. This is not a lengthy job, but it does tend to be a dirty one, and it has to be done so often that it can be rated something of a nuisance. However, it is expensive to replace the A-frames, king-pins, bushes and fulcrum pins, which all wear rapidly unless serviced properly. A previous owner may have neglected this area, so before purchasing any of the cars, check the condition of these vital, parts. To do this, it is necessary to jack up the front of the car, and preferable to have an assistant who can rock and lift the wheel so that you can watch for signs of movement between the various parts. If the wheel simply lifts on the king-pin, it may be a matter of tightening the nut at the top of the king-

pin. If, after doing this, there is still vertical movement, it may be necessary to remove shims from the top of the king-pin (if there are any) or add shims to the underside of the top trunnion. The cork washer in the bottom of the stub axle is very prone to disintegrating, allowing water and dirt to enter the bottom bush. If this happens, wear will be rapid. However, it is easy to slide the king-pin off the stub axle, and it is well worth doing it annually (MOT time, perhaps) to check that the washer is intact and that everything is receiving its quota of grease. It is important to ensure that the grease penetrates both the swivel-pin bushes and each end of the fulcrum pins.

When topping up the steering box, do not forget the steering idler on the opposite side of the car. A thrust screw and locknut on top of the steering box allow wear to be taken up. The steering boxes are either of cam-and-peg or worm-and-nut arrangement. With the former, end-play on the inner column can be eliminated by removing shims from behind the plate at the lower end. If necessary, the peg can be driven out of the rocker shaft and turned through 90 degrees before replacing it. This provides a fresh face to bear on the cam. The felt bush at the top of the inner column must be kept soaked in oil, otherwise it will dry out, shrink and produce a slackness between the inner and outer columns. Early A40s had a steering idler that was a threaded fit into the idler body. A30s, A35s and later A40s had an idler with removable shims under the top cover. Any vertical movement of the idler shaft can be eliminated by removing some of the shims.

The brakes, too, demand a little more attention than those on a modern car. On the A30 and A35, the master cylinder and rear frame cylinder are underneath the car. Therefore, they are vulnerable to whatever delights are thrown at them from the road. Being out of sight, they are easily forgotten. Both cylinders are getting scarce and expensive, so it is as well to aid their preservation by changing the brake fluid regularly and by applying generous amounts of brake grease inside their rubber boots to keep out the weather. Resleeved master cylinders are available. After replacing an A30/35 master cylinder, the brakes (and brake lights) may remain on when the pedal is released. If this happens, it means that the pushrod between the pedal and the master cylinder requires adjusting so that the master cylinder piston can return to its stop. If it cannot do so, the system will remain pressurized, because the piston will be covering the bypass port, preventing the fluid from returning to its reservoir.

Even A30s and A35s have to stop for avalanches—Susten Pass, 'Eurovisit Switzerland', in 1985

The efficiency of the braking system, particularly on the A30, A35 and A40 Mk I, falls off rapidly if the rear brake expanders and balance lever are not free. The rear stirrup and handbrake mechanism must be adjusted correctly, but provided these points are attended to, the system works well enough, and the handbrake is absolutely first class. Although the A40 Mk I retained the A35's hydromechanical rear brakes, the Mk II went fully hydraulic. All the A40 Farinas have pendant pedals which allow the master cylinder to be sited under the bonnet.

If oil is discovered on the rear brakes of any of the cars, it probably means that the wheel-bearing oil seal requires replacing. Once the hub has been removed, it is a simple job to press out the bearing, pop in the new oil seal and press the bearing in again.

One of the pleasures of owning an A30/35 or A40 is that they are neither so valuable nor so rare that one can be accused of vandalism when resorting to modifications that make the car more suited to present-day road conditions. Enthusiastic owners have been modifying these cars since the day they were built. Today's owners seem to be divided fairly equally between those who wish to preserve their cars in original condition and those who prefer varying degrees of modification. Happily, there are not too many who seek to modify the external appearance of the cars. Even those who do might claim, with some justification, that they were doing their bit by adding variety to rally fields, which otherwise would be full of almost identical Austins.

The simplest way of making a dramatic improvement to the roadholding of all the cars is to fit radial tyres. Without them, the cars do not corner nearly as well, raised white lines and other road-surface irregularities calling for constant correction at the wheel. With radial tyres, the irregularities no longer cause the car to leave its allotted path, making for more relaxed driving. Normally, a 145 × 13 in. radial tyre is recommended to replace a cross-ply 5.20 × 13 in. tyre. If slightly higher gearing is required, a 155 × 13 in. tyre will fit with plenty of clearance at the rear of an A30/35 or A40, but with saloon versions of the former, the larger tyre may catch the front wheel arches on turning. Whether it does so will depend on the state of the front springs and dampers. The A40 will accept 165 × 13 in. tyres, but they are really too wide for the rim and are not recommended.

There are many routes to improved braking on A30/35s and A40s. The simplest and most effective improvement for the two earlier cars is to fit A40 Farina front brakes. This is an easy task—the parts only require swapping over. The A30 or A35 front brake drums, hubs and 7 in. backplates are removed. The 8 in. backplates from an A40 are bolted on, complete with the A40's wheel cylinders and wider brake shoes. After replacing the original hubs, all that remains is to fit the A40 brake drum. Braking will have improved considerably, and it will be much easier to adjust the front brakes using the A40's micram adjusters. Properly maintained, the original rear brakes will be quite adequate.

Fitting a servo to any of the cars works wonders. It does not give you any more braking, but it means you can stop the car easily without having to push your feet through the floor. The change is more dramatic in the A30 and A35, because the pendant pedals of the A40 already provide extra leverage.

A servo can be fitted under the bonnet and a vacuum pipe run to it from an adaptor on the inlet manifold. For the hydraulic connections, it is a matter of feeding the output from the master cylinder to the input on the servo and then taking the output from the servo back to the line feeding the wheel cylinders. After fitting a servo, some owners prefer to fit harder brake linings.

A30/35 owners have performed all manner of conversions to replace the original under-floor brake master cylinder. Some have merely fabricated brackets that allow the use of a cheaper and more readily obtainable under-floor cylinder, but others have gone the whole hog and used the complete A40 pedal-box assembly. This provides hydraulic operation for both brakes and clutch, and it puts the master cylinders in a much more accessible position under the bonnet.

When a 1275 cc Spridget engine is fitted to an A30/35 or A40, it may well be worth fitting the Spridget disc brakes, too. Provided the Spridget king-pin is used, this is another bolt-on job. Those who have done it claim that braking is not unbalanced, even when retaining the rod-operated rear brakes of the earlier cars, but others prefer to modify the rear brakes to A40 Mk II specification. If a front anti-roll bar is fitted, it will be necessary to fit the discs so that the calipers are at the rear and to re-route the brake pipes.

A significant improvement to the roadholding of the A30/35 and A40 Mk I can be obtained by adding a front anti-roll bar from the A40 Mk II or Spridget. When fitting, it is essential to build strong locating points where the anti-roll bar is gripped under the front chassis rails. Some A40 Mk I owners convert their cars to take telescopic rear dampers as on the Mk II. Uprated front dampers are available for all models.

Owners who wish to add more pep to their cars are spoilt for choice. Where an increase in power is contemplated, however, it would be as well to consider some or all of the braking and handling modifications mentioned previously. All models can be improved by selecting from the variety of second-hand engines and transmissions which are readily available for the A-series-engined cars.

It is a simple matter to drop the 948 cc engine into an A30, retaining the original gearbox. The A30 owner may also wish to consider swapping to the 848 cc unit of the later A35 vans. The A30 gearbox is rather weak, but it is possible to modify its internals to the A35's ratios. This gives the advantages of the later box without having to alter either the floor of the car or the gear lever. Quite a few A30s have had the front end of their transmission tunnel cut out and replaced by one from an A35, allowing the use of the remote-control gearboxes.

A35s and A40s with 948 cc engines will readily accept the 1098 cc engine and gearbox. It is preferable to fit the complete unit, but the 948 cc gearbox can be retained if the 948 cc flywheel and clutch are switched to the larger engine. Trouble can be experienced if a 948 cc gear lever finds its way on to a 1098 cc box. Changing gear becomes difficult, and the car may jump out of reverse due to the dome on the gear-lever retaining plate being slightly smaller on the 1098 cc box. A 948 cc owner who wishes to use the later 1098 cc box (or the box from the 848 cc A35 van) can do so, and gain further benefit by fitting the larger clutch and corresponding flywheel at the same time.

Where a 1098 cc engine has been fitted to an earlier car, it is sensible to use either the 4.2:1 or 3.9:1 differential and gain in both economy and quietness of running. A35s with a 948 cc engine are also found to be perfectly happy with a 4.2:1 differential. Differentials are easily swapped from car to car, but before installing a later differential (e.g. the 4.2:1, 3.9:1 or 3.7:1) to earlier axles, it will be necessary to drill a combined level and filler hole in the rear of the axle casing. The hole can be closed with a plug like that on the steering-box filler. With the many possible combinations of engines, differentials and rear tyre sizes, you can tailor any car to suit your needs almost exactly. The author's own A35 has a 1098 cc engine which performs very happily and willingly, even though it is allied with a 3.7:1 differential from a Wolseley 1500. This arrangement gives, for example, a true road speed of 54.5 mph at only 3000 revs and allows the 30-year-old car to take long-distance continental motoring in its stride. For the same road speed, a standard A35 saloon would require 3700 revs.

Those interested in engine tuning can have a field day. Several books have been written on tuning the A-series engine and, no doubt, there will be others to come. However, David Vizard's weighty, but very readable, *Tuning the A-series Engine* should provide more than enough ideas for most people.

Cars with the Zenith carburettor can be improved by fitting the $1\frac{1}{4}$ in. SU carburettor and manifold from the A40 Mk II or later A35 vans. There are other sources, but these have the required throttle linkage. The Spridgets provide a useful source of twin carburettors and appropriate manifolds, should these be required.

Most owners of 1098 cc engined A40s seem happy with the original engine. Those wishing to upgrade from the 948 cc unit are often tempted to go straight to the 1275 cc Spridget engine and gearbox. Indeed, several A30 and A35 owners have done likewise, either because they revel in particularly rapid motoring, or because they use the vehicle for towing a trailer or small caravan. Once again, the differential chosen will depend on how the car is to be used. The earlier flywheels cannot be used on the 1275 cc engine.

On the electrical side, the most common modifications are to alter the polarity to negative earth, to fit an alternator, and to modify the headlights with either a sealed beam or halogen conversion kit. Owners of A30 and A35 saloons can improve on their original windscreen wipers by fitting the motor and drive rod from the later A35 vans. This motor is more powerful and fits on the inner wing, so it is more accessible than the earlier units that are hidden away under the front bulkhead. Some owners fit an electric fan to achieve faster warm-up, more power and quieter running.

The snags involved in these and many other possible modifications are very few indeed, and you do not have to go far in car club circles to find those who are willing and able to help in weighing up any scheme you might be proposing.

Yes, the cars have always been modified. Not always by boy racers or tearaways, either. One of the first A30s to be modified was done by royal command. Not only was Bob Grice responsible for testing Austin prototypes, but he was also responsible for the BMC cars in the Royal Mews. The Duke of Edinburgh had taken an interest in the baby of the Austin range when he visited Longbridge in December 1955. Not long after, in early 1956, Bob was instructed to produce an A30 for the royal household. The Duke's visit to Longbridge had coincided with the unrest at Suez, and it was felt that the royal household should 'fly the flag of economy' by using economical cars. An A30 was produced to show-quality finish. With white paintwork, red leather upholstery, limousine-type carpets and burr walnut fascia, it looked a treat. The long A30 gear lever was replaced with a shorter, stouter, chromed version with a white knob. Before it reached the palace, the crisis was over and the small car was required no longer—Longbridge had a one-off car on their hands. There was a fairly rigid tradition that one-offs

David James and family of Brisbane with their full-house of A30, A35 and A40. *Courtesy David James*

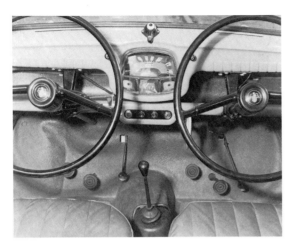

His and hers? Not really. Simply an A35 kitted out as a
driving-school car in April 1958. *Courtesy Austin Rover*

and prototypes had to be destroyed, but Bob Grice
did get permission to use the car, provided it never
reached the open market. Registered SOH 256, it was
used by his family over several years, but in the end
he had to keep his promise of seeing it crushed when
he had finished with it.

There were not many other A30/35 or A40
variants produced at the factory. An A40 had been
widened by 3–4 in. and one or two A35s were fitted
with dual controls, including twin steering wheels,
but that was about it.

As soon as private owners got their hands on the
cars, it was a different matter. We have seen how
they were modified for racing or rallying, but as well
as that, cars could be found rebuilt into anything
from dumper trucks to dragsters. Modified A40s
acquired names such as *Meaner Farina* and *Heavy
Breathin'*. Those in the know rated *The Dorset Horn*,
a much-modified, Pontiac-powered, fibreglass-
bodied, yellow A35 as 'one of the biggest crowd
pleasers in drag racing', chants of 'We want the
Horn' preceding its exciting runs at Santa Pod Raceway. Another competitor at Santa Pod used to push-
start his A-series-powered dragster, known as *Uncle
Scrumble*, in fine style. A blue A35 pick-up with yellow pin-stripes, buttoned upholstery and pine-
wood-lined pick-up bed was used to coax the dragster into life on the strip. At the National Street Rod
Association's rod run at Little Billing in 1979, you
could have seen a Swedish A35 pick-up complete
with 5.7-litre Chevrolet V8 engine and automatic
box. At the Shotton Steel Works, you could have
found them converting a couple of A30 vans into

tipper trucks. Yes, if you looked in the right places,
you could find A30s, A35s and A40s with every con-
ceivable modification, from spats to spoilers, from
de-seams to top-chops. In Australia, an A30 was
even converted into a lawn mower. However, the
prize for the zaniest A30/35 ever must surely go to
the push-me/pull-you car that was constructed from
the front ends of an A30 and an A35. It caused the
Sunday Independent of 9 February 1969 to ask, 'Did
you ever see anything like it in your life!' The car
was used as an advertising medium by Westwood
Motors of Plymouth. Its range was limited somewhat, because (under the vagaries of the Road Traffic
Act and the Vehicle Construction and Use regulations) it was not allowed to have a special fuel tank
fitted, so petrol had to go in the radiator. Then, as
now, people had fun with their baby Austins.

Today, there are few people making outrageous
modifications to their A30s, A35s or A40s. Some
models are getting too scarce to modify. AS3s seem
very thin on the ground now. A35 pick-ups are considered to be rare, but how many AP6 A35 Countryman versions have you seen? How many A30, A35
or A40 vans are still in their original condition,
without added side windows? An A30 or A35
Countryman is a desirable vehicle, but unconverted
vans are becoming something of a rarity. It is hoped
that those coming across an original van will recognize this and consider keeping it in its original state.
Some perceptive folk have already done so, combining their hobby of running a period vehicle with a
sign-written van that advertises their business. For
those contemplating purchase take note: many a
converted A30/35 van is advertised as a Countryman, but the genuine article will have a chassis number prefixed by AP4, AP5 or AP6.

As the cars have become rarer, they have become
part of the classic-car movement, which has done
a great deal to foster the restoration of even bread-
and-butter cars of the 1950s and 1960s. Enthusiasts
of quite modest means are able to take part in an
interesting hobby. It does not really matter whether
an old car is being run out of necessity or nostalgia—
it can still be fun.

Equally, a quick flip through a few contemporary
issues of *The Austin Magazine* is enough to establish
that original purchasers of A30s, A35s and A40s
were well satisfied with their choice. The cars were
providing them with reliable and economical motoring, and they were more than happy to proclaim it.

With some, it went further than that. Even when
new, the A30 in particular had certain intangible
qualities which led many a family to adopt their

Brisbane City Council plumbing inspector Ken Diggles, and the ride-on mower he built from his A30, made the front cover of *Practical Welder*. *Courtesy Commonwealth Industrial Gases Ltd*

A lady in drag. In 1984, with a 7-litre Ford Galaxy engine installed in her A30, Stephanie Milam took it to the Santa Pod Raceway dragstrip. Her figures for the quarter-mile were 12.81 seconds at 108.1 mph. *Courtesy Stephanie Milam*

RIGHT This 'push-me, pull-you' car was built by David Thomas for Westwood Motors in 1969 from the front ends of an A30 and A35. The car was used as an advertising gimmick, attending many motoring events under its own steam.
Courtesy Sunday Independent

baby Austin as a family pet. The lively A35 earned similar loyalties, and although the A40 Farina was a little less dinky than the A30 or A35, there is little doubt that it was (and still is) cherished by many an owner.

Good though these cars were to their original owners, one can argue that those owning them today may be reaping even greater benefits. Writing to *Woman's Own* in 1985, a Mrs Seed from Wigan declared, 'I'm middle-aged and slightly overweight, yet men turn to stare at me and chat me up in car parks. What is my secret? For 22 years I have been driving about in a 1958 A35—which men of all ages find irresistible!' Yes, in these days of uniformity,

there is a pleasure in owning something a little different, but there is far more to it than that.

Recently, I had a phone call from a chap who had bought a Metro and wanted to sell his A30. Could I advise him what to do? Certainly: 'Sell the Metro, put the money in the bank, and run your A30 on the interest.' It raised a laugh, and between us we did manage to find a new home for the A30, but I was not pulling his leg. What I suggested was perfectly feasible. Although the Metro is an excellent car, and there may well be circumstances where it is preferable to an A30, A35 or A40, the latter cars require such a relatively small investment that it leaves their owners quids-in towards running costs.

LEFT **Zoe rides again. A purposefully-modified A40, now purposefully restored, creates much interest at the A40 Farina Club's Nottingham Weekend in July 1986**

BELOW **A40 Farinas gather at Nottingham University for their annual rally in July 1986.** *Courtesy Tim Hinton*

Another major cost of motoring does not exist for owners of well-maintained A30s, A35s and A40s. Their depreciation costs are nil.

When running an older car as daily transport, it is prudent to stock a few of the more difficult-to-obtain spares—at least those which could put the car off the road. Many mechanical items are interchangeable between the A30, A35 and A40, as well as with those from Minors, Sprites and Midgets, so almost everything is (and, with a few exceptions, will remain) available. More often than not, one can find mechanical spares at prices considerably lower than the equivalent parts for a modern car, so it is not too costly to build up a reasonable stock.

Body panels are a different matter. There are still some lucky finds to be had, but they are becoming few and far between. Some panels are being remade, while the most vulnerable parts of others are being produced as repair sections.

The way to keep up to date with spares availability—a changing scene, year by year—is to join the appropriate owners club. After several years of attempting to stock and trade in spares, many clubs are finding that it is better to offer an efficient spares information service. The A40 Farina Club was one of the first to develop this approach, and the A30-A35 Owners Club were happy to model their spares information service along similar lines. Mem-

ABOVE Spares for your A40 Farina—only one of the attractions of a national rally. *Courtesy Tim Hinton*

TOP Netherlands 1984. Henk Busscher (left), organizer of many a splendid 'Eurovisit', obliges the photographer, as the author (right) discusses spares with Marek Czajkowski who had just arrived from Poland. It is not easy to keep an A35 running in Warsaw, so Marek was delighted with this gift of spares from UK club members. *Courtesy Anne Sharratt*

bers of both clubs receive a spares information booklet, which contains all the major sources of spares and which is updated as necessary. There is a growing list of permanent suppliers of spares and services to which members can turn for assistance. Club magazines and newsletters are another means by which members are put in touch with bargains.

If, like some, you only run your A30, A35 or A40 because 'it's the only bloody car I can afford', the cost of your petrol to a national or local club rally will usually be recouped by bargain purchases of spares. At such events, you will often find that elusive item of trim, or a seat or seats to match your car's interior. Several local groups hold monthly meetings, and once you get to know the 'likely lads' in your area, a phone call before any such meeting will usually produce the spare you want or some idea of where it can be obtained.

Of course, the clubs have much more to offer. For a very modest annual subscription, you become part of a body of people who not only have a genuine interest in your car, but who have, collectively, an immense fund of expertise. Club publications contain many useful technical articles. In the event of being beaten by a particular job, even those members living in remote places are only a phone call away from those who can shed light on their problem.

Both the Austin A30–A35 Owners Club and the A40 Farina Owners Club hold an annual national rally and AGM where purists and concours fanatics can indulge themselves fully, either as onlookers or participants. Those interested in cars which have been modified mechanically will be able to find many of like mind.

Figures supplied by the Society of Motor Manufacturers and Traders show the number of A30s, A35s and A40s still 'on file' at Swansea on 31 December 1985:

A30	6658
A35	5190
Total A30/35	*11,848*
A40 948 cc saloon	1870
A40 948 cc Countryman	210
A40 1098 cc saloon	2406
A40 1098 cc Countryman	552
Total A40	*5038*

These figures do not include A30/35 vans, as these are lumped together with Minor vans in the Swansea records under the heading 'Austin Morris 5 & 6 cwt

ABOVE **Port Richey, Florida, in 1986. Cath Sharratt (left) meets Polly Bubanovich and her A35. On the right are Bob and Millie Koto of Boynton Beach, with whom the author and his wife were staying**

LEFT **You may have to stand on your head to see the point of this unusual formation of A30s and A35s at the club's 1982 national rally**

vans', of which there are 7200. Surely the vast majority of these must be Minors.

Figures supplied by the Associazione Nazionale Fra Industrie Automobilistiche in Turin show that in 1984 there were still 2159 Innocenti A40s in use in Italy. Numbers of each model were: A40—493; A40C—276; A40S—521; A40SC—869. These figures apart, it is impossible to estimate how many cars still exist abroad, but even those in this country give the A30–A35 Owners Club and the A40 Farina Club plenty of scope for expansion. Membership numbers are at present in the region of 1500 and 700 respectively. For club officials, of course, more members mean more work. Club members who can offer a hand in any capacity will usually have it gently, or even not so gently, snapped up.

The classic-car scene is developing internationally, which adds interest and variety to club life and club publications. Where distances are vast, communication is mainly by post, although gradu-

ally we may see more instances of clubs and club members playing host to each other on a reciprocal basis from one side of the globe to the other. In Europe it is a relatively easy matter to pop to and fro between each other's countries. Members from Poland, Sweden, France, Germany, Austria, Switzerland, Belgium and Holland have all managed to meet their British counterparts under the auspices of the 'Flying A', either at national and local rallies in England, or on the several splendid 'Eurovisits' of recent years.

The A30, A35 and A40 Farina are very definitely practical classics. They are cars that are still capable of covering many thousands of miles in a year, including continental motoring; cars for which the strong club scene is of tremendous assistance with advice and spares; cars which are a real alternative to fast-depreciating modern machines; cars which have earned themselves the name 'The Affordable Classics'. Cars to enjoy.

APPENDICES

TECHNICAL DATA

Dimensions	Length*	Width	Height	Track**	Wheelbase
A30 saloon	11 ft 4$\frac{3}{8}$ in.	4 ft 7$\frac{1}{8}$ in.	4 ft 10$\frac{1}{4}$ in.	3 ft 9$\frac{1}{4}$ in./ 3 ft 8$\frac{3}{4}$ in.	6 ft 7$\frac{1}{2}$ in.
A35 saloon	11 ft 4$\frac{3}{8}$ in.	4 ft 7$\frac{1}{8}$ in.	4 ft 11$\frac{1}{4}$ in.	3 ft 9$\frac{1}{4}$ in./ 3 ft 8$\frac{3}{4}$ in.	6 ft 7$\frac{1}{2}$ in.
A30/35 Countryman	11 ft 5$\frac{7}{8}$ in.	4 ft 8 in.	5 ft 3 in.	3 ft 9$\frac{1}{4}$ in./ 3 ft 8$\frac{3}{4}$ in.	6 ft 7$\frac{1}{2}$ in.
A30/35 van	11 ft 5$\frac{7}{8}$ in.	4 ft 8 in.	5 ft 4 in.	3 ft 9$\frac{1}{4}$ in./ 3 ft 8$\frac{3}{4}$ in.	6 ft 7$\frac{1}{2}$ in.
A35 pick-up	11 ft 8$\frac{1}{2}$ in.	4 ft 7$\frac{1}{8}$ in.	4 ft 10$\frac{3}{4}$ in.	3 ft 9$\frac{1}{4}$ in./ 3 ft 8$\frac{3}{4}$ in.	6 ft 7$\frac{1}{2}$ in.
A40 Mk I	12 ft 0$\frac{1}{4}$ in.	4 ft 11$\frac{3}{8}$ in.	4 ft 9$\frac{1}{4}$ in.	3 ft 11 in./ 3 ft 11 in.	6 ft 11$\frac{1}{2}$ in.
A40 Mk II	12 ft 0$\frac{1}{4}$ in.	4 ft 11$\frac{3}{8}$ in.	4 ft 9$\frac{1}{4}$ in.	3 ft 11 in./ 3 ft 11 in.	7 ft 3$\frac{1}{16}$ in.

*Without overriders.   **Front/rear.

De luxe models Length of A40 Mk I with overriders is 12 ft 2 in. Length of A40 Mk II with overriders is 12 ft 1 in. due to overriders being wider apart and not on the most forward part of the curved bumper.

	Engine capacity	Bore × stroke	Compression ratio	bhp @rpm	Torque (lb ft @ rpm)
A30	803 cc	57.9 × 76.2 mm	7.2:1	28 @ 4800	40 @ 2200
A35	948 cc	62.94 × 76.2 mm	8.3:1 or 7.2:1	34 @ 4750 or 32 @ 4600	50 @ 2000 or 48 @ 2200
	1098 cc	64.58 × 83.72 mm	7.5:1	45 @ 5100	57 @ 3000
	848 cc	62.94 × 68.26 mm	8.3:1	34 @ 5500	44 @ 2900
A40 (Zenith carburettor)	948 cc	62.94 × 76.2 mm	8.3:1*	34 @ 4750	50 @ 2000
A40 (SU carburettor)	948 cc	62.94 × 76.2 mm	8.3:1*	37 @ 5000	50 @ 2500
A40	1098 cc	64.58 × 83.72 mm	8.5:1**	48 @ 5100	60 @ 2500

* 7.2:1 available.   ** 7.5:1 available.

Model	Final-drive ratio	Road speed (mph/1000 rpm)
A30 saloon (to C 1018)	5.143:1 (7/36)	12.62
A30 saloon (C 1019 on)	5.125:1 (8/41)	12.66
A30 saloon (C 43,849 on)	4.875:1 (8/39)	13.30
A30 Countryman/van**	5.375:1 (8/43)	12.67
A35 saloon	4.55:1 (9/41)	14.26
A35 pick-up*	4.55:1 (9/41)	14.72
A35 Countryman/van* (948 cc)	4.55:1 (9/41)	14.72
A35 van* (1098 cc)	4.22:1 (9/38)	15.94
A35 van* (848 cc)	4.875:1 (8/39)	13.80
A40 Mk I and II 948 cc saloons	4.55:1 (9/41)	14.26
A40 Mk I* and II 948 cc Countryman	4.55:1 (9/41)	14.72
All A40 Mk II with 1098 cc engine	4.22:1 (9/38)	15.30

* 5.60 × 13 in. tyres.   ** 5.90 × 13 in. tyres.   All other models with 5.20 × 13 in. tyres.

PRODUCTION DATA BY MODEL

Most of this data has been compiled from the microfilm and production ledgers at BMIHT. Archivist Anders Clausager gave much kind assistance in this operation, but the author is responsible for the accuracy of the figures produced.

All dates refer to build dates, and these may differ considerably from dispatch dates or registration dates.

Pre-numbered bodies were fed down the production line in any order and allocated sequential chassis numbers (car numbers) on the final assembly line. Body numbers may be out of sequence with chassis numbers. For example, in a batch of A40 Mk I cars with 50 consecutive chassis numbers, the highest and lowest body numbers differed by 11,757. This lack of sequence makes choosing the first body number to use in any year a matter for debate. Usually, it will be possible to find a higher body number in the previous year's production. Things average out, however, and the total numbers attributed to any model are not affected.

Figures for individual models have been calculated from their body numbers. Overall production figures have been calculated from the chassis numbers, after allowing for any gaps noted in the ledgers.

CKD units were not allocated body numbers in the Longbridge records (only chassis numbers), so figures for these have been calculated by subtracting the number of vehicles built at Longbridge from the highest chassis number of that series, after allowing for any known discrepancies.

Model identification

Early A30s had their body and chassis identification plates at the rear of the engine bay. Body numbers of most of the vehicles are also to be found in that position. A40 body numbers are either below the wiper motor at the rear of the engine bay, or on the bonnet-lock panel at the front. What Austin called the 'car number' is what most people, including registration authorities, normally called the 'chassis number'. (These days, it is called the Vehicle Identification Number or VIN.)

Prior to 1934, all Austins had both a car number and a chassis number (which were different), but from then on, the two became identical. The car/chassis number of later A30s and all A35s and A40s is found on a plate fastened to the left-hand front door pillar. This is the number which should be used on the registration documents under the heading VIN/chassis/frame number.

On any car/chassis plate: S = four-door saloon; 2S = two-door saloon; P = Countryman (or W = A40 Countryman); V = van; K = pick-up.

Traditionally, the letter A in Austin prefix systems was used to denote 'small car'. The cubic capacity of the engines used in the A30, A35 and A40 gradually increased from 803 cc to 1098 cc, but all fell within the capacity class that was denoted by the prefix A in the car/chassis number.

The final number before the car serial number, e.g. 3, 4 or 5, etc, denotes the model series. For example: AS3 = early A30; A2S4 = A30 two-door saloon; AS5 = A35 four-door saloon.

Note: The A30 began as an AS3 (or Series 3) because AS1 and AV1 were the Austin Eight saloon and van models of the 1945–47 period. AS2 was never used but may have been allocated to that narrow-track, short-stroke version of the A40 Dorset, which could have been A2S2, but was not put into production. There was no AS7, because the number 7 was allocated to the early Austin Mini as A-A2S7.

For new models introduced in 1958 or later, a second letter A was added in front of the first. The new A signified 'Austin', and became necessary after BMC went over to a unified prefix system based on Austin practice. For example: A-A2S6 = A40 Mk I saloon; A-AW9 = A40 Mk II Countryman with 1098 cc engine.

Although the A35 van was originally an AV5, the extra A appeared on the chassis plates of A35 vans (as A-AV5) after A35 saloon production ceased. Although the records sometimes refer to AV6 and AV8 vans, in both cases all chassis plates are stamped A-AV6 or A-AV8. It is assumed that chassis plates of the later AP5 Countryman and all AP6 Countryman models will follow suit as A-AP5 and A-AP6, but as there are none on club records this has not been verified.

On BMC cars from the mid/late 1960s onwards, a suffix letter after the car/chassis number denotes the assembly plant: A for Austin is Longbridge, M for Morris is Cowley, G for MG is Abingdon. Late A-AV8 A35 vans had this A suffix to their car/chassis number, as did the A40 Farina Mk II from chassis number 166,000 onwards.

Engine numbers are found on a plate at the right-hand front end of the cylinder block. Engine type is shown by a prefix before the number:

8AB = A35 van 848 cc
8AG = A35 van 848 cc later models
9 = A35 948 cc early models
9A = A40 Mk I, Zenith carburettor, early models
9AB = A35 948 cc later models with Lucar (push-on) electrical connections
9D = A40 Mk I, Zenith carburettor, later models
9DB = A40 Mk II 948 cc, SU carburettor
10AB = A35 van 1098 cc
10D = A40 Mk II 1098 cc
10DD = A40 Mk II 1098 cc with positive crankcase ventilation

These prefixes are found in front of the letter U (for centre floor gearchange) and the H or L (for high or low compression).

A30 engines did not conform to the above pattern, nor did those of early A35s. The 803 cc engine numbers were prefixed 2A, as were 948 cc A35 engines during much of the first year of A35 production.

In August 1954, a unified car/engine number system was introduced, which meant that, from then on, the cars had the same number for the engine and the chassis, but with different prefixes. The first A30 with a unified car/engine number was car number 73,000. The last A30 with different chassis and engine numbers was car number 72,036; the numbers from 72,037 to 72,999 were not issued. The unified car/engine number system was used on all A30s from then on, and also on the early A35s from 1956 to 1959. The last A35 with a unified car/engine number was car number 205,402 in August 1959. After another break in the number series, production was resumed from car number 206,001, and from then on engine numbers differed once again from car numbers. Some of the numbers between 205,402 and 206,001 were issued for engines but not for chassis.

It will be seen that no AS3, no AV6/AP6, no A-AV8, and none of the A40 Farinas will have the same car/chassis and engine number.

On the A35s with unified car/engine numbers, and possibly also on the A30s with such numbers, there will be a further three letters in the car number prefix. Typically, these extra letters are HCS or LCS. HC or LC means that the vehicle was fitted with a high- or low-compression engine respectively. The S seems to denote that a synchromesh gearbox was fitted, as other Austin models of the period, fitted with either an overdrive or an automatic gearbox, had the letters O or A in this place. Therefore, typical A35 prefixes of the 1956–59 period may be:

For saloons—A2S5-HCS or AS5-HCS
For the Countryman—AP5-HCS
For the commercial models—AV5-LCS or
AK5-LCS

Note that most saloon and Countryman models of the A30/35 had high-compression engines, and most vans and pick-ups had low-compression engines.

Note: C = car or chassis number; B = body number; E = engine number.

A30   Model AS3 May 1952–October 1953
Chassis numbers 101–31,749

C 101–113	Pre-production prototypes.
C 114	First car recorded in production records.
C 118	First car dated in production records (3 May 1952).
C 29,897	Continuous production ceased.
C 30,001–30,228	228 CKD cars sent to Australia.
C 31,749	Last of 12 AS3 saloons built after introduction of AS4.

C 25,631	Experimental AS4 built for Earls Court Show 1953.

Production figures AS3:

29,897 minus (100 + 1*) plus (228 + 12) = 30,036 (includes approximately 4427 CKD).

*Experimental AS4.

By the end of 1952, approximately 4000 cars built. January–October 1953, 26,036 built. The total is accurate; the approximation refers to year-end split, as no dates on record cards.

A30   Model A2S4 and AS4 October 1953–September 1956
Chassis numbers 29,898–224,327
Model AV4 August 1954–September 1956
Chassis numbers 68,714–223,093
Model AP4 August 1954–September 1956
Chassis numbers 73,987–223,678

C 29,898 B 231	First A2S4 (marked in records as having 7/36 rear axle, but see text).
C 29,920	First dated car in records (5 November 1953).
C 31,745 B 400,102	First AS4.
C 68,714 B 50	First van (31 August 1954), called AV3 initially in records.
C 73,987 B 572	First Countryman (8 September 1954).
C 76,205 B 1	Confirms start number of bodies for AP4/AV4 (16 September 1954).

Series 4 production

	A2S4	AS4	AP4/AV4	CKD	Total
October 1953–December 1954	37,912	18,720	1200*	7577	65,409
1955	32,311	30,741	12,300*	9516	84,868
January–September 1956	18,290	5075	15,508*	4077	42,950
Total	88,513	54,536	29,008	21,170	193,227**

143,049

*Very approximate year splits, but totals correct.   **Plus one experimental AS4.

AV4 production did not start until August 1954. All 1954 AV4/AP4 were Briggs-bodied. The 12,300 AV4/AP4 of 1955 consist of approximately 4800 Briggs bodies and 7500 Fisher & Ludlow bodies. Research by Anders Clausager of BMIHT has so far unearthed in the records a Briggs-bodied A30 van with body number 5868 (out of a contract believed to be for 6000 vans). The last Briggs-bodied van to be assembled at Longbridge would seem to have been AV4 143,591 (body number 5716), which was turned out on 8 August 1955. During June and July a mixture of Briggs- and Fisher & Ludlow-bodied vans had been turned out. The Fisher & Ludlow body numbers seem to have started at 1001, the first Fisher & Ludlow van being assembled at Longbridge on 3 June 1955 as AV4 129,963 (body number 1020). Very few Briggs-

bodied AV4/AP4 seem to have survived. Three AP4s have turned up, two in Australia and one in the UK. They have a 'Briggs of Dagenham' body plate at the rear of the engine compartment.

Note: After chassis number 73,000, all A30s had same car and engine number. Highest car number issued prior to that was 72,036. The 963 car/chassis numbers not issued have been subtracted from the 1954 figures. No separate model figures can be given for October–December 1953, but total of all models produced in that period was 6664. Total A30s produced in 1953 (AS3 plus Series 4) was approximately 26,136 plus 6664 = 32,800.

Total Series 4 production = 193,228.
Total A30 production, 1952–56 = 223,264 (includes 25,598 CKD).

A35 Model A2S5 and AS5 September 1956–
August 1959
Chassis numbers 103–205,108
Model AV5 September 1956–
February 1962
Chassis numbers 204–282,531
Model AP5 October 1956–
February 1962
Chassis numbers 357–282,527
Model AK5 November 1956–
December 1957
Chassis numbers 392–78,987

101 and 102 were engines dispatched to Don Hawley in the development department.

C 123 B 87,578	A2S5 in Spruce green/beige, Earls Court (2 October 1956—first day of continuous production).
C 171–C 203	Not allocated. Of the saloons prior to C 171, only three were four-door versions.

C 103	First two-door car, Capri blue, Paris Show (7 September 1956).
C 204	First A35 van (13 September 1956).
C 357	First A35 Countryman (11 October 1956).
C 392	First pick-up (14 November 1956).
C 78,987	Last pick-up (22 November 1957, but C 77,574 built 23 December 1957).
C 203,980	Last four-door car (12 August 1959).
C 205,108	Last two-door car (26 August 1959).
C 282,531	Last AV5 van (15 February 1962).

Series 5 production

	A2S5	AS5	AP5/AV5	AK5	CKD	Total
To December 1956	5484	1562	3693	280	8	11,027*
1957	42,720	12,297	19,941	195	3173	78,326
1958	38,363	9007	21,797		6178	75,345
1959	13,717	6095	28,787		2518	51,117**
1960			27,574		1443	29,017
1961			34,133			34,133
January–February 1962			2431			2431
Total	100,284	28,961	138,356	475	13,320	281,396

The highest body number of a pick-up is 491, but only 475 pick-ups were completed.

Longbridge-built A35 saloons total 129,245.

Total Series 5 production 281,396 (includes 13,320 CKD).

*33 chassis numbers not allocated have been subtracted.

**1000 chassis numbers not allocated have been subtracted.

A35 van	Model AV6 February 1962–September 1962 Chassis numbers 101–13,396 Model AP6 March 1962–September 1962 Chassis numbers 2101–10,954

C 154	Lowest body number (15 February 1962). New body number 101.
C 13,396	Last AV6 van (17 September 1962).
C 2101	First AP6 Countryman (13 March 1962).

C 101	First AV6 van (14 February 1962). B 162,451 in old series (new body number 102 and engine number 204).

Total production AV6 = 13,222 (155 exported).
Total production AP6 = 74 (13 exported).
No CKD.

A35 6-cwt van	Model A-AV8 (1098 cc) September 1962–May 1966 Chassis numbers 13,401–62,548 Model A-AV8 (848 cc) October 1963–February 1968 Chassis numbers 35,316–73,315

C 13,401	First A-AV8 (18 September 1962). B 12,696 E 101.
C 35,316	First 848 cc van (25 October 1963). B 34,654 E 102.
C 62,548	Last 1098 cc van (19 May 1966).
C 73,315	Last 848 cc van (6 February 1968). B 72,775 E 14,330 (highest chassis number, highest 848 cc engine number).

848 cc engine ran from E 101–14,330 = 14,230.

Total of 848 cc vans = 14,230.
Total of 1098 cc vans = 45,685.

Total A-AV8 = 59,915.

No CKD.

A-AV8 production

	1098 cc	1098/848 cc	848 cc
September–December 1962	8398		
1963		16,379	pilot production from October at C 35,316
1964		12,782	
1965		8068	
1966	last 1098 cc 19 May 1966	7611	
1967			6482
January–February 1968			195
Total	8398	44,840	6677

Total A35 production

Longbridge-built (A2S5) two-door saloons	100,284
Longbridge-built (AS4) four-door saloons	28,961
Longbridge-built AV5/AP5	138,356
AK5 (pick-up)	475
CKD (AS5, A2S5, AV5, AP5)	13,320
AV6 (van)	13,222
AP6 (Countryman)	74
A-AV8 (1098 cc van)	45,685
A-AV8 (848 cc van)	14,230
Total	354,607

Note: All AK5, AV6, AP6 and A-AV8 were Longbridge-built—i.e. no CKD.

**A40 Mk I   Model A-A2S6 saloon
June 1958–September 1961
Chassis numbers 101–169,711
Model A-AW6 Countryman
September 1959–September 1961
Chassis numbers 41,473–169,712**

C 101   First saloon (2 June 1958). B 101 E 116 (XOC 241 to experimental department).

C 41,473   First Countryman (23 September 1959). Dispatched CKD to Sydney.

C 50,471   First non-CKD Countryman (28 September 1959). To publicity department.

C 63,801   Lowest body number Countryman B (F)1 (30 November 1959). Fisher & Ludlow body.

C 169,712   Highest chassis number Countryman (21 August 1961). To Singapore (but A-AW6 169,651 completed 21 September 1961).

C 169,711   Last saloon (28 September 1961).

Production figures A40 Mk I

	A-A2S6(A)	A-A2S6(F)	A-AW6(A)	A-AW6(F)	CKD	Total
June–December 1958	7395				1247	8642
1959	40,802			306	20,762	61,870
1960	43,227	5272	7105	7529	3928	67,061
January–September 1961	12,370	7905	9577		2187	32,039
Total	103,794	13,177	16,682	7835	28,124	169,612
		116,971		24,517		

(A) denotes bodies built at Longbridge.

(F) denotes bodies built at Fisher & Ludlow.

CKD total 28,124 (3196 of these were Countryman models).

Total Mk I saloons = 116,971 + 24,928 CKD = 141,899.

Total Mk I Countryman = 24,517 + 3196 = 27,713.

Total A40 Mk I = 169,612.

**A40 Mk II Model A-A2S8 saloon
948 cc   August 1961–September 1962
Chassis numbers 101–50,200
Model A-AW8 Countryman
October 1961–September 1962
Chassis numbers 261–49,545**

C 101   First saloon (29 August 1961). B 120 E 113.

C 261   First Countryman CKD (dispatched 7 October 1961).

C 401   First Countryman (non-CKD) (12 September 1961). Paris Show. B 101.

C 49,545   Last Countryman (17 September 1962).

C 50,200   Last saloon (17 September 1962).

Highest body number of Countryman B 49,544.

Highest body number saloon (Longbridge) B (A) 19,751 (19 September 1962).

Highest body number saloon (Fisher & Ludlow) B (F) 14,048 (19 September 1962).

One Longbridge body used for an A-A2S9 to be subtracted in calculating total A-A2S8.

At changeover to 1098 cc engine, 223 chassis numbers were not allocated and must be subtracted in calculations, i.e. 46,777–46,780; 47,430–47,450; 49,152–49,173; 49,360–49,370; 49,506–49,550; 49,901–49,900; 50,151–50,170.

Production figures A40 Mk II 948 cc engine

	A-A2S8		A-AW8	CKD	Total
	(A) Body	(F) Body			
August–December 1961	5601	3487	3197	818	13,103
January–September 1962	14,049	10,461	9255	3009	36,774
Total	19,650	13,948	12,452	3827	49,877

33,598

Total Mk II (948 cc) Countryman = 14,744 (12,452 + 2292 CKD).

Total Mk II (948 cc) saloons = 35,133 (33,598 + 1535 CKD).

A40 Mk II 1098 cc

Model A-A2S9 saloon
September 1962–November 1967
Chassis numbers 50,201–172,897
Model A-AW9 Countryman
September 1962–November 1967
Chassis numbers 50,251–172,360

C 50,201 First saloon (18 September 1962).
C 50,251 First Countryman (18 September 1962).
C 172,360 Last Countryman (14 November 1967).
C 172,897 Last saloon (20 November 1967).

Chassis numbers 172,891–172,896 not allocated—to be subtracted in calculating total production.

Longbridge-assembled saloons

Body (A) 19,752 to 29,088 (8 August 1963).
Body (F) 14,048 to 78,829.
By 8 August 1963, this last body series was at 31,323, and where bodies were not marked (A) or (F) in ledger, it was impossible to tell them apart.

Approximate total Longbridge-assembled saloons = 74,119—consisting of 9337 (A) bodies + 64,782 (F) bodies.

A40 production totals

	Saloon	Countryman	Total	Total
Mk I	141,897	27,715		169,612
Mk II				
948 cc	35,133	14,744	49,877	
Mk II				172,568
1098 cc	80,605	42,086	122,691	
Total	257,635	84,545		342,170

Longbridge-assembled Countryman models

Body 12,570–21,428 (finished 8 August 1963).
Body (F) 7840–34,509.

Approximate total Longbridge-assembled Countryman = 35,529—consisting of 8859 + 26,670 (F) bodies.

CKD total = 13,043 (122,691 less 109,648 bodies).

CKD Countryman models 6557 (counted in ledger).

CKD saloons 6486.

Total Mk II 1098 cc saloons = 74,119 + 6486 = 80,605.

Total Mk II 1098 cc Countryman models = 35,529 + 6577 = 42,086.

Annual production figures all Mk II 1098 cc

September–December 1962	13,750
1963	40,050
1964	29,179
1965	15,967
1966	12,259
1967	11,486
Total	122,691

These figures on the left include the CKD figures, as well as the Longbridge-assembled cars. They do not include Innocenti A40 figures in any form.

Production figures for Innocenti A40

A40 Berlina (Series 1)	November 1960–January 1962	10,213
A40 Combinata (Series 1)	December 1960–January 1962	6444
A40 Berlina 950 cc (Series 2)	February 1962–December 1962	6828
A40 Combinata 950 cc (Series 2)	February 1962–January 1963	9979
A40S Berlina 1100 cc	December 1962–April 1965	6861
A40S Combinata 1100 cc	December 1962–February 1967	27,381
Total		*67,706*

Guide to first chassis number for all models and years

A30 AS3 saloon

1952	114
1953	4000

A30 AS4/A2S4 saloon

1953	29,898
1954	36,700
1955	96,510
1956	181,378

A30 AP4 Countryman

1954	73,987
1955	96,499
1956	181,391

A30 AV4 van

1954	68,714
1955	96,515
1956	181,379

A35 AS5/A2S5 saloon

1956	103
1957	12,423
1958	89,826
1959	164,834

A35 AK5 pick-up

1956	392
1957	10,130

A35 AP5 Countryman

1956	357
1957	11,181
1958	90,740
1959	165,958
1960	217,101
1961	247,651
1962	280,101

A35 AV5 van

1956	204
1957	11,163
1958	89,489
1959	164,866
1960	216,951
1961	245,968
1962	277,160

A35 AP6 Countryman

1962	2101

A35 AV6 van

1962	101

A35 A-AV8 van

1962	13,401
1963	21,799
1964	38,178
1965	50,960
1966	59,028
1967	66,639
1968	73,121

A40 Mk I A-A2S6/A-AW6 saloon and Countryman

1958	101
1959	8753
1960	70,613
1961	137,674

A40 Mk II A-A2S8/A-AW8 saloon and Countryman 948 cc

1961	101
1962	13,204

A40 Mk II A-A2S9/A-AW9 saloon and Countryman 1098 cc

1962	50,201
1963	63,951
1964	104,001
1965	133,180
1966	149,147
1967	161,406

MODIFICATIONS BETWEEN MODEL CHANGES

This information has been obtained from Austin service journals with the kind help and permission of BMIHT and Austin Rover.

C = car or chassis number; E = engine number; B = body number.

Months given refer to actual build dates.

Model A30 (AS3) four-door saloon—October 1951 (true production from May 1952)—October 1953, chassis numbers 101—31,749.

C 234 LH and 315 RH—Dowel fitted to gearbox front cover.

E 474—Parallel compression rings fitted to second groove of piston to improve lubrication of cylinder bore.

E 475—Improved oil pump introduced to prevent misalignment of the driving shaft.

C 599 LH and 601 RH—Gearchange lightened by altering cone angles of gears.

E 855 (C 992)—New hubs fitted. Wheels secured with studs and nuts rather than set screws.

C 1019—Axle ratio changed from 5.143:1 (7/36) to 5.125:1 (8/41).

C 1051 LH and 1060 RH—Petrol pipe changed from left to right of vehicle.

C 1264 RH and 1268 LH—Thread on swivel axle changed from BSF to UNF.

B 1457—New-type interior mirror with three-point fixing to improve rear visibility.

B 2006—Heater switch, when fitted, positioned on fascia centre panel, replacing trafficator switch. Trafficator switch moved to outer right- or left-hand lower edge of fascia panel and mounted on bracket.

B 2202—Bucket seats increased in width.

B 2709—Dual wipers fitted.

C 2768 RH and 2794 LH—Headlamp with non-split rim fitted.

C 2790 LH and 2847 RH—Twin stop- and tail-lamps standard fittings. Twin reflectors and centrally-placed stop- and tail-lamp discontinued. Central number-plate lamp fitted.

C 3030 LH and 3275 RH—Worm-and-nut steering gear fitted as alternative to peg-and-cam.

C 4979 RH and 5048 LH—Spare-wheel mounting moved from centre to right-hand side of rear-seat panel to increase boot capacity.

E 6290—Engine sling brackets increased from 3 in. to $3\frac{1}{2}$ in.

C 6666 RH and 6682 LH—New type of ignition switch with barrel lock and keys replaces knob type.

C 8655 LH and 8656 RH—Shape of brake drums modified to attain closer proximity to road wheel to prevent water entering adjustment holes. Two set screws fitted to ensure drum fits securely to hub during brake adjustment with wheel removed.

E 9622—Dynamo lubricated with felt pad rather than grease-packed lubricator.

E 9960—Fan and water-pump pulley strengthened to eliminate risk of breakage.

B 9989—Master-cylinder inspection plate increased in size and fitted with rubber seal in place of felt to prevent water entering vehicle.

B 10,749—Strap-type door-pull fitted to all doors.

C 13,675 RH and 13,676 LH—Brass and rubber bush replaces oilite bush at gearbox end of clutch-pedal shaft for silent operation. New bush should only be used at gearbox end of shaft.

E 13,862—New joint washer between oil pump and crankcase to reduce risk of incorrect assembly.

B 14,780—Front-seat cushion inner valance modified to clear tunnel better. Seats now handed.

B 14,830—External hinges used on boot lid. Combined boot handle and lock fitted to replace locking key. Prop rod introduced to support open lid.

C 15,779 RH and 15,786 LH—New rear-axle gear-carrier assembly with reduced offset of bevel pinion from crown-wheel centre.

E 17,957—New flywheel ring gear introduced to improve security of gear.

B 20,186—Rear seat redesigned to improve access and increase legroom.

E 20,961—Petrol pump fitted with priming lever.

E 21,520 (C 21,314 RH and 21,408 LH)—Ignition coil mounted on dynamo instead of dash panel to comply with ignition-suppression regulations.

B 24,120—Prop rod for boot lid moved from left to right of boot.

C 29,437 RH and 29,385 LH—Second-speed synchronizer modified to hold first-speed wheel firmly in engagement and stop tendency of early cars to jump out of gear under heavy load.

June 1953—Exterior sun-visors introduced. Retail price, £3 16s 0d. Underside painted non-reflecting matt green ready for use, top in red-oxide primer.

August 1953—4-watt side-light bulbs instead of 6-watt to cut current consumption—particularly when parked.

September 1953—Front and rear door casings made from hardboard instead of millboard to obviate the risk of distortion due to moisture absorption.

November 1953—Non-lockable petrol filler cap fitted. Lockable cap only available as extra.

Model A30 (AS4) four-door saloon and A30 (A2S4) two-door saloon—October 1953– September 1956, chassis numbers 29,898–224,327.

C 40,505 (A2S4) and C 40,979 (AS4)—Brake adjustment holes in drums circular and same size as holes in road wheels. Rubber plug used to seal both holes and to be put in place after tightening wheel on drum.

C 43,849 (A2S4) and C 43,898 (AS4)—Final-drive ratio raised to 4.875:1.

March 1954—Wing-joint mouldings only available off the roll rather than ready-cut lengths.

Engine 49,357 onwards—Modified carburettor incorporating a new type of discharge nozzle and choke tube to reduce tendency to ice-up.

C 49,778—New propshaft with larger universal joints. New bevel pinion flange on rear axle to accept propshaft.

E 56,573 onwards—Longer, stepped dowels used to locate clutch on flywheel. Larger holes in flywheel to receive dowels.

October 1954—Rear reflectors fitted to conform with new lighting regulations.

C 64,411—New horn of improved performance.

From now on, the modifications also refer to AV4 and AP4 (when applicable).

Model A30 (AV4) 5-cwt van—August 1954– September 1956, chassis numbers 68,714–223,093.

Model A30 (AP4) Countryman—August 1954– September 1956, chassis numbers 73,987–223,678.

AS3 models and AS4s prior to C 73,000 had engine numbers differing from the chassis number. From C 73,000, all A30s have unified chassis/engine numbers.

C 70,376—Pressurized radiator introduced.

E 75,588—Third parallel compression ring replaced by tapered version to improve oil consumption.

C 79,639—Hole in swivel axle for upper bush increased in diameter to same as that for lower bush to facilitate production. Inside diameter of bush unaltered.

E 102,987–103,000 and 103,547 onwards—Fuel trap fitted to vacuum ignition control pipe.

C/E 123,335—Oil-filled ignition coil for longer life.

E 127,918–128,000 and 128,066 onwards—New cylinder-block drain tap requires no washer.

C/E 138,909–139,000 and 139,139 onwards—26JS carburettor replaced by 26VME.

E 152,491—New distributor housing with UNF threads in place of BSF.

E 172,130–173,000 and 173,100 onwards—Gear selectors altered to improve gearchange.

C/E 207,412 A2S4, 208,467 AS4, 211,845 AV4, 212,299 AP4—Solid steering cross-rod introduced to replace tubular type. Track-rod ends now have female thread.

Body numbers A2S4, 77,918, AS4 451,860, AP4 21,018, AV4 21,754—New front bucket seats.

Model A35 (AS5) four-door saloon and A35 (A2S5) two-door saloon—September 1956–August 1959, chassis numbers 103—205,108 (A2S4) and 112–203,980 (AS4).

Model A35 (AP5) Countryman—October 1956–February 1962, chassis numbers 357–282,527.

Model A35 (AK5) pick-up—November 1956–December 1957, chassis numbers 392–78,987.

Model A35 (AV5) 5-cwt van—September 1956–February 1962, chassis numbers 204–282,531.

Body numbers (A2S5) 93,504, (AS5) 455,631—Rubber mats introduced to replace front carpets in blue, green or red rubber to match trim. This took place in late 1956 after production of 4500 A2S5 and 630 AS5.

February 1957 (all models)—Simple door-pull introduced to replace escutcheon and pull-strap.

February 1958 (AV5)—Scuttle and sill-side carpets replaced by scuttle casing in hardboard.

C 93,507—Improved dip-switch introduced to eliminate dead spot which could occur between full-beam and dipped-beam.

C/E numbers, high-compression 106,712 and low-compression 106,588—New clutch-driven plate introduced to obviate any roughness in the transmission. Plate can be identified by green mark on its hub.

AS5 106,769 RH and 106,071 LH, A2S5 106,762 RH and 105,991 LH, AV5 107,135 RH and 108,016 LH, AP5 107,812 RH and 108,150 LH—Rubber seating pads positioned on either side of rear springs in place of original fibre pad seating.

C/E AP5 208,743 LH and 209,634 RH, AV5 210,216 RH and 210,320 LH—22-amp C40/1 dynamo fitted to replace previous 19-amp unit. New dynamo has larger air vents and cooling fan of increased diameter. New control boxes fitted to suit high-output dynamo at body number AP5 94,021 and AV5 9400.

AV5 218,191 RH and 217,642 LH, AP5 217,110—Stronger flanged section at base of rear road-spring seat to improve rigidity.

Models AV6, AP6, A-AV8 (1098 cc and 848 cc) had no major modifications that are not dealt with in the text or under Paint and Trim Colours (Appendix 4).

Model A40 Mk I (A-A2S6) saloon—June 1958–September 1961, chassis numbers 101–169,711.

Model A40 Mk I (A-AW6) Countryman—September 1959–September 1961, chassis numbers 41,473–169,712.

B 2007–'A40' flash on boot lid replaced by 'Austin' to left of handle and 'A40' to right of handle. Second strap added to support boot lid.

B 5162—Single-mounting windscreen washer with double jet replaces two separate jets.

C 11,073—Self-cancelling indicators with timer introduced.

B 18,081—Windscreen wipers sweep through larger angle.

B 20,695—Sealing rubber fitted to rear bonnet drain channel to prevent engine fumes entering car via fresh-air grille.

B 20,760—Petrol-tank filler grommet altered to improve sealing.

B 26,269—'Flying A' removed from bonnet.

C 27,042—Sound-insulation board fitted to front bulkhead. Roof light fitted on driver's side to replace courtesy bulb under fascia. Rear trim panels extended to rear of body. Hinged boot floor fitted in place of spare-wheel cover.

C 27,579 RH and 27,338 LH—Accelerator-shaft seal modified to improve dust sealing.

C 28,797 RH and 28,132 LH—Improved ignition switch fitted.

C 35,553—Rubber dust-excluder ring no longer fitted to headlamps.

A2S6 44,447 RH and 44,412 LH—22-amp C40/1 dynamo fitted to replace previous 19-amp unit. New dynamo has larger air vents and cooling fan of increased diameter. New control box fitted to suit high-output dynamo at body number A2S6 33,698.

B 50,918—Sun-visor of improved design.

B 53,774—Choke knob incorporated on moulding for heater-control panel.

Body numbers (A2S6) 56,525 and (A-AW6) 1329—Clip added at joint of dash panel and toeboard to secure heater control cable. To improve operation of cable and to eliminate vibration and possible fouling against the brake pipes and electrical equipment.

B 59,635—Improved rear number-plate light.

B 60,709 RH and 61,513 LH—Finger-pull fitted to glove box in place of quick-release catch.

C 67,093 RH and 67,151 LH—Strengthened seat for front springs.

C 82,696 (A2S6) RH and 81,637 (A2S6) LH, also C 87,811 (AW6) RH and 88,520 (AW6) LH—Steering idler with push-on cap replaced by one with cover bolted to body.

C 82,888 RH and 82,231 LH—Rubber bushes fitted to both pins of rear shackle. Grease nipples deleted from upper bushes.

86,350 (body number 60,541) (A2S6) and 86,430 (body number 2385) (AW6)—New windscreen wiper arms and blades fitted to prevent scratched windscreen. Rigid bayonet fixing prevents transverse movement of previous hook fixing.

C 129,107 A2S6 and 128,618 AW6—Air cleaner redesigned to allow movement of air intake towards exhaust manifold in winter to prevent icing of carburettor.

Model A40 Mk II (A-A2S8) 948 cc saloon—August 1961–September 1962, chassis numbers 101–50,200.

Model A40 Mk II (A-AW8) 948 cc Countryman—October 1961–September 1962, chassis numbers 261–49,545.

A2S8 and AW8—Where steering side rods were fouling the front wing valance aperture on full lock, it was suggested that service agent should enlarge the aperture in the required position by cutting away the offending metal and remaking the flanged edge.

Model A40 Mk II (A-A2S9) 1098 cc saloon—September 1962–November 1967, chassis numbers 50,201–172,897.

Model A40 Mk II (A-AW9) 1098 cc Countryman—September 1962–November 1967, chassis numbers 50,251–172,360.

A2S9 and AW9—In early cars, instances were reported of the brake pipes from the four-way connection to the front brake hoses fouling the steering box and the apertures in the front wings. The cure was to reposition the brake pipes. There were also instances of the speedometer cable rubbing against the pipes from the brake and clutch master cylinders. The cure was to re-route the speedo cable to midway between the clutch and brake cylinders.

B 22,226 (saloon)—Framed interior driving mirror introduced.

B 51,842 (A-A2S9) and B 20,295 (A-AW9)—Wood-grain fascia introduced.

C 152,302 (A2S9) and 151,710 (AW9)—Shallower, two-stepped hub cap replaces three-stepped type.

C 159,315 (A2S9) and 161,047 (AW9)—Plastic battery tray replaces board type.

PAINT AND TRIM COLOURS

Information gained directly from the production records at BMIHT. Colours, listed by model and year of manufacture, given thus: body colour/trim colour.

A30 saloon (AS3 four-door)

May–July 1952 (cars 114–344)
Cotswold beige, Dove grey and Austin Seven grey— all with brown trim, Powder blue/beige trim.

From mid-July 1952
Selsey blue, Sedgemoor green, Sandown fawn, Shaftesbury grey—all with beige trim. Black/beige added in late autumn at C 2214.

Colours for Coronation Year 1953
Initially, the same colours as end of 1952, although black was available with beige or red trim. First black/red car was C 9422.

Coronation colours introduced in late April: Coronet cream/red, Windsor grey and Balmoral blue/blue, Sandringham fawn and Buckingham green/tan. Black/red or tan trim. This range continued until the end of AS3 production in October 1953.

A30 saloon (AS4 four-door) and A30 saloon (A2S4 two-door)

1953 and 1954
The same range continued into AS4 and A2S4 production, but most of the AS4s produced in 1953 were in black.

In late 1953 and early 1954, several A2S4 (A30 two-door saloons) were produced with contrasting roofs. For example: Coronet cream with red or Sandringham fawn roof; Balmoral blue with Windsor grey roof; Chelsea grey with medium blue roof; Sandringham fawn with Coronet cream roof; medium blue with Chelsea grey roof; Windsor grey with Balmoral blue roof.

(Australian *Monthly Motor Manual* of March 1953 quotes A30 colours available there as: Fern green, pastel green, light grey, pastel blue, beige and black.)

The Coronation colours continued until late October 1954, when the following appeared: Tweed grey/red, Spruce green/beige, Chestnut/beige, mid-blue/beige, black/red or beige trim. The odd car or two were produced in Chelsea grey/red.

1955
Same range continues, except Chestnut disappears and mid-blue becomes Reef blue. Chelsea grey came into full use at the end of June.

At the end of October, a completely new range of colours appeared: Tintern green/green, Cardigan grey/red, Conway blue/beige, black/red or beige trim.

1956
The above continued in use, except that at the beginning of the year, Cardigan grey was replaced by Tweed grey/red. In February, Streamline blue was introduced and Chelsea grey/red and Spruce green reappeared. The latter now had green trim in place of beige. These seven colours continued in use to the end of A30 production, but further trim options appeared, giving 14 different colour and trim combinations. They were: black/green, red or beige trim; Tweed grey/red trim; Chelsea grey/red or green trim; Tintern green/green or beige trim; Spruce green/green or beige trim; Conway blue/blue or beige trim; Streamline blue/blue or beige trim.

A considerable number of A30s were trimmed in hide to special order, although it was only a very small proportion of total production. The normal trim was in leathercloth

A30 van (AV4) and A30 Countryman (AP4)

August 1954 onwards
The first four vans were in green/tan, but from then on, they were in green, grey or primer, all with brown trim.

The first Countryman was produced in red and cream with red trim for the Earls Court Commercial Show. Otherwise, the Countryman was produced in the same colour and trim as the van, except for an occasional Countryman in cream.

1955

These colours continued until February, when the range for van and Countryman became: Campbell cream, Windsor grey, Westminster green or primer. All had brown trim.

By the end of March, fawn trim was introduced for all Countryman models.

In August, County cream replaced Campbell cream.

1956

The same range continued into 1956, but Spruce green was added at the end of June.

A35 saloon (AS5 four-door and A2S5 two-door)

1956

Island blue, Streamline blue, Capri blue, Spruce green, Tintern green, Court grey, Tweed grey, Chelsea grey, black.

Unless to special order, the trim was mainly blue with blue cars and green with green cars. Normally, grey cars were trimmed in red, but could also have green or blue trim. Some black cars had green or fawn trim, but most were trimmed in red. Combinations such as Spruce green/beige, or Capri blue and Streamline blue/red, were produced to special order.

Blue twill and green twill trim were used on blue and green A35 saloons respectively from early on, although at first in very small numbers. A few black cars were also turned out with green twill.

1957

Spruce green, Tweed grey, Court grey, Island blue and black continued all year.

Palm green and Speedwell blue replaced Capri blue, Streamline blue and Tintern green in mid-February. The first Speedwell blue car was built on 5 February 1957 for the Geneva Show.

Trim combinations were as before, although there were more cars in Spruce green/beige, but these were only produced up to March. Blue and green cars with matching twill trim were quite common right through to the end of A35 saloon production. The twill was mainly used with Island blue and Spruce green cars, but it could also be found with Palm green and Speedwell blue versions. Palm green cars were much less common than those in Spruce green.

In June 1957, five saloons were turned out in two-tone paintwork. Three of these were works cars. There were three Old English white saloons with a contrasting colour of either Tweed grey, Berkshire green or Sunset red. The last had scarlet trim. A black saloon was turned out with contrasting Mardi Gras red duo-tone paint and scarlet and black trim.

1958

Same colours and combinations as late 1957, although a few black cars were being turned out with tan, terracotta or grey trim to special order.

1959

Same colours and combinations as 1958, except that although most black cars were turned out with cherry trim, a steady trickle had terracotta, and a few had tan or grey trim.

No more than a dozen A35 saloons were produced with hide trim during the entire production run—all were to special order. The normal trim was of pvc-coated fabric.

Wheels: A35 saloons, in all body colours, were specified to have Court grey wheels.

A35 pick-up (AK5) 1956–57

All home-market pick-ups in Tweed grey/cherry red. Export colours—Tweed grey and County cream/cherry red, Spruce green/green, Island blue, Streamline blue and Speedwell blue/blue trim.

A35 van (AV5) and A35 Countryman (AP5)

1956

The majority of very early A35 vans were in Westminster green or Windsor grey. Other colours were County cream, Tweed grey and Spruce green. Quite a few vans were produced in other colours to special order, and others were turned out in primer. All early vans had brown trim, except one or two to special order.

The Countryman colours were those of the van, but Countryman models were trimmed in fawn, except to special order.

1957–February 1962

A few Westminster green vans were produced at the beginning of 1957, but by the end of January, the colours were: County cream, Tweed grey, Spruce green or Island blue. These colours continued until the end of AV5 production.

The beginning of 1957 saw the introduction of co-ordinated trim for the vans. County cream and Tweed grey/cherry, Island blue/blue, Spruce green/green. Vans with brown trim continued in production, but in fewer and fewer numbers, and in March 1957 brown trim was dropped. A black van with cherry trim was built for the Paris Show on 4 September 1957.

The Countryman used the same colours as the van, but continued with its fawn trim until March 1957, when Spruce green/green began to appear. Other Countryman models were produced in the co-ordinated trim combinations of the vans to special order.

The Countryman gradually appeared in the same co-ordinated trim as the vans during 1958, and by March the fawn trim had been dropped. One or two black/red trim Countryman versions were produced to special order.

During 1960 and 1961, large numbers of A35 van bodies were painted at the Morris bodies plant at Coventry.

A35 Mk II van (AV6) and Countryman (AP6) February 1962–September 1962

Two of the earlier colours continued—Tweed grey/cherry and Spruce green/green. Two new colours appeared—on day three of AV6 production (16 February 1962) Farina grey/cherry was introduced, and Florentine blue/blue came in three days later.

The AV6 Countryman was turned out with co-ordinated trim, but black trim appeared on the vans with Florentine blue on 27 March 1962, and with Spruce green on 2 May 1962. The black trim spread to Tweed grey and Farina grey vans on 15 June 1962.

A35 van (AV8) September 1962–February 1968

Spruce green, Tweed grey, Farina grey and Island blue, all with black trim. There was also a steady stream of vans produced in Glasso French grey/black trim.

The first batch of ten 850 cc engined AV8 vans was turned out in Special grey/black trim for Saunders of Worcester.

In July 1966, four vans were turned out in Snowberry white with black trim. A further example was built in August 1966.

A40 Mk I saloon (A2S6) and Countryman (AW6)

All had a black roof, unless ordered in the optional monotone exterior. Wheels either in cream or pale grey.

Farina grey/tan trim, or Tartan red trim with Farina grey piping, or Ocean blue trim with Farina grey piping; Tartan red/black trim with Tartan red piping; Horizon blue/blue trim; Sutherland green/grey trim with Sutherland green piping; Ocean blue/grey trim with Ocean blue piping; black/red, blue, grey or tan trim.

Only about a dozen Mk I A40s were produced to special order with hide trim.

A few early cars were produced in Horizon blue/tan trim, but only for a short period. There were some odd cars in the very first batch. Two cars were produced in Cloud grey: 102 was trimmed in red and dispatched to Capetown on 25 July 1958; 106 was trimmed in tan and dispatched to Canada on 30 July 1958. Two cars were produced in Willow green with tan trim: 103, which went to Rotterdam on 16 September 1958, and 107, which went to Dar es Salaam on 1 August 1958. The only basic saloon produced in the first 50 was in Cloud grey with red trim, and this went to Zurich on 31 July 1958. Only five Willow green and five Cloud grey cars were produced. All were in the first 20 cars and all went abroad.

Apart from these oddities, and car number 8509, which was produced in 'Special grey' with Dove grey hide for Sir Leonard Lord on 30 December 1958, all production cars conformed to the original list of six colours with black roofs. Cars were only produced with optional monotone exteriors from mid-1959 onwards.

In November 1960, one car was produced with a special paint try-out. This car, A2S6 135,159, was in Surf blue with a Farina grey roof and Horizon blue trim. In June 1961, five cars were produced in special paint try-outs, and some of the colours would be seen later on the Mk II cars. They were all saloons: 155,379 was in Cumulus grey with a Snowberry white roof and Hazelnut trim; 155,382 was in Agate red with a black roof and Cardinal red trim; 156,007 was in Embassy maroon with a black roof and Biscuit trim; 156,037 was in Blue Royale with an Ocean blue roof and Ocean blue trim; 156,040 was in Persian blue with a Farina grey roof and Horizon blue trim. All, except the Blue Royale car, are recorded as having Snowberry white wheels and instrument board.

A40 Mk II saloon (A2S8) and Countryman (AW8)

Duo-tone upholstery (i.e. with Damask silver panels) was common to de luxe and basic models. A contrasting roof colour was standard on de luxe models, but had to be ordered on basic models.

Horizon blue/black roof had trim in Damask silver/Horizon blue. Agate red/black roof had trim in Damask silver/Cardinal red or Damask silver/Satin beige. Fern green/Snowberry white roof had trim in Damask silver/green or Damask silver/Cumulus grey. Embassy maroon (no contrasting roof available) had trim in Damask silver/Satin beige or Damask silver/Cumulus grey. Cumulus grey/Snowberry white roof and black/Cumulus grey roof had trim in Damask silver/Cardinal red or Damask silver/Cumulus grey. Snowberry white/Cumulus grey roof had trim in Damask silver/Cumulus grey, Damask silver/Cardinal red or Damask silver/Horizon blue.

In spring 1962, from A-A2S8 (body A10,086), A-A2S8 (body F5554) and A-AW8 (body 5544), the seats took on a ladder pattern in monotone colours of green, Cardinal red, Cumulus grey, Satin beige and black.

At the very beginning of Mk II production, some cars were produced with Hazelnut trim. This applied to some Cumulus grey cars with Snowberry white roofs and to some black or Snowberry white cars that had Cumulus grey roofs. In October 1961, the Hazelnut trim ceased, but it reappeared later on the 1098 cc cars.

A40 Mk II saloon (A2S9) and Countryman (AW9)

All trim continues in monotone. Wheels in Snowberry white, cream or pale grey. Exteriors monotone or duo-tone as below.

Monotone

Cumulus grey* with Cardinal red or Cumulus grey trim; Agate red* with Cardinal red or Satin beige trim; Horizon blue* with Horizon blue trim; Snowberry white* with Cumulus grey, Cardinal red or Horizon blue trim.

Embassy maroon with Satin beige trim; black with Cardinal red trim.

Black with Satin beige or Hazelnut trim.**

Duo-tone

Cumulus grey/Snowberry white roof with Cardinal red trim (or Cumulus grey trim*); Agate red/black roof with Cardinal red trim (or Satin beige or black trim*); Horizon blue/black roof with Horizon blue or black trim; Fern green/Snowberry white roof with green trim**; Snowberry white/Cumulus grey roof with Cardinal red trim (or Cumulus grey or Horizon blue trim*); Embassy maroon/black roof with Cumulus grey trim*; black/Cumulus grey roof with Cardinal red or Hazelnut trim.

*Export only.
**Home market only.

Apart from the changes listed below, the same colour combinations were available to the end of A40 production.

On 8 August 1963, a saloon was turned out in Glen green with a Snowberry white roof. It was a paint try-out, and in December 1963, Glen green was brought in as a replacement for Fern green. Glen green was for the home market only, and the cars were in monotone or with a Snowberry white roof. Only Satin beige trim was available with Glen green.

On 5 March 1964, a car was produced with a monotone Embassy maroon exterior and another with monotone Horizon blue exterior; both had black trim.

Hazelnut trim reappeared on 6 March 1964 in a black car with Cumulus grey roof, but only about half a dozen similar cars were produced.

On 1 June 1964, a Countryman was turned out in monotone 'new' maroon and Satin beige trim. This colour became known as 'Maroon B' and replaced Embassy maroon from June 1964 onwards. Maroon B cars were available in monotone with Satin beige trim. Cars in Maroon B were available for export with a black roof and Cumulus grey trim.

By November 1964, very few cars were being turned out in Cumulus grey trim, and by December 1964, the trim choice was Cardinal red, Horizon blue or Satin beige.

BMC paint codes for colours used on A30, A35 and A40 Farina

Speedwell blue	BU 1
Florentine blue	BU 7
Island blue	BU 8
Ocean blue	BU 16
Horizon blue	BU 17
Reef blue	BU 19
Capri blue	BU 20
Streamline blue	BU 21
Conway blue	BU 22
Palm green	GN 3
Spruce green	GN 13
Sutherland green	GN 19
Tintern green	GN 20
Westminster green	GN 32
Fern green	GN 39
Glen green	GN 40

Court grey	GR 1
Cardigan grey	GR 2
Tweed grey	GR 4
Farina grey	GR 11
Chelsea grey	GR 15
Dove grey	GR 26
Cumulus grey	GR 29
Tartan red	RD 9
Chestnut	RD 12
Embassy maroon	RD 21
Agate red	RD 22
Maroon B	RD 23
Old English white	WT 3
Snowberry white	WT 4
County cream	YL 6
Black	BK 1

CLUBS

Austin A30–A35 Owners Club

Roger Driver,
Orchard End,
Wilmington,
Polegate,
East Sussex,
BN26 5SQ

A40 Farina Club

Michael Smith,
15 Heath Avenue,
Penarth,
South Glamorgan,
CF6 1QZ

Classic Saloon Car Club

Peter Deffee,
7 Dunstable Road,
Caddington,
Luton,
Bedfordshire

Austin A30–A35 Eigenaren Club

Dick van Arum,
Oosteinde 37,
2611 VB,
Delft,
Netherlands

Austin Motor Vehicle Club of New South Wales

Peter Jones,
26 Leichhardt Street,
Ruse,
NSW 2560,
Australia

Australian Austin A30 Car Club

Tom Bacon,
21 Radio Street,
Maidstone 3012,
Victoria,
Australia

Austin Motor Vehicle Club of Queensland

Terry Jorgensen,
34 Desgrand Street,
Archerfield,
Brisbane,
Queensland 4108,
Australia

Austin Seven Club of South Australia

Jean Gilbert,
5 Culley Street,
Clarence Park,
South Australia 5034,
Australia

INDEX